# INVISIBLE SOJOURNERS

# INVISIBLE SOJOURNERS

## African Immigrant Diaspora in the United States

John A. Arthur

Westport, Connecticut
London

**Library of Congress Cataloging-in-Publication Data**

Arthur, John A., 1958–
    Invisible sojourners : African immigrant diaspora in the United
States / John A. Arthur.
        p.   cm.
    Includes bibliographical references and index.
    ISBN 0–275–96759–X (alk. paper)
        1. Africans—United States—Social conditions.   2. Immigrants—
United States—Social conditions.   3. Africans—Migrations.   4. African
diaspora.   5. United States—Emigration and immigration.   6. Africa—
Emigration and immigration.   I. Title.
E184.A24 A74   2000
    305.896′073—dc21            99–054445

British Library Cataloguing in Publication Data is available.

Library of Congress Catalog Card Number: 99–054445
ISBN: 0–275–96759–X

First published in 2000

Praeger Publishers, 88 Post Road West, Westport, CT  06881
An imprint of Greenwood Publishing Group, Inc.
www.praeger.com

Printed in the United States of America

The paper used in this book complies with the
Permanent Paper Standard issued by the National
Information Standards Organization (Z39.48–1984).

10 9 8 7 6 5 4 3 2 1

# Contents

# Preface

America is a nation of immigrants. More than half of the foreign-born population of the United States came to the United States between 1980 and 1994. Immigrant flow into the United States since 1981 to 1995 has more than doubled. Part of the new global migration of skilled and unskilled people leaving areas of low capital formation and economic development for highly advanced economies, the Africans who have settled in the United States during the last twenty years represent the largest number of Africans in more than two hundred years to settle in America. Between 1974 and 1995 alone, Ethiopian migration to the United States increased from 276 to 5,960—an increase of over 2,000 percent. The increase in the same period for Nigeria was from 670 in 1974 to 6,818 in 1995—an increase of over 900 percent (Gordon, 1998: 94).

The cultural polyphony of Africans has become a noticeable aspect of the urban landscape of major metropolitan centers across the United States. Throughout America, African immigrants make significant contributions to the cultural and economic enrichment of this country. Their contributions in the areas of medicine, higher education, and engineering have been chronicled in major newspapers. Largely invisible and unknown to many Americans, these Africans are becoming some of the continent's most educated and dynamic people.

Their passage to the United States takes the form of a chain migration; often they leave Africa for another destination, work for a few years, and then save enough money to undertake the journey to America. Africa's colonial contacts with the West, the agitation for political self-determination, the Cold War, the economic and political dislocation following independence, the capitalist penetration into Africa, and the configurations of United States immigration laws have all facilitated the immigration of Africans to the United States. This diaspora will persist with further economic globalization and the gradual removal of international barriers to the free movement of people, goods, and services.

This book is about the niche that Africans are carving in the new global migration. It does not seek to test hypotheses or formulate theoretical statements about international migration to the United States. Its primary goal is to coax out the forms, patterns, and meanings associated with the migratory transfer of Africa's human capital to this country. A secondary goal is to give voice to the migratory experiences that reveal how the Africans negotiate the formation of ethnicity, racial identity, and the multifaceted relationships that they forge with the members of the host society.

I approached this book from the sociological perspective that the dynamics and the social construction of African immigrant identity are inextricably linked with macro-historical forces that transcend the shared experiences of the African diaspora. Consequently, I have provided an in-depth discussion of the interplay of geopolitical, cultural, and economic factors influencing the immigrants' individual and collective experiences both in Africa and in their new homeland. Throughout the course of this book, I have tried to give a voice to the multiple dimensions of the African immigrants' experiences in the United States. Using an ethnographic approach enabled me to probe extensively into the thought patterns of the immigrants. The probe yielded in-depth introspective remarks from the immigrants about the reasons why they left Africa, their acculturation to life in America, the benefits of their migratory experiences, their moments of joy or sadness, and their approaches to the future. Where possible, I have used verbatim statements from the immigrants without disclosing their identities. My hope is that, by bringing out the sociological contents of the immigrants' lives, I am adding to the understanding of fundamental features of the migratory experiences shaping immigrant histories in this country.

The African immigrants in the United States do not constitute a monolithic entity. They are as varied in their cultures as the countries in Africa that they represent. They are divided by language, religion, class, and nationality. But they remain united in their journey to America to pursue cultural and economic goals. Many of Africa's young dream of the opportunity to come to the West. Those who succeed in doing so consider themselves very fortunate. Fiercely kinship-oriented in their world view, the Africans who come here share the economic benefits of their migratory experience with their entire extended families. In so doing, these African immigrants become agents of social change in their home countries—sharing pieces of the material and non-material culture of this nation with people living in both peripherally and centrally located towns, cities, and villages all over Africa. They are active in the social, cultural, economic, and political development of their home countries, sojourning in America, waiting patiently for conditions to improve at home, and then repatriating.

Writing a book requires the cooperation, assistance, and encouragement of many individuals and organizations. With generous grant support from the University of Minnesota and its College of Liberal Arts, I spent three years collecting and analyzing the data for this book. I thank the University of Minnesota and the College of Liberal Arts very much for their support and for the wonderful environment that they provide for scholarship. This book would not have become a reality without their institutional commitment to the research enterprise. I gratefully acknowledge Lori Moogard and Nicole Rostveit, my undergraduate research assistants, who aided in the data collection and analysis. My heartfelt thanks to them. Absolutely essential was the assistance given to me by Darlene Lind, secretary in the Department of Sociology and Anthropology at the University of Minnesota. The following individuals were invaluable in assisting me during the data collection phase of this project: Dr. Masami Suga, Refugees Studies Center; Wendy Treadwell, Machine Readable Center; and statistical consultant Dr. Karl Krohn, all affiliated with the University of Minnesota.

I am eternally grateful to the African immigrant groups for granting me access to their cultural universe. Sincere thanks to the leaders of the immigrant associations who made it possible for me to identify my respondents. I am also indebted to the individual immigrant and refugee families who graciously welcomed me to their homes. I enjoyed our moments together.

I cannot end without special appreciation to Jackie Stewart, director of institutional research at Augusta State University in Georgia; Nancy Disch, former social science librarian at the University of Minnesota; and Bruce Mork, Department of Sociology and Anthropology, University of Minnesota. To Jackie, Nancy, and Bruce, I say sincere thanks for listening as the ideas for this book unfolded, for reading earlier drafts, and for their constant encouragement and advice.

I have drawn heavily on what I have learned from my colleagues over the years, and I stand in their debt. Special thanks to Drs. Sharon Kemp, Jay Laundergan, and John Bower for their support and for the intellectual insights that they provided. I remain grateful to LeAne Rutherford, assistant professor, Instructional Development Service, University of Minnesota. Finally, I express my appreciation to my family for their enduring support. Their presence, coupled with the motivation they provided throughout my education, has sustained me throughout my career in academe. Sincere thanks to all. In designing the questionnaire, I found the survey items originally developed by Harry Pachon and Louis DeSipio in their study of Latino immigrants (1994) very helpful. Also helpful were the questions deposited in the National Opinion Research Center (NORC) dealing with general immigration issues, compiled by the Roper Center for Public Opinion Research.

# Chapter 1

# Introduction: African Immigrants in the New Global Migration

As early as the 1500s, the African slave trade had already brought thousands of Africans to the New World. In what became known as the Middle Passage, Africans were exported from their homelands to the Americas to develop and sustain plantation agriculture and to work the mines of South America in a new and unfamiliar environment (Thompson, 1987). Starting in 1619, the first wave of Africans who settled in what was to become the United States of America came to these shores involuntarily. The Africans were indentured for specified periods, but as the economic advantages of their forced labor became clearer, the period of servitude soon came to be expanded to the duration of their lives. The Africans brought not only their labor, but skills and knowledge in areas useful to the white settlers. In Africa, the captives had been farmers, builders, artisans, craftsmen, healers, and, yes, even rulers.

Immigration has ebbed and flowed, ebbed and flowed. The earliest black immigrants living in the American colonies totaled about fifty-eight thousand. The largest numbers settled in Virginia, South Carolina, and Pennsylvania (Bennett, 1975). During the entire period of the first African diaspora to America, the slave trade brought between ten and twenty million Africans. After the trade in human cargo was abolished in the 1800s, few Africans came to the United States. Between 1891 and 1900, only three hundred and fifty Africans came. From 1900 to 1950, however, during the period of colonial rule in Africa, over thirty-one thousand Africans immigrated to the United States (Gordon, 1998). No matter the era of their immigration, in their triumphs and struggles, Africans have contributed immensely to shaping America.

Today, the African diaspora in the United States continues, as thousands of African immigrants voluntarily come to the United States to seek a better life for themselves. As part of the group of immigrants referred to as the "new Americans," the Africans form a small percentage of the total immigrant population in the United States. According to Immigration and Naturalization Service (INS) data, during the 1960s, the African immigrants comprised about 1 percent of all immigrants who were legally admitted. By the end of the 1970s, their share of the total immigrant population had increased to 2 percent (Wong, 1985). In the 1980s and 1990s, they formed 3 percent of those legally admitted.

The African immigrants are coming to the United States principally from Nigeria, South Africa, Liberia, Cape Verde, Egypt, Ghana, Kenya, Liberia, and the Horn of Africa (mainly Ethiopia, Somalia, and Eritrea). Data provided by Gordon (1998) reveal that Nigerians alone now constitute 17 percent of the African immigrant population in the United States. They are followed by Ethiopians, who account for another 13 percent. According to data from the INS, prior to 1971, the majority of the immigrants from Africa came to the United States from the northern part of the continent, mainly from Egypt and Morocco. African immigration to the United States from North Africa has slowed while immigration from Sub-Saharan Africa has increased. The African immigrants are part of the international migration of talent, otherwise known as the brain drain, from the less developed to the post industrial societies of the world (Glaser, 1978; Gordon, 1998; Grubel and Scott, 1977). The majority of the African immigrants have experienced urban life and transnational migration prior to arriving in the United States.

The numerical trend of Africans living in the United States has, with some exceptions, been increasing. The 1970 census showed there were about 61,463 Africans living in the United States. By 1980, their number had increased to 193,723—a threefold increase. The 1990 census counted more than 363,819 Africans. Between 1970 and 1990, the number of Africans living in the United States increased fivefold (Census of the United States, 1970–90). For fiscal year 1995–1996, the number of Africans who were admitted as permanent residents increased by 27 percent (U.S. Immigration and Naturalization Service, 1993–1996).

For many of the African immigrants, the journey to the United States involves a transnational migratory pattern. Leaving because of Africa's worsening economic and political problems, or to pursue education, or to reunite with family members, these immigrants typically reach the United States in stepwise fashion, sometimes living in several other countries before managing to secure a visa for their ultimate destination in the United States. Relative to other immigrant population groups such as Hispanics or Asians, the African immigrants have a low rate of naturalization. Many consider themselves sojourners in the United States, intending to return home when economic and political conditions improve.

The cultural polyphony of the Africans is becoming more noticeable in major metropolitan centers such as New York City, Washington, D.C., Atlanta, Houston, and Los Angeles. Though few in number compared to other immigrant groups in the new migration to the United States, the Africans' contributions to the American immigrant quilt have been noteworthy in the areas of educational attainment, multilingual characteristics, strong kinship and family structure, ethnic business formation, and unfettered ambition to become successful. Many of the Africans have become economically more successful than they had been in Africa. They are more likely than native-born blacks to be employed and live in multiple income households even though they earn less than native-born Americans overall (Butcher, 1994). The variances in income among all immigrant groups, however small or large, is sometimes attributed to differential endowments and earnings-related attributes of immigrant populations (Dodoo, 1991a/b/c; Bashi and McDaniel, 1997). In the case of African immigrants, entry to labor markets, earnings, and mobility has been influenced largely by education, language proficiency, and entrepreneurial initiative. Internal differentiations exist among the African immigrants. A growing number of them, especially those without educational credentials, find themselves restricted to menial and low-paying jobs where they are subjected to exploitation. Like Polish, Irish, Armenian, and Hungarian immigrants at the beginning of the twentieth century, the African immigrants with limited job skills and little education find themselves at the low end of a segmented labor market. Through continuing education and self-improvement, many of them do not stay at the bottom tier of the labor market for very long. Over time, many are able to move into desirable jobs where they receive better wages with fringe benefits.

Acculturated but not assimilated, the Africans engage the host society selectively, confining their activities to carefully constructed zones, mainly educational and economic, that are vital for their survival in this country. For the majority of the immigrants, education is seen as the pathway to social mobility and economic advancement. Some come to America as students on nonimmigrant visas; upon the completion of their education, if they have skills that are in high demand, they are able to find employers who petition the INS to admit them as permanent residents under the third preference category of the immigration law.

Like native-born American blacks, African immigrants recognize that racial stratification is very important in shaping their individual and collective destinies in the United States. Coming from countries where blacks are in the majority and control every aspect of social organization, the immigrants approach the black and white racial divide with extreme caution, sometimes disengaged, distanced, and reluctant to participate fully in the affairs of the host society. At home, the major sources of intergroup conflicts are ethnic differences. In the United States, they are confronted with racial categorization and its economic and cultural results. Thus, for a large number of African immigrants, the status that they attempt to claim vis-à-vis the dominant society is that of "foreigner." By stressing their national or continental origins, the Africans hope that they will receive better treatment from whites than African-Americans receive (Bryce-Laporte, 1973; Model, 1991). The status "foreigner" is seen as less derogatory and culturally more valuable than the status "black." In spite of this attempt to negotiate their cultural identity with the dominant white society, the majority of the immigrants come to recognize that no matter what they do, they are never able to insulate themselves from white racial stereotypes and discrimination against people of African origins. In the United States, they are lumped together with black Americans, and to assert their difference, the Africans stress their accents and sojourner status. This has not spared them either. But even though most of the African immigrants strongly disapprove of the way white America has treated and continues to treat its citizens of African ancestry, they stay in America for monetary reasons (Apraku, 1991).

This study documents the African immigrants' perspective of the international migratory process and reveals how they define, interpret, and negotiate the contours of cultural identity in an American society that is characterized by diversity and plurality. The study delineates the factors that spur international migration from Africa and examines the settlement patterns of African immigrants in the United States. In addition, the forces that influence the relationships that the immigrants form with the host society and the relationships that they form with other members of the African diaspora will be examined. Further, the study explores the social and legal processes involved in the transformation from African immigrant cultural identity to American citizenship.

The study also focuses on the social and psychological aspects of the immigrants' experiences in the United States, how they cope with interethnic conflicts, racial animosities, cultural denigration, and economic marginality. Portraits of immigrant family structure, labor force and economic participation, social networks, and community organizations are also presented. In addition, the way the immigrants construct patterns of gender and sex roles, including socialization and child-rearing practices, will be elucidated. The social and cultural intricacies involved in how second-generation immigrant children define their cultural and ethnic identities are examined within the nexus of race and ethnic relations in the United

States. Intergenerational schisms among immigrant families and the social and cultural continuities that undergird these conflicts are highlighted.

This study will be appreciated by researchers working in the areas of African and African-American studies as well as by students of race and ethnic relations more generally and by those who seek to understand the global dimensions of the continuing African diaspora. There are also broader lessons of the human spirit. It is the convergence of ideas and the collective will of the guest and the host to sustain each other that sometimes define the cooperative character and the commonalities of the human spirit. In this regard, the immigrant experience may reveal as much about the host culture as about the cultures of the immigrants.

The growing presence of African immigrants in the United States provides yet another opportunity to learn about the peoples and cultures of Africa. Although the number of Americans who visit the African continent is increasing, most Americans are more apt to learn about African cultures and peoples as a result of the growing visibility of African immigrant communities in the United States. In the nation's capital, in New York City, and in other major urban centers across the country, African immigrants are defining their cultural identities and presence. African immigrant restaurants and businesses are being formed. African professionals are working in various capacities in America. Whether African immigrants are working as merchants in New York City, professors at major institutions of higher learning, or taxi drivers in Minneapolis–St. Paul, the documentation and profiling of their collective and individual experiences provide further enrichment and enlargement of the American quilt. Their presence provides us with the opportunity to highlight the peoples and cultures of Africa. The knowledge gained by an understanding of the experiences of African immigrants in the United States can help to erase the doubts and apprehensions that Americans in general may have about Africa and possibly open up avenues for better relations between the peoples and governments of the United States and Africa.

The mass migration of skilled workers out of Africa to the developed economies of the world is at a crisis stage. From 1960 to 1989, an estimated seventy thousand to one hundred thousand highly skilled Africans left the continent to settle in Europe and the United States (Gordon, 1998: 86). African governments do not have the database to provide them with information on the extent of the brain drain. More importantly, these governments have yet to assess the deleterious impact of this drain on their social, economic, and cultural development. Consequently, there are no policies in place to stem this tide. Secondary school and university students across the African continent focus their ambitions on leaving, upon the completion of their studies, to seek economic opportunities in other parts of the world. The majority of those who are leaving the continent in search of greener pastures in the West and elsewhere are young, well-educated, skilled professionals, most of whom have been educated at the expense of the emerging middle-class tax-paying public. The colonial and post-colonial policies that have persistently favored urban over rural Africa in economic and industrial development schemes have left the rural areas impoverished and economically depressed. The urban bias in the distribution of economic resources is a major determinant of rural out-migration. Those living in the rural areas eventually become part of the global movement of labor from places of low economic and industrial concentration to areas of the world where wages are high and economic opportunities more abundant. Similar patterns of social and economic development have also triggered the migration of skilled and unskilled migrants from the Caribbean basin and Latin America in the new migration to the United States and Canada (Mortimer and Bryce-Laporte, 1981).

Africa's brain drain is taking place as the continent stands at the crossroads of economic development and Africans clamor for the establishment of democratic institutions and political accountability. Africa's dilemma stems from the fact that the colonial and post-colonial policies of economic, political, and cultural development have been framed from a Euro-American perspective that offers little or no relevance to the needs of the people on the continent. For instance, the rapid expansion in secondary and postsecondary education since 1945, although essential for economic and cultural development, was undertaken without any assessment of how school leavers would be incorporated into the labor market. The inability of the labor market to absorb school leavers has resulted in massive underemployment and unemployment. Unable to find jobs, both skilled and unskilled workers are compelled to search for jobs in Western countries. In Africa's current situation it is imperative for the continent to adopt measures to retain its best and brightest.

The continent faces gigantic social, economic, and political problems. For Africa, the past three centuries have been marked by deferred dreams and unmet needs. The road to economic and political stability in post-independence Africa has been a very difficult one. Problems abound in the areas of inadequate food production, destruction of the ecosystem caused by deforestation, civil strife, coups and counter-coups, dictatorships, and political corruption. Corruption involves the whole population and operates according to vertical relations of inequality. It is deleterious to the macro-development of Africa and makes rational economic activity impossible (Chabal and Daloz, 1999).

In spite of its enormous social, economic, and political problems, Africa cannot be ignored for long, especially by the United States, for a number of reasons. Nearly thirty-three million blacks (about 13 percent of the American population) trace their ancestral origins to Africa. The cultural affinity and identification of black Americans with Africa is increasingly being strengthened through economic, social, cultural, and political contacts with the motherland as black Americans seek their historical roots. Black Americans played a role in ending apartheid in South Africa by putting pressure on United States companies to divest themselves of their economic interests in South Africa. What is more, the economic potential of Africa is immense. With an estimated population of nearly half a billion, which is growing at approximately 3 percent annually, the future economic possibilities of Africa as a potential market for American manufactured goods are enormous in light of intensified competition among the major industrialized nations for access to global markets.

## IMPACT OF U.S. IMMIGRATION LAWS ON AFRICAN IMMIGRATION

Generally, immigrants come to the United States seeking economic advancement, political freedom, and the opportunity to fulfill life-long dreams and ambitions. For past and present immigrants, the laws regarding entry to and settlement in the United States are a continuum of qualitative and quantitative restrictions. In general, U.S. immigration laws have alternated between acceptance and restriction depending upon internal public sentiments and external geopolitical considerations such as the Cold War.

The immigration of Africans to the United States has been facilitated, in part, by the 1965 Immigration Act, the 1980 changes in laws related to refugees, the 1986 Immigration Reform and Control Act (IRCA), and the 1990 Immigration Act. Beginning with the 1965 Immigration Act, the national origin and quota system for admitting immigrants has been phased out. Family reunion provisions were strengthened by the 1965 act and, above all, visas for prospective immigrants from the Western Hemisphere were limited to a preference system by which no one country in that hemisphere could have more than twenty thousand visas. The 1965 act introduced the labor certificate and occupational preference and non-preference provisions under which persons (irrespective of which hemisphere they come from) with skills considered in high demand by the U.S. Department of Labor could be issued immigrant visas. The labor certification provision required that the foreign-born applicant being considered for employment must receive remuneration and emoluments comparable to those given to others in the sector or field of employment in which the employment is being sought.

The 1965 act also made it possible for children of nonimmigrants born in the United States to file visa petitions for their parents to be legally admitted into the country. For about a decade, many pregnant women entered the country illegally and gave birth to children and later used their United States–issued birth certificates to apply for citizenship. In 1976, the 1965 Immigration Act was amended so that undocumented parents of U.S.-born children could not apply for citizenship until their children reached the age of twenty. Furthermore, in abandoning the national origins quota system, which for years had favored Northern and Western Europeans, U.S. immigration laws in 1976 made it possible for Africans to obtain visas to come to the United States to pursue education, reunite with families, or even market their skills (Jones, 1992).

One of the dominant issues in U.S. immigration policy during the 1970s was that of refugees fleeing civil wars, natural disasters, and despotic or communist regimes across the world to seek asylum and refuge in America. Notable during this time were the refugees fleeing areas of conflict in Hungary, Cuba, Southeast Asia, the Soviet Union, Africa, and the Middle East.

During the 1970s, U.S. immigration laws defined a refugee in narrow terms as someone fleeing from a country with a communist government or from the Middle East, and the admission of refugees into the United States took place outside the normal immigration mechanisms. The attorney general of the United States was granted the power to parole into the United States any person for urgent reasons or for reasons in the public interest (Section 212 [d] of the 1952 Immigration Act). In the Refugee Act of 1980, the United States changed its definition of a refugee to conform to the United Nations protocol on refugees and provided for fifty thousand visas annually for them. The act allowed the president to admit refugees in excess of the fifty thousand limit only after consultation with Congress.

Africans have benefited from the reconfiguration of U.S. policies on refugees. According to 1994 figures, 6,078 Africans were admitted to the United States as refugees. In 1995, this increased to 7,527. Data from the Immigration and Naturalization Service for 1996 showed that a total of 128,565 persons were granted refugee or asylee status. Africa's share of that total was 5,464 or 4 percent. The majority of Africa's refugees and asylum seekers are from Ethiopia, Somalia, Sudan, Eritrea, Ghana, and Liberia (U.S. Immigration and Naturalization Service, 1996: Table 6).

During the late 1970s and 1980s, illegal immigration into the United States and the large numbers of undocumented workers attracted a great deal of attention from the government, immigration interest groups, mass media, and ordinary citizens. Proposals that would make it illegal for employers to hire undocumented aliens were submitted by a cabinet committee appointed by President Jimmy Carter in March 1977, but Congress took no action. In 1981, a select commission recommended to the President that undocumented aliens who had been living in the United States be given legal status and, simultaneously, that laws affecting immigration and refugees be made more restrictive. The commission further recommended that the number of those eligible for preference visas as relatives of U.S. citizens be expanded and the number of immigrants accepted from any one country be further limited.

The IRCA was passed by Congress in 1986. Designed to slow illegal immigration from Mexico and other Central American countries, this legislation had the approval of a number of government commissions set up by Presidents Ford, Carter, and Reagan (Martin and Midgley, 1994). In response to public pressure fueled by anti-immigration fervor, particularly from California, Congress decided to reform the immigration laws. The IRCA sought to impose fines and other penalties on employers who knowingly hired undocumented aliens. The 1986 reform required employers to verify the work eligibility of prospective job applicants by checking social security cards, United States passports, driver's licenses, state-issued identification cards, or alien registration cards. Employers convicted of hiring illegal aliens would be subject to penalties including fines ranging from $250 to $10,000 and terms of imprisonment depending on the number and persistence of offenses (Bouvier and Gardner, 1986).

The immigration reforms of 1986 also made it possible for undocumented Africans then living in the United States to become permanent residents. It provided legal status through an amnesty offered to illegal aliens and workers without proper work permits. The 1986 reform led to the adjustment of the status of about two million immigrants, a majority of whom were living in the United States prior to 1982. In recognition of the possible impact of the immigration reform on the supply of agricultural workers, exceptions were granted to agricultural workers under the Replenishment Agricultural Worker (RAW) program to allow them to stay if shortages of labor occurred in the agricultural sector. An overall assessment of the 1986 immigration reform legislation reveals that it has not curbed illegal immigration into the United States. However, the legislation succeeded in its efforts to legalize the status of undocumented workers and their families (Martin, 1994).

After decades of relatively open immigration policies, public opposition to legal and illegal immigration to the United States grew. Four years after the passage of the IRCA, public discontent with immigration policies came to the fore with the passage of the 1990 Immigration Act. This act provided the opportunity for adjustment to legal status for millions of illegal aliens. The act also required employers to check proof of eligibility for employment of all prospective employees—citizens and non-citizens alike. To discourage illegal immigration, the law also imposed fines on employers who hired illegal aliens.

The 1990 act also contained two major provisions that had a significant impact on African immigration to the United States. First, the act made it possible to increase the total number of immigrants admitted on the basis of skills for employment in the United States. Second, to promote diversity among the immigrants admitted, a program was launched to increase the admission of immigrants from countries and regions of the world with a low representation of immigrants. In 1995 alone, about 37 percent of the visas under the diversity initiative program were allotted to Africa (Gordon, 1998).

The 1990 Immigration Act failed to have any significant impact on illegal immigration to the United States through the states bordering Mexico in the Southwest (California, Arizona, and Texas) and the main entry point in the Southeast (Florida). As the number of illegal immigrants has increased, so has the level of anti-immigration fervor. During the summer of 1994, the saga of the Haitian and Cuban refugees fleeing repressive regimes and crumbling economic systems in search of greater political and economic freedoms increased national awareness of the extent of public discontent with illegal immigration.

In California, the discontent with illegal immigration and the allegedly high cost of providing services to illegal aliens led to the passage of Proposition 187, which would deny state social services to children of illegal immigrants. Acting on the premise that the control of the nation's borders is a federal responsibility, Florida became the first of five states—the others being California, Arizona, Texas, and New Jersey—to sue the federal government to demand payments (about $1.5 billion) for services rendered to illegal aliens during fiscal year 1993. On December 20, 1994, a federal judge in Miami ruled that he could not force the federal government to reimburse the State of Florida, saying that he recognized "a tremendous financial burden due to the methods in which the federal government has chosen to enforce the immigration laws," but that he lacked the authority to compel the federal government to reimburse the state.

## SOURCES OF DATA AND DESCRIPTION OF STUDY

The data for this study came from three sources—the Census of the United States (1970, 1980, and 1990), Immigration and Naturalization Service (INS) data including Immigrant Tape Files (1980–1993), and a field survey of African immigrants living in four American cities—Charlotte, Washington, D.C., Atlanta, and Minneapolis–St. Paul.

The Census Bureau, in its headcount, asks questions that distinguish between native and foreign-born residents. These data are used to determine the number of foreign-born persons in the United States population. From the three censuses, I was able to obtain demographic and economic data on immigrants of African descent who have settled in the United States. In the census, migration information is obtained by asking people where they lived at a certain time. For example, the census of April 1, 1990, asked where people had lived on April 1, 1985. The census data were supplemented with the Integrated Public Use Microdata Series (IPUMS) data, which are also extracted from the census.

The IPUMS data include twenty-three high-precision samples of the American population taken from eleven censuses. They also include a series of representative samples of individuals in the United States. The samples are independent, and it is not possible to trace the individuals responding to each census over the years. The inherent advantage of the IPUMS data is that they provide information in broad areas including demographic, cultural, educational, and labor force participation characteristics. Variables selected for analysis include location, household, economic, workforce, education, place of birth or country of citizenship, and migration characteristics.

The INS data files proved helpful in identifying immigrants of African descent lawfully admitted to this country. The data provide a wealth of information on immigrant characteristics such as age, sex, marital status, country of birth, port of entry, month and year of admission, educational attainment, occupation and labor force participation, and place of residence. Other valuable demographic information in the INS data files includes class of admission (refugee, immediate relative, preference category) and countries of chargeability. Using data from multiple sources, both qualitative and quantitative, I was able to develop a rich, complex sociological description and analysis of the experiences of Africans who have settled in the United States. One of the principal objectives of this study was to compile detailed and comprehensive statistical data on immigrants of African ancestry. The goal was to gather and analyze both qualitative and quantitative information about the immigrants describing the demographic and contextual aspects of their experiences.

In addition to the data on immigrant social and demographic characteristics, data were also collected on a broad range of issues concerning immigrants' individual and collective attitudes and perceptions about their experience in this country. The instrument used included questions to assess the motivations for migration, the role of extended family members in the migratory decision-making and sponsorship process, and the micro- and macro-structural contexts surrounding the expectations and outcomes of migration. Immigrant adjustment and adaptive mechanisms upon arrival at their destinations have been emphasized, including the relationships that the immigrants form with members of the host society and with other immigrant groups. Emphasis is placed on the intricate networks of support, mutual benefit societies, and transnational ties that nurture the immigrants and provide them with psychological, cultural, and at times economic buffers against the hardships of a dramatically new culture.

Both qualitative and quantitative analyses have been used. Though the quantitative approach enabled me to examine inter-variable correlations, it was the qualitative approach that offered the most insight into the immigrants' social and cultural universe. Structured (mail or telephone interviews) and unstructured participant observer interactions with the immigrants (whether at national day celebrations or weddings) enabled me to witness social events as they occurred and to learn about the symbolic meanings surrounding these activities.

Initially my plan was to survey a representative sample of African immigrants in the United States. Contacts were made with African diplomatic missions in New York City and Washington, D.C. representing thirty-six African countries, with the goal of establishing a sampling frame from the lists of Africans registered with their countries' missions and embassies. These listings turned out to be badly out-of-date, often not updated since the 1980s. Therefore, I concentrated on four cities with sizable African immigrant communities—Atlanta, Minneapolis, the District of Columbia, and Charlotte, North Carolina.

The primary data came from a survey administered to 650 African immigrants residing in those four cities. I used a non-probability, snowball sampling approach in each of the four. Through social networking, I used channels of contact to identify potential respondents. Beginning with contacts established with African immigrant-owned businesses such as ethnic food stores, African taxi drivers in the nation's capital, ethnic restaurants, national immigrant associations (for example, the benevolent and mutual aid associations formed according to national identities), and religious organizations whose memberships were entirely African, I was able to identify areas of the four cities where the immigrants resided. From the ethnic stores, taxi drivers, and immigrant associations, I obtained flyers announcing coming social activities—wedding ceremonies, parties, ethnic festivals, national independence day celebrations, child-naming ceremonies, and funerals involving various African immigrant groups.

To gain entry into the world of the immigrants and access to potential respondents, I engaged in the social and cultural activities sponsored by various African immigrant groups. Access to the groups and their associations enabled me to obtain a listing of the memberships of various associations. Once the listings were made available, I forwarded letters to potential respondents about the study. Also, immigrant friends that I had come into contact with while attending immigrant-sponsored social events made announcements about the study on my behalf. As an immigrant from Ghana myself, I did not encounter much resistance in establishing contacts with respondents and gaining entry into their individual and collective worlds. By participating in social functions ranging from a child-naming ceremony in Atlanta to worship at all-Ghanaian churches in Georgia, Northern Virginia, and Maryland, and through the referrals made by owners of ethnic stores, I identified potential respondents.

I developed a register containing information such as the addresses and telephone numbers of the immigrants. Considering that Africans do not constitute a monolithic and culturally homogeneous group, I expanded the social network approach to target immigrants from diverse places and cultures in Africa. I sent letters to over eight hundred immigrants announcing the study, explaining its significance, and encouraging people to participate. I was overwhelmed by the enthusiastic response that I received. In all, 994 immigrants returned a slip indicating their willingness to participate in the study. From this number, I chose 650 immigrants to be interviewed and/or surveyed.

I pretested the survey instrument in Minneapolis–St. Paul. A total of thirty-five immigrants from Ethiopia, Eritrea, Ghana, and Somalia participated in the pilot test. This resulted in a number of changes in the instrument. The final interviews, by telephone, mail, and in the field, were carried out over a two-year period. The data collection processes, especially the field surveys, were approached with one principal goal in mind—to collect data on aspects of the immigrant experience not captured by the official data on immigrants, especially during the time when legal status was being adjusted for permanent residency in the United States.

Social scientists have always found negotiation of entry into the subjective and objective worlds of respondents to be a daunting task. My access to the respondents was facilitated by my own status as an African immigrant. The task of maintaining the balance between this status and the status of a researcher involved in studying the immigration experiences and the culture of fellow Africans was a difficult one. The African immigrants in my study were from different nationalities and cultures. I found myself sometimes separated by language and by a lack of knowledge and understanding of the various cultural nuances I observed at social gatherings. On a few occasions, I had to disengage myself from clusters of African immigrants who were communicating in a language unknown to me. I tried to join in the conversation by changing the medium of communication to English or to a language or dialect I knew the immigrants spoke. Often, I failed. Some immigrants would switch their medium of communication from an African language only after I disclosed my identity to everyone in the group and explained my presence. Even this did not guarantee complete acceptance and access to information. But that did not sway me from my principal goal of maintaining critical phenomenological judgment during the data collection process.

Some of the immigrants were reluctant to provide me with detailed information about their status. Immigrants do not easily divulge information about their status to strangers for fear the immigration authorities will be alerted. I, therefore, had to be "checked out." Despite statements by the respondents that, overall, they have been treated fairly by immigration officials, there seemed to be an underlying sensitivity to issues of immigration and a deep-seated mistrust of the obtrusiveness of the INS as a government agency.

Access to the homes of immigrants did not mean unlimited rights to chat informally with everyone in the household. Usually, there was a spokesperson, a male, who took it upon himself to answer all the questions. Females, teenage children, and elderly immigrants wanted to share their immigrant experiences with me, but they were restricted in what they had to say by the spokesmen. Once outside of the family environment during social activities and events, I noticed that the women were more at ease and chatted with me more freely. Questions regarding family financial decision-making, fertility behavior, expectations of women's role, and relations with American-born blacks were often considered sensitive and protected domains among the immigrants.

## ORGANIZATION OF STUDY

Structurally, my study is divided into nine chapters. Chapter 2 discusses the causes of African migration to the United States. To provide a broader context for an understanding of the process of African migration to the United States, an analysis of internal regional population mobility is included. A complex process of stepwise or chain migration is delineated. Aspects of the migratory decision-making process, the flow of information between the place of origin and intended destination, the role of education, the perceived advantages of migrating to the United States, and the problems encountered in preparing to come to the United States are presented.

Chapter 3 describes the demographic characteristics of the African immigrants. The characteristics of immigrants by age, marital status, income, and educational attainment are described. The objective is to delineate patterns of African immigration as determined by place of origin, nationality, country of birth, port of entry to the United States, class of admission status, and geographic and residential settlement pattern after entering the United States.

Chapter 4 provides a description of African refugees. The chapter highlights the experiences of one refugee family living in Minneapolis–St. Paul. It traces that family's saga from its home in Ethiopia, the political conditions leading to the displacement of population in the Horn of Africa, the settlement of some of the refugees in the United States, and the experiences of some of the refugees.

Chapter 5 focuses on the nature and content of intra-immigrant relationships and the ways in which the immigrants forge connections with the members of the host society. Immigrant relationships with other African diaspora populations are examined. The cultural connections, networks, circles of friendships, and shared bonds are highlighted. This chapter stresses the ways the immigrants maintain their unique cultural identities and the ways these cultural identities are manifested. The significance of immigrant associations in assisting the immigrants to cope with and adjust to conditions in their new, adopted country is also examined. Questions about the role of these immigrant associations in linking the immigrants to their national countries while providing the immigrants with the social, cultural, or economic anchors that they need will be addressed.

The structure of African immigrant families, kinship and household composition, educational attainment, and business formation are examined in Chapter 6. Chapter 7 examines the immigration experiences of women and children. The structure of the relationships that the women form with their husbands and among themselves is highlighted. The chapter gives voice to the gender contexts that define the individual and collective struggles of the women. Child-rearing and socialization practices, expectations of children, intergenerational conflicts, and the new generation's construction and interpretation of cultural identities will be discussed.

The pathways African immigrants follow to become American citizens are explained in Chapter 8. This chapter also examines the long-term future aspirations of the immigrants, including the contested decisions that are made about retirement and repatriation. Chapter 9 summarizes the major findings, the measures that the African countries can implement to curb the African brain drain, and the future of African emigration to the United States.

# Chapter 2

# Causes of African Migration to the United States and the Dynamics of the Post-Arrival Adjustment Process

The voluntary migration of Africans to the United States is an arduous, complex, and varied process. It is often characterized by multiple stages. Compared to other immigrants coming into the United States from Asia, Europe, or Latin America who follow a direct migratory pattern, African immigrants follow a chain or multistage transnational migratory pattern, usually leaving Africa to work in other countries for a while, saving enough money to show proof of financial security at a U.S. consulate, and then undertaking the journey to the United States. For most of the Africans currently living in the United States, the migratory process began with intra-African or rural to urban migration. For both skilled and unskilled Africans, the principal motivation behind this migratory behavior is usually to pursue education or to find employment in the urban centers of economic and cultural activities where wages are higher than in the rural areas.

The history of the African continent is rich in movements both across and within national boundaries. These movements have been promoted by trade, warfare, pastoralism, slaving, and evangelization. For example, the age-old seasonal wanderings of Fulani-speaking peoples throughout Western Africa seeking water and pasture for their livestock are legendary.

In the twentieth century, intra-African migration of labor has been characterized by movement to the centers of mineral, oil, and industrial production. The primary determinant that has driven this process is the expansion in economic and industrial activities brought about, in recent years at least, by two main factors. First, African governments have promoted private over public ownership of economic and industrial production. This has resulted in the privatization of inefficient state-owned corporations and industrial monopolies. Government-initiated liberalized tax incentives have made it possible to invest in indigenous enterprises. The promotion of private over public enterprise has increased the demand for labor in the urban centers where the majority of economic and industrial production activities are located. Second, the globalization of trade and the growing dispersion of economic activities from core to peripheral countries, from areas of high capital formation to emerging capitalist economies, has affected internal migration in Africa. In post-colonial Africa, global trade has created a demand for both skilled and unskilled labor. This demand has fueled the migration of labor to sites of economic and industrial production. Labor migration has become the principal form of capitalist penetration in Africa as a whole.

Three periods in intra-African labor mobility can be discerned. The first notable movement of labor in the twentieth century was to the Maghreb: Tunisia, Morocco, Libya, and Algeria. This movement developed in the period before 1939 and lasted until after World War II. The second stream of migration flowed toward major agricultural and industrial employment centers in Ghana, Gabon, the Ivory Coast, and Nigeria. The stream of labor to these countries started toward the end of the 1950s, at the time when many African countries were gaining their independence. With the attainment of political independence, new opportunities opened up for workers of all types to assist in economic and industrial development. A third and presently unfolding movement of labor is to the southern part of the continent, especially to the expanding economies of Botswana, Zimbabwe, Lesotho, Mozambique, Angola, and South Africa. The end of apartheid in South Africa, the war in Angola, the independence of Zimbabwe (formerly Southern Rhodesia), and the establishment of democratic political institutions have ushered in a period of relative economic prosperity in the entire region of Southern Africa. Buoyed by their booming economies, South Africa and Zimbabwe have become preferred destinations for skilled Ghanaians, Nigerians, and Liberians. In addition, there is a movement of skilled and unskilled workers from the mid-section of the continent (Rwanda, Burundi, and the Congo) to Southern Africa.

In each phase of intra-African labor movement, the motivation to migrate has been determined by national and international labor policies that have encouraged the recruitment of cheap labor from places with a large pool of unskilled labor to areas of labor shortage. The forces that have shaped the nature of intra-African migration have been examined by several researchers (Todaro, 1969; Arthur, 1991; Mabogunje, 1970; Amin, 1974a, 1974b; Zachariah and Conde, 1981; Todaro and Stilkind, 1981). These authors have called attention to the inequality in the distribution of economic development projects between capital cities and rural areas; the higher wages migrants earn in the urban centers compared to the rural areas; and the development of urban systems in Africa. Before and after independence in 1957 from Great Britain, Ghana experienced an influx of labor from Nigeria, Togo, Chad, Liberia, Mali, and Burkina Faso. Migrants came to Ghana to work in the cocoa industry and the gold and bauxite mines. Most of the migrants were absorbed into the local culture and were more or less considered citizens. However, in 1969, Prime Minister Kofi Abrefa Busia issued the Aliens Compliance Order, which expelled all the immigrants from Ghana. Hardest hit by the expulsion order were Nigerians, most of whom had lived in the country for decades.

Since the 1950s and 1960s, the temporary or permanent movement of labor across Africa's borders has intensified. The discovery of oil and the expansion of economic and industrial activities in Nigeria triggered a wave of migration to that country. Workers from Ghana, Togo, and Benin flocked to oil-rich Nigeria during the 1970s and early 1980s. The subsequent expulsion of the majority of these workers by the Nigerian government triggered an international crisis because of the massive numbers of displaced immigrants who had to be returned to their homes. Unable to accommodate over one million Ghanaians, as well as nationals of Benin and Togo, Nigeria decided in 1983 to expel all the foreign migrant workers, giving them fourteen days to leave. The misery caused by the expulsion led to reactions from the international community. The United States and Great Britain described the expulsion as a violation of every imaginable human right. The government of Ghana saw the expulsion as a retaliation by the Lagos regime for the earlier expulsion of Nigerians from Ghana.

Historically, the peoples of Africa have moved freely with little or no regard for international barriers. This was certainly the case before European colonization and political aggrandizement. The 1885 Treaty of Berlin and the scramble for Africa by the Western powers led to the arbitrary establishment of colonial boundaries by the European colonizers. The creation of the colonial states was intended to serve the political and economic interests of Europe. Little or no regard was given to African ethnic and cultural configurations in the drawing of boundaries. This utter disregard for Africans and their political institutions by Europeans has been one of the major causes of ethnic conflicts and tensions in the region today.

In the post-independence era, intra African migration became restricted as each country attempted to formulate policies designed to preserve jobs for its own citizens, especially during periods of economic stagnation and political instability. With the formation of regional and continental multilateral economic unions (for instance, the Economic Commission of West African States and the East African Economic Bloc), the barriers to the free movement of people, goods, and services have been lowered. But on the whole, such multilateral economic organizations have failed to develop sustained economic, industrial, and cultural development programs to improve the lives of Africans. The result is that many of Africa's young and better educated people are forced to look beyond the continent to fulfill their economic aspirations. In addition, political civilities have eroded. Political terror has resulted in hundreds of thousands of Africans having to flee. Internal conditions, primarily economic and political, have been driving people out of Africa to all corners of the world (Apraku, 1991).

Aside from the slaves who left from Goree Island and other slave shipping points along the Atlantic coast for the Middle Passage, few Africans left the continent before the middle of the twentieth century. Historically, African immigrants to the Western world targeted those European countries that had colonized Africa during the nineteenth and early twentieth centuries, especially Britain and France. Following the end of World War II in 1945, things began to change. In the middle and late twentieth century, the sustained voluntary migration of Africans has been to the United States.

## REASONS FOR COMING TO THE UNITED STATES

The African immigrants who were surveyed cited four main reasons for coming to the United States. These are the desire to pursue postsecondary education, to reunite with family members, to take advantage of economic opportunities, and, finally, to escape from political terror and instability.

For the majority of African immigrants living in the United States, the first cultural contact with America is through the education system. Education is the cultural capital that most African immigrants bring with them to the United States. Educationally, three streams of Africans are coming to the United States. The first stream includes those who have completed tertiary education at the university, technical, or teacher-training levels prior to their arrival in the United States. Those arriving with postsecondary education tend to pursue graduate level education. The next group consists of those who have completed advanced secondary school education (General Certificate of Education, Advanced Level) in Africa. Once in the United States, the majority of these immigrants tend to pursue vocational-technical education in professional and non-professional studies leading to the award of an associate's degree. Both of these streams of Africans see education as the proven path to high social mobility. For those specializing in the sciences and in business, a graduate degree opens the possibility for professional careers with fringe benefits. The third stream of Africans coming to the United States to pursue educational goals consists of those without a secondary school diploma. Though education features prominently in their career goals, the problems they encounter upon arrival are varied and difficult to surmount. The problems include inadequate finances, lack of language proficiency, and lack of support from institutions of learning. According to the survey data, the majority of this group of Africans (over 83 percent of them) who come to this country to further their education drop out of school, lose their student visa status, and join the ranks of day laborers in the urban immigrant underground labor economy.

For the majority of the immigrants who pursue higher education, the desire to do so can be traced to the importance that African families attach to education and also to the European colonial stress on meritocracy and credentials as prerequisites for access to civil service jobs. Particularly for rural African youths, the completion of primary school education provides the impetus to leave the rural areas to seek wage employment in the urban sector. It increases the possibility of being sponsored by the family to leave for urban areas to pursue further education. This opportunity enhances the prospects of engaging in international migration.

Following in the tradition of their European colonizers, upon attaining political independence, various African countries embarked upon educational programs to raise the literacy level of their citizens. Primary and secondary schools proliferated. In addition, technical and teacher-training institutions and universities were set up. African institutions of higher learning have focused mainly on bachelor's level education with only a few institutions providing postgraduate opportunities. For those desiring to pursue higher education, the United States, Canada, and England are the preferred destinations.

The survey data show that nearly 86 percent of the African immigrants who participated in this study had completed a high school education before coming to America. Of this number, 60 percent had completed university or some postsecondary education and came to the United States to further their education at various institutions of higher learning. The majority of African immigrants currently living in the United States entered the country with student visas (a nonimmigrant status), completed their education, and then overstayed their visas.

Family reunification was another reason mentioned by African immigrants for coming to the United States. Nearly 40 percent indicated that they came to the United States to reunite with family members. Under current U.S. immigration laws, naturalized citizens and permanent residents are permitted to submit visa applications for their immediate relatives for the purpose of family reunification. The study revealed that many African immigrants sponsor relatives to come to the United States to pursue advanced education. Approximately one-third of the respondents indicated that relatives had sponsored them to come.

Family members in the United States usually sponsor relatives from Africa who have good prospects of pursuing advanced education at the postgraduate professional level. This means that at a minimum, family members require that prospective candidates for sponsorship must have a secondary school education. Prospects for sponsorship are brighter for those who have completed postsecondary education. It is expected that those who are sponsored will later assist other extended family members. Within the African extended family system, migration for the purpose of pursuing educational goals, especially in the United States, is considered rational behavior, an investment in the family's human capital with the expected result of increasing net family earnings. Families are likely to sponsor family members to go to destinations that will bring the maximum financial benefit. The expectations placed on the migrants by extended relatives are, thus, very high. The migratory experience is not only for the benefit of the individual migrant; it has a collective importance for the migrant's extended family as well. This increases the pressure on the migrant to succeed financially and, if possible, send money home, assist relatives with the capital to operate a small business, or sponsor younger family members to come to the United States.

It has been shown that Africans emigrate to the United States to pursue higher education and to reunite with their relatives. In addition, economic factors feature prominently. Africans leave their home countries because they are "pushed" out by poor, deteriorating economic conditions. They are "pulled" to the United States because of the economic opportunities available in this country (Lee, 1966). Africans come to the United States to improve their standard of living and to enhance their human capital potential. Like other immigrants, Africans select destinations where the expected net benefit of migration will be greatest. Migration is, therefore, viewed as a cost-benefit calculation, a personal investment that will be made only if the returns are justified (Borjas, 1989). The expected gains to be derived from the place of destination are culturally perceived and defined within the constraints of such factors as social, cultural, and psychological costs of migration, level of existing information about the intended place of residence, access to labor markets, and presence or absence of kin group members who have successfully undertaken the journey. The economic motivation for African migration to the United States is based on the neoclassical paradigm of utility-maximization. In this perspective, migration from developing to developed countries is seen as human capital investment. Migration also stems from the over-dependence of developing countries on institutions of higher education in the developed countries to provide advanced education for their best students. According to Ong, Cheng, and Evans (1992), the students sent abroad from developing nations to be educated in developed countries, upon graduation, become part of the international labor market, seeking jobs in the advanced economies.

The immigrants also provided information about the economic conditions in Africa spurring their migration to America and other Western countries. Deteriorating economic conditions, crumbling infrastructure, poor sanitation, lack of housing, and lack of quality healthcare impose constraints upon Africans seeking a better life for themselves and their families. Agricultural stagnation and deforestation, coupled with drought, have led to a dwindling of food production in Sub-Saharan Africa. The acreage under agricultural production is shrinking due to vagaries of weather, aging farmers, falling world commodity prices, lack of agricultural machinery, and poor marketing and distribution systems. The result is that farmers cultivate only for subsistence, growing enough to feed themselves and their families.

Africa's economic dependency on Western capital, coupled with pressures from international donor countries for structural adjustments as a precondition for aid, has restricted economic and industrial development. The direct result of this is capital inefficiency, economic policy decisions devoid of pragmatism, and, above all, cultural and political patrimonialism, often a principal source of corruption. The beneficiaries of the resulting disorder and precarious conditions have been Africa's rulers, who enrich themselves at the expense of their citizens and use their ill-gotten wealth to consolidate their power and wage political terror. The devolution of political institutions and the insidious process of governmental legitimation of violence as a means of conflict resolution is manifested in fear and insecurity, which ultimately drive the internal and international migration of people to safe havens.

Models of colonial economic development are also a major factor in the migration of Africans to the United States and other industrialized nations. During the colonial period, most of the colonized countries specialized in the production of raw materials to feed the factories of Europe and America. Local processing of raw materials was not stressed by the colonialists. This model of economic development led to the impoverishment of countries that are well endowed with natural resources. Even when the colonialists established local companies to process raw materials into finished or semi-finished goods, the goal was still to feed the industries of the West. The few industries that were established in Africa were located in the urban areas. The rural areas that produced the bulk of the raw materials were left out of the economic process. Economic and cyclical fluctuations in the rural economies, coupled with the deterioration in rural living, triggered out-migration to the urban centers. Uneven economic development between rural and urban economies is a major factor in both internal and international migration.

The patterns of rural-to-urban migration in Africa are inexorably linked to the international migration of Africans to Western Europe and North America. The results of the survey show that internal migration in Africa is a strong correlate of African migration to the United States. The journey to national and international urban centers inside and outside Africa initiates the migrants into the culture of migration. For many young Africans, expectations of moving to the United States are high. Such expectations have even become part of adolescent culture.

The perceptions that inhabitants of emerging countries associate with life in the United States and other Western nations are also a determinant of migration. When they visit home, African immigrants living in the United States and other European countries talk about a different kind of world from that of Africa. Africans and other citizens of developing regions view the United States as the land of immense economic opportunity, liberty, and freedom. This has created a "going abroad to the United States" syndrome in all levels of African society, particularly among youths, urbanites, and educated people. The vision of life created by returnees is that of an America where it is possible to survive on minimum wages and where the monthly minimum wage is more than the average African worker makes in a year. The chance to experience the culture of economic materialism in America is a compelling force motivating some Africans to undertake the journey to the United States.

The principal beneficiaries of this migration and the brain drain of Africa's talents are professionals and those with postsecondary education or marketable skills. The stark reality is that the labor markets and economies of Africa have not been able to expand to absorb and sustain college graduates in gainful employment. The result is massive underemployment and unemployment among graduates and professionals. Secondary school and university graduates are, therefore, forced to look for better economic opportunities overseas. A class has emerged whose needs are yet to be met at home. Education has created hopes and aspirations, opening up vistas of economic and cultural opportunities, the fulfillment of which Africans pursue vigorously in the West because blocked economic and industrial development prevents the achievement of even moderate increases in the standard of living at home.

Research on African emigration to Great Britain and North America shows that some African countries, Ghana and Nigeria particularly, have become major exporters of educated people and trained artisans to other countries. The exodus of educated Ghanaians has been substantial since independence in 1957. The exact number of those who have left is not known since African countries do not keep adequate data on emigration. But estimates suggest that the Canadian city of Toronto alone has over twenty thousand Ghanaians working in various professional and non-professional occupations (Peil, 1995).

The African brain drain to the West, as indicated earlier, takes the form of a migration in stages, which first takes the migrant to another African country or to destinations where it is relatively easy to obtain papers and where work is plentiful. The first stage of the migration process becomes part of a broader strategy aimed at improving one's standard of living in a given destination. Potential immigrants first travel to Saudi Arabia, Libya, Kuwait, Malaysia, Singapore, Brazil, the Caribbean, and

Eastern Europe. After finding work and saving some money, the migrants then apply for admission to a university or college in the United States, pay their tuition for one academic year, and place sufficient funds in their bank accounts to qualify for a student visa.

For the majority of Africans who arrive in the United States to pursue educational goals, fields of study are carefully chosen to reflect areas of the U.S. labor market in need of qualified workers. There is little emphasis on the arts and humanities. Business administration and the sciences, especially computer science, engineering, and medicine, are preferred choices of study. Even those who arrive from Africa with baccalaureate degrees in the social sciences and the arts often switch to graduate programs in business administration, law, and computer science.

Prospective immigrants' perceptions of the place of destination becomes crucial in determining which town or city to choose. Perceptions of the intended place of destination are articulated within informal social networks of friends and relatives and also are dependent on access to information. The potential to earn higher wages in the United States compared to the wages received in Africa serves as a "pull" factor that attracts immigrants. Prospective immigrants are confident that no matter what the unemployment rate or existing immigration laws restricting employment of nonimmigrant visa holders, they will find employment, even if it is illegal, because the menial jobs most Americans will not perform are becoming more plentiful every year.

The past and present political climate in Africa has been a major determinant of the decision to leave. The political landscape of Africa is dominated by war, civil strife, and social fragmentation. Persisting political conflicts in Rwanda, the Congo, Liberia, Somalia, Sierra Leone, Sudan, Burundi, and Nigeria illustrate the political fragility in the region. Those who can escape seek political asylum as refugees. But considering the number of trouble spots in Africa and the sheer numbers of people who are displaced, very few are able to come to the United States to be resettled. Cuban, Chinese, Eastern European, and Soviet political refugees have been received with open arms, unlike refugees of African ancestry fleeing political terror in Haiti or Africa. The number of Africans who are granted political asylum or given refugee status is minuscule. Those who came to the United States to seek political asylum or refugee status form less than 2 percent of the survey respondents. The majority of these are from a handful of countries: Ethiopia, Somalia, Eritrea, Liberia, Ghana, Sierra Leone, and Nigeria.

Political instability and the violent victimization of political foes are major causes of emigration among Africa's elite. One-third of the Africans who participated in this study indicated that they know of Africans who have come to this country within the last five years because of political violence. Other respondents mentioned relatives or friends who have fled to other countries as a result of the destabilizing effects of war, civil unrest, genocide, and dictatorship.

The worsening political conditions have not made life any easier for most Africans. With the exception of a handful (notably the Ivory Coast, Gabon, Botswana, Zimbabwe, Cameroon, and Senegal), African countries are mired in political degeneration as democratic institutions are replaced by despotic, tyrannical, and kleptomaniac regimes that have no respect for human rights or the political and economic well-being of their citizens. The ascendancy of the military as an alternative to civilian rule has been a total failure. Military governments have increased the continent's social, cultural, political, and economic woes. Due to their ineptness, both military and civilian regimes have been unable to generate new ideas or mobilize their citizens for national integration and development. When attempts have been made to reform social and political organizations, the results have been dismal. Ghana and Nigeria are examples. Under civilian and military regimes in the two countries, various land tenure reforms have been announced. The goal is to minimize absentee ownership and give farmers, the backbone of the economies of the two countries, access to land to maximize production. But the impact of these reforms on agricultural production has been minimal at best. The result is the depression of the rural economies and the mass rural-to-urban movement of young men and women in search of competitive and diminishing economic opportunities.

As indicated earlier, African immigration to the United States has also been influenced by changes in United States immigration laws. Changes in 1965 abolished the national quota system that had restricted the number of citizens from each country who could immigrate to the United States. The new law allowed up to 120,000 immigrants to be admitted legally into the country every year. This law made it relatively easier for immigrants with legal status to sponsor their immediate relatives. In addition, legislative changes made in the 1986 IRCA accorded many Africans already in the United States an opportunity to adjust their status to that of legal residents, making them eligible after five years to become citizens and, hence, affording them the opportunity to sponsor relatives to come to America. According to Joseph Takougang, the Immigration Reform and Control Act resulted in the addition of more than 39,006 Africans to the immigrant population in the United States between 1989 and 1992. This figure excludes those Africans who are married to American citizens and those who acquired permanent residency before 1986, using other provisions in immigration law (Takougang, 1995).

## CONSTRAINING FACTORS AND PREPARATIONS MADE BEFORE LEAVING AFRICA

The process involved in undertaking international migration is a long and arduous one. Cultural, physical, economic, and structural factors inhibit or facilitate the predeparture process. Certain factors influence the decision to go or stay. These may include coping with the temporary separation from family, language barriers, and the financial cost of the travel. Exit permits (in the case of some countries), passport and immigration requirements, and health certification and criminal background checks are only a few of the internal and external requirements that may present problems to the prospective traveler. These requirements serve to pre-select prospective travelers at the points of origin.

A potentially constraining factor encountered by prospective immigrants from Africa is securing a passport. As social, political, and economic conditions have deteriorated in Africa, it has become imperative to have a passport because the political and social environment can become chaotic at any time. One has to be ready to flee to another country, legally or illegally.

The process of applying for and obtaining a passport is rife with corruption, cronyism, and abuse by government officials and self-appointed passport brokers who charge exorbitant fees. For passport seekers who are poor and who do not have any connections in the Ministry of Foreign Affairs or the central Passport Office, the process is even more frustrating and cumbersome. African governments use the passport as a tool of political control. Passport applicants are often subjected to the whims of officials at passport offices because there is no administrative accountability.

Throughout his reign as head of the military government in Ghana, General Ignatius Kutu Acheampong made it very difficult for professionals and students who were embroiled in political conflict with the government to obtain passports and travel documents. Sometimes, obtaining the forms entailed enormous financial costs, and prospective applicants might well end up offering bribes. In the same country, the government also levied taxes on applicants for passports. The government claimed that the tax was meant to defray the cost of the repatriation of Ghanaian citizens abroad should they be deported. But the general public perception was that this tax was another scheme designed by the government to restrict the number of people who were issued passports. Payment of this levy, however, is a small price for the chance of leaving the country. In short, the long-term payoff outweighs the initial investment.

For those who reside in the rural areas, additional financial costs can be incurred in traveling long distances to the capital city to file the passport application. In Ghana, regional administrative centers do accept passport forms from applicants for transmission to the capital city of Accra for processing. But most people prefer to bypass their regional passport office and travel to the Accra office where at least they can be sure that the forms have been received. Processing is another problem, involving multiple trips to the city to check the status of the application. An underground economy of passport brokers has become a thriving enterprise. For exorbitant fees, these brokers collect and file applications at the passport office and act as intermediaries between the office and the applicant.

For those who are fortunate enough to receive their passports, the pressure to leave begins to mount. Among Ghanaians, this pressure is dealt with by embarking on a trip to Togo, the Ivory Coast, Liberia, Libya, or Nigeria in search of a temporary or permanent job. This marks the first stage in a long and arduous process of making it to the West (mainly the United States, Great Britain, and Canada) and to distant places in Asia.

In an African social and political culture where documents can be manufactured at will, not all potential travelers have to subject themselves to administrative ineptitude and become caught up in the bureaucratic thickets. Passport and custom controls involving intra-African travel are fraught with corruption. Underpaid, overworked, and poorly trained, immigration and customs officials have also become victims of Africa's economic paralysis. To survive economically, they are compelled to demand bribes from businessmen and women who travel across national boundaries transporting essential commodities and provisions for sale at high profit margins. For those travelers who are willing to pay their way, it is easier to cross national borders and establish residency in other countries with or without a passport or visa. Upon reaching their destination, it is also possible for them to use the large-scale underground documents industry in Africa's big cities to gain access to birth certificates, which can then be used to apply for passports. Once a passport is obtained, the link to the international community is established.

Worthy of mention in obtaining a visa is the role of the unofficial middlemen, the visa brokers. For a fee, sometimes more than six months' wages, they provide prospective visa applicants with the necessary forms. Although the visa forms are free, not everyone has the time to wait in line from dawn for the American consulate to open. Visa brokers are willing to assume this responsibility. They also coach prospective visa applicants on how to fill out the forms and what to expect from consular officers.

Two other factors facilitate the preparatory process when leaving Africa to come to the United States. The first is the presence of relatives or friends there. Prospective immigrants choose destinations in the United States where relatives and friends are already settled. The majority of the immigrants who participated in the survey settled in such places. Having a network of relatives and friends living at the intended place of settlement eases the post-arrival anxieties of the newcomers and facilitates their transition into the host society.

A second factor facilitating the preparatory process involved in migratory decision-making is access to a flow of information from America. Although other channels of information flow from the United States to Africa and vice versa, most prospective immigrants prefer to rely on information provided by relatives. Fewer than 15 percent of the survey respondents obtained information about their intended place of destination from the U.S. Information Services or from the local library. Another 27 percent corresponded directly with their intended college or university of study without a relative or a friend serving as an intermediary. Included in this group are those who have already completed college or university training or at least completed the General Certificate of Education at the Advanced Level. But generally, relatives and friends act as sources of information about prospective colleges and universities, request and pay for application fees, and register the prospective migrant for the Scholastic Aptitude Test and the Test of English as a Foreign Language.

Relatives and friends also assist the prospective immigrant to qualify for a visa. They may be called upon to deposit money in a bank and then obtain a statement of the financial status of the visa applicant. Sometimes, they prepay the tuition for a semester at the intended institution of learning. They may also furnish the American consulate in the home country with a copy of a W-2 form showing income earned or a copy of an income tax statement. The purpose is to convince the consulate that sufficient funds are available to support the applicant. The process of qualifying for the visa can take weeks, if not months. Evidence suggests that some relatives or friends who cannot meet the stringent financial requirements for obtaining a visa from an American consulate will combine resources, deposit money in a single account, and use that as proof that the applicant will not become a public responsibility or charge. Usually after the visa is granted, the money is given back to the individual contributors.

For those who do not take the educational route to secure access to the West, employment in those African countries with currencies that are convertible to the U.S. dollar or the British pound is the preferred route. This factor explains, in part, the stream of Ghanaians who flocked to Nigeria to work in various capacities at the height of the oil boom in that country, as that country's currency, the naira, achieved parity with and even surpassed the U.S. dollar in value during the 1980s. Money saved is converted to dollars and later used as evidence of financial support in the visa application process for entry into the United States.

To improve upon the chance of obtaining a visa for the United States, prospective nonimmigrants may apply for a tourist visa to travel to a country whose application process is not too stringent. Once the visa is approved, a brief visit to the issuing country is undertaken. A formal visa application is then filed with the U.S. consulate. Some visa applicants believe that their chances are enhanced if they have previously honored the visa requirements of other countries. The cost of this strategy is prohibitive. But most of the immigrants who have engaged in this practice justify the additional costs because it enabled them to secure their visa to enter the United States.

## POST-ARRIVAL EXPERIENCES AND THE ADJUSTMENT PROCESS

Beginning immediately upon arrival in the United States, the adjustment process is influenced by a number of factors. These include access to immigrant networks and information, the presence of relatives and friends, immigrant education, age, class, marital status, fluency in English, attitude to risk, predetermined expectations, and even luck.

The newcomers must learn the expectations of American culture if they are to survive and adapt to life in their new country. Most are fortunate enough to be socialized by immigrants who arrived earlier. Upon arriving in the United States, the immigrants settle in cities with large concentrations of African immigrant or ethnic minority populations. The settlement areas are chosen to enable the new immigrants to tap into existing networks of support and interpersonal bonds that previous immigrants have formed among themselves. The networks of support assist the newly arrived. They provide access to temporary housing, job opportunities, possibilities of self-employment, and knowledge of the city.

The networks of support available to assist newly arrived immigrants in adjusting to their new environment are crucial in easing the uncertainties that the immigrant may encounter. But equally important are the financial resources available upon arrival. The majority of those surveyed indicated that they had entered the United States with less than $300 in traveler's checks. Only 7 percent of those who participated in the study entered the United States with $300 or more at their disposal. Among this group are those immigrants who had engaged in trans-African migration or held various jobs in the oil-rich gulf states and elsewhere prior to migrating to the United States. Even when they arrive with substantial financial resources, African immigrants utilize the mutual aid or benevolent organizations that have been established.

Undocumented aliens also use these networks. The challenge posed to the immigrant networks by those arriving without proper documentation is even greater. The first challenge is to provide the undocumented alien access to the underground labor market where papers are not scrutinized. For those who arrive solely for work, this marks the beginning of an uncertain, risky, and sometimes long and frustrating process of legitimizing one's status. In addition, the lack of proper work papers renders aliens susceptible to exploitation and abuse by employers who subject them to unfair and unsafe working conditions. Usually, undocumented aliens do not complain for fear the employer will report them to the immigration authorities.

Accounts of this exploitation were heard from African immigrants who once worked in poultry processing plants and on peach farms in the central Savannah River area of Georgia and the Carolinas. Despite the denigration and harsh realities that accompanied the daily work routines of the migrant laborers, the general consensus was that compared to working conditions and wages in Africa, those in America were better. When letters are written to relatives in Africa, the saga of working in poultry processing plants and toiling in rattlesnake-infested peach farms harvesting fruits is never mentioned. A portion of the money earned, no matter how meager, is remitted home to support relatives. The newly arrived immigrants endure deplorable work conditions but at the same time remain hopeful that something better will come along. And for those who started their immigrant experience laboring in the poultry and peach industries, times have indeed changed for the better. Having acquired legal status, they put behind them the emotional, physical, and economic cost of what they had to endure to survive in the early stages of their immigrant experience in America. Many enroll in general education classes and later in vocational and technical institutions. A few are able to attend area universities and later pursue postgraduate education.

The initial months and years after arriving in the United States thus present traumatic challenges to most of the immigrants from Africa. A strong determination to succeed, coupled with an admirable work ethic, enables many of them to overcome their fears of failure. When hopes begin to dissipate and times get rough, immigrants will usually provide comfort and solace to each other. Repatriation to Africa is never an option. One immigrant who used to work on a peach farm in Edgefield County in South Carolina said: "Leaving to go back home would amount to an admission of failure, a disappointment to relatives. Better to endure in silence than pack and go home." Another immigrant faced with a similar problem retorted: "What do I have to go back to Africa for? I would simply become part of the collective suffering being endured by members of my family. I labored picking peaches here so that they can, at least, have something, no matter how small."

The adjustment process is even more difficult for those who arrive with children. While this is not the norm, a handful of women immigrants who had immigrated with their children were encountered. Two women talked about their experiences when they arrived nearly two decades ago in the United States without proper documentation. The women traveled the tri-state area of North Carolina, South Carolina, and Georgia with their children, then aged eleven and fourteen, eking out an existence picking fruits and vegetables.

Though literate, the women had not completed secondary school in Africa. The children were not enrolled in school in America. They worked alongside their mothers on the farms. Their first break in America came when an elderly woman in a nearby trailer park home offered to take care of the children while the women worked. The elderly woman enrolled the children in school, and six months later, she was able to assist the women in landing child-care jobs in an affluent suburb even though they did not have proper documentation. Good fortune came to the two women when a general amnesty for undocumented aliens was announced by the U.S. government. The two did not waste time in applying for the amnesty. With their status legalized, the two women went back to school and trained as licensed nurse practitioners. Looking back on those trying years and almost in tears, they expressed their gratitude to America for giving them the chance to dream. When I inquired how this experience had affected their lives, the older of the women said: "I cannot estimate the total impact. It's beyond me. My children are doing great. I am doing very well. I am able to assist other immigrants, even strangers. I think the spirits of my departed ancestors were present in our midst. Somehow, I think they were able to influence things and set the course of events." A last comment about this experience of accomplishments came from the second woman, whose testimony was compelling and philosophical. She said: "The experience we described changed the way I look at children today in society, especially the immigrant child. Most of them labor alongside their parents working back-breaking jobs instead of going to school. But their little spirits tell them that it is okay to labor and sow in tears and one day reap in joy."

For those African immigrants who have little education or lack legal status, labor force participation begins with employment in the menial, low-paid sectors of the economy. But over time, some of them are able to move into the mainstream using self-help, entrepreneurial innovation, and education. Their movement and incorporation into mainstream society is facilitated by strong kinship bonds and networks of economic aid.

In examining all the factors that motivate Africans to come to the United States, one thing seems certain. African immigrants come to the United States in search of opportunity and the yearning desire to fulfill unmet needs for themselves and for their families in Africa. They come with ambition, resilience, and a strong work ethic. To the majority of the African immigrants, America offers tremendous possibilities and opportunities. Assiduous and resilient, the Africans are determined to succeed in America. Once here, the network of friendship and kinship that they forge with one another enables them to carve out a niche for themselves, surmounting obstacles together and sharing in each others' triumphs and successes.

In this chapter, the economic, social, political, and legal factors that influence the emigration of Africa's young to the United States have been described. The cumbersome preparatory processes, especially the dynamics involved in the visa application process, have been highlighted. From an examination of the evidence presented, the following conclusions are offered.

First, the voluntary trans-Atlantic migration of Africans to the United States is linked to the high intra-African mobility of skilled and unskilled labor. The desire to emigrate, especially among Africa's young, is so intense that a burgeoning underground group of "experts," usually locals, operate kiosk-based businesses that profit from every aspect of the immigration process. Second, the Africans are transnationals. They come to the United States from all over the world following a complicated process of stepwise migration. Third, economic reasons and family reunification outweigh other considerations in migrating to the United States. Next, is the desire to pursue higher education. Fifth, African migrants to the United States use complex networks of information flow via family members and friends, communicating the conditions awaiting newcomers upon their arrival. Such associational networks have become an institutionalized feature of international and internal migration in Africa. They are replicated and sustained in America.

The immigrants contribute to the development of Africa and to the development of America as well. Their presence enriches the cultural fabric of American society. Hundreds serve as college professors and high school teachers. Hardly any major city in the United States exists today without its complement of African churches, language schools, and ethnic stores. The nearly five hundred thousand African nationals in the United States, led by Nigerians, Egyptians, Ethiopians, South Africans, Ghanaians, and Liberians, are unusually accomplished (African Profiles International, 1996: 14). Their remittances to Africa assist in the establishment of small businesses, provide funds for the education of family members, and enable many Africans to gain access to Western consumer items. Immigrants returning to Africa become agents of social, political, economic, and cultural change. They bring innovations, challenge old assumptions, and seek new ways to strengthen the African resolve to become truly self-sufficient and independent. Their individual and collective contributions to the development process in Africa are enormous. And the governments of Africa recognize their contributions.

# Chapter 3

# Portrait of the African Immigrants in the United States

The end of the Second World War brought political independence to many African countries. As one nation after another gained independence, Africans were fired up with vigor, optimism, and high hopes for the future. One era, foreign domination and colonization, was about to end. A new era that would put Africans in charge of their own affairs once again was about to dawn. For Africans everywhere, the attainment of political independence revived hopes that in due course, economic independence would also be realized, and Africans would once again be in control of their own destinies.

The newly independent countries embarked upon ambitious social, cultural, and economic development programs designed to improve the living standards of the majority of their people who were living in poverty and deprivation. A major component of the national reconstruction program was Africanization. This process involved harnessing the human and natural resources of Africa to solve the continent's myriad problems. It emphasized the necessity for economic self-reliance to meet the needs of an exploding population.

The East African nation of Tanzania illustrates Africa's push toward economic self-reliance and political strength. Independence from Great Britain came in 1961. But before Great Britain took over Tanzania, Germany had ruled it in accordance with the decision of the Congress of Berlin in 1885. The leader of the newly independent nation, Julius Nyerere, did not waste time; he launched an ambitious political and economic experiment in African socialism known as *ujamaa*. In what is now known as the Arusha Declaration of 1967, Nyerere declared that independence cannot be real if a nation depends upon gifts and loans from others for its development (Nyerere, 1968). The implementation of *ujamaa* led to major structural changes in Tanzanian society. The state assumed control of every aspect of economic production. The government stressed the development of agriculture in the rural areas as well as the establishment of socialist villages where nearly 90 percent of the population resided. Under the socialist village concept, farming was undertaken by groups of people who lived as a community, worked as a community, marketed their products together, and undertook the provision of local social services.

In Africa's development efforts, expatriates were to be replaced by a cadre of indigenous Africans capable of assisting in the gigantic task of nation-building. The task was an arduous one. It involved, in part, the containment of ethnic strife and the integration of minorities into the nation-state. Several countries, notably Ghana and Nigeria, embarked upon massive educational and cultural programs in which their best students and civil servants would be sponsored for education in England, the United States, Canada, Scandinavia, China, the Soviet Union, and the Eastern bloc.

The African countries used their own resources in conjunction with bilateral and multilateral international aid to sponsor thousands of students for study abroad. Hard-earned foreign reserves were expended to pay for the education of Africans abroad. The expectation was that the trained Africans would return home and contribute to the social, economic, cultural, and political development of their countries. The African governments felt that the contributions of the educated class to the continent's reconstruction effort were vital if civil and democratic societies were to be created and national unity forged. Their success in placing Africa on the road to economic prosperity would demonstrate that Africans were capable of self-government. It would demonstrate not only that Africa's quest for political and economic independence was legitimate but that Africans have the capacity and resources to become major players in the world's political and economic forums.

The hard lesson that the newly independent nations learned, less than fifteen years after most of them had gained independence, was that political self-determination did not ensure economic self-determination. The cords of political colonization had been severed only to be replaced by economic imperialism and global capitalism. The monocultural economies of the emerging nations during and after the colonial period had become overly dependent on the industrialized countries with their massive capital resources. Most, if not all, of the African nations continued in their colonial status as suppliers of agricultural raw materials and minerals to the industries of the West. Little emphasis was placed on the processing of raw materials into finished or semi-finished products for local consumption or for export. To make matters worse, economic and industrial development projects stagnated due to inadequate foreign reserves, debt, fiscal mismanagement, and political corruption. But Africa's economic woes did not prevent the Eastern and Western blocs from seeking its allegiance in matters of international politics. As the Cold War intensified, the formation of military alliances and the supply of armaments became more important to the participants in the Cold War than the bread-and-butter issues confronting Africa.

The opportunities offered by Western and Eastern countries to train Africa's future leaders must be explained within the geopolitics of containing or expanding communism. After World War II, Africa became a contested terrain in the Cold War between East and West. The formation of the Organization of African Unity (OAU) added to the political importance of Africa as a participant in the political chess game between the capitalist and socialist spheres of influence. The United States and Russia, key participants in the Cold War, pursued the loyalty of Africans in world assemblies, especially in the United Nations.

Cultural, economic, political, and military treaties and exchanges were established between the United States, Britain, China, the Soviet Union and its Eastern bloc satellites, and various African countries. The cultural component of these bilateral and multilateral pacts and exchanges made it possible for Africans to receive scholarships to study abroad in the West and the East. Non-governmental organizations from the West and East also contributed resources to train Africans to serve in various capacities. The Chinese government offered technical advisors and made capital available for Tanzania to construct its rail system. Oil-rich Angola solicited and received Cuban military and economic assistance in its fight for political and economic self-determination. Nkrumah's Ghana sought massive economic and political assistance from both the West and the East. Consequently, Africa became drawn into the East-West confrontation over economic and political ideologies.

Meanwhile, the African countries counted on their citizens, who had been granted the opportunity to study abroad, to return home and contribute to national development efforts. Initially, some of the students returned and served in various capacities. Modest socioeconomic, industrial, and cultural developments occurred, raising the living standards of some Africans, especially the urban residents and the educated class. Aspirations were renewed. Invigorated by a growing number of educated professionals and elite members, a small middle class emerged. The expectations were that, with sustained economic and industrial development, basic amenities (pipe-borne water, transportation, electricity, healthcare, and housing) would become accessible to all. It appeared that Africa was on a promising course of economic and political advancement.

But something went awry, especially in Sub-Saharan Africa. Persistent problems brought upon by political instability, corruption, economic mismanagement, coups d'état, civil unrest, and deterioration of infrastructures led to disillusionment and despair. These problems triggered the migration of the educated, the professional class, the civil servants, and those with relatives or other contacts abroad. Even unskilled workers began to cast their eyes to distant lands in search of better economic opportunities. The brain drain in Africa had commenced. Beginning more than fifty years ago, this brain drain is still evolving as thousands of Africa's best and brightest, including unskilled workers, seek economic advantages far away from home. The consequences of the brain drain have yet to be examined in detail, and policies to ameliorate the problem have yet to be put in place by African governments.

For a majority of the people of the region, forced to eke out an existence on a per capita income under $700 a year, intra-African migration and migration to the oil-fields of the Middle East and the tiger economies of Asia have become the norm. The poverty, the political corruption, and the arbitrary manner in which the Western countries had drawn up the borders of Africa during their scramble for the region ignited intra-ethnic wars and conflicts, further destabilizing fragile political institutions. Minority groups and political dissenters are frequently silenced. Africa's most vulnerable population groups—women and children—often become the victims of political terror, genocide, and ethnic cleansing. These problems are exacerbated by drought, low agricultural production, rising fertility levels, and the inability of governments to offer economic or political security.

Africa and Africans suffered and are still suffering as a result of these dislocations. International aid and World Bank assistance have yet to filter down to the common person. Usually, foreign aid has served only to redistribute wealth among the well-to-do, leaving the rural dwellers even more disillusioned and impoverished. Unable to cope, Africans are leaving their countries and engaging in legal and illegal migration, mainly to the West. The result is that the continent's most productive people are leaving in droves to search for employment in countries other than their own. They have recreated their communities and cultures in the capitals and major cities of the developed countries. The United States, Great Britain, Canada, Germany, and Australia are the major countries of destination for the African immigrants. Throughout urban Africa, the declared ambition of young men and women is to emigrate to America or to any Western country.

While there has been a substantial amount of both academic and non-academic interest in immigrants from Asia, Europe, and Latin America, there is a paucity of research on the thousands of Africans who are coming to the United States. Who are they? What are their demographic and household characteristics, countries of origin, and settlement patterns? Under what provisions of the immigration laws are they admitted for entry to this country? This chapter uses INS and census material and field inter-views of 650 African immigrants in Atlanta, Charlotte, Washington, D.C., and Minneapolis–St. Paul to present a sociological portrait of the African immigrants in the United States.

## THE AFRICAN IMMIGRANTS IN OFFICIAL IMMIGRATION FILES

Between 1950 and 1990, most of the immigrants who were legally admit-ted to the United States came from five countries—Mexico, the Philippines, China, Korea, and Vietnam. Together, these countries accounted for 85 per-cent of the total. Asia and Latin America have, thus, emerged as the princi-pal countries exporting immigrants to the United States, replacing the dominance of Western and Eastern European immigrants at the beginning of the nineteenth and early twentieth centuries.

The voluntary migration of Africans to the United States is a recent phenomenon. Compared to immigrants from other regions and countries who come to the United States to seek better economic conditions, the number of African immigrants remains small. In 1995, the Africans com-prised only 6 percent of all immigrants who were legally admitted. Be-tween 1820 and 1993, the United States admitted a total of 418,425 Africans as permanent residents. In comparison, in 1993 alone, 345,425 Asians were given permanent residency (Wynn, 1995). An analysis of the INS data for the period 1980 to 1993 reveals that a total of 249,759 African immigrants were lawfully admitted to the United States. The number of legal African immigrants admitted rose from a low of 13,981 in 1980 to a high of 24,826 in 1992, an increase of approximately 80 percent. The INS data showed that the number of legal African immigrants increased dur-ing the middle 1980s. Of the total number of 249,759 immigrants admitted between 1980 and 1993, about 6 percent (13,981) were admitted in 1980. By 1985, this number had increased to 17,117 or almost 7 percent of the total of all those admitted (U.S. Immigration and Naturalization Service, Immi-grant Tape Files, 1980–1993).

The INS collects data on immigrants who petition to become permanent residents. A considerable amount of social and demographic information can be gleaned from official immigration data about the characteristics of Africans who have been legally admitted to the United States since 1980. These people either arrived in the United States with a valid immigrant visa issued by the U.S. Department of State (new arrivals), or they were al-ready in the United States in a temporary status and adjusted to legal per-manent residence by petitioning the INS.

The INS compiles data about immigrants whose status is adjusted. In-cluded in the social and demographic information are year of legal immi-gration, port of entry, month of admission, class of admission, country of chargeability, age, country of birth, occupation, country of last permanent residence, marital status, gender, nationality, type of case (specifies whether the immigrant is a new arrival or adjustment), issuance of labor certification, nonimmigrant class of entry, city of intended residence, and zip code of intended residence. A number of these variables have been selected for analysis.

Data from the INS from 1980 to 1993 provided some information about the gender and the marital status of African immigrants. Of the 237,842 cases for whom data were available, 65 percent were married as opposed to 32 percent who were single. The rest were widowed, divorced, or separated. Male immigrants outnumbered females by 60 percent to 40 percent (U.S. Immigration and Naturalization Service, Immigrant Tape Files, 1980–1993).

Information is also available on the labor force and occupational characteristics of aliens who petition the INS for permanent residence in the United States. For aliens qualifying for immigration based on their job skills (third and sixth preference principals), "occupation" describes the employment that the prospective immigrant will perform once admitted to the United States. For all other aliens, "occupation" refers to their employment in their country of last residence or in the United States. Categories are also provided for aliens not in the labor force at the time of adjustment of status (homemakers, students, retirees, and unemployed people).

INS occupational groupings for African immigrants admitted by the immigration authorities between 1980 and 1993 show, by far, that students and children formed the largest group (12 percent of those who indicated an occupation). This was followed by housewives (11 percent), and people in service occupations (10 percent). Executives, administrators, and managers comprised slightly over 4 percent; administrative support (including clerical) workers approximately 4 percent; and operators, fabricators, and laborers another 5 percent. Immigrants working in sales or marketing formed under 3 percent. Postsecondary teachers, physicians, nurses, technologists, and technicians (except health technicians) made up 1 percent of the total. Engineers, surveyors, and mapping scientists comprised less than 2 percent, while immigrants who listed precision production, craft, and repair occupations made up 2 percent. Unemployed or retired persons comprised 13 percent. Six percent did not report any occupation.

Data on immigrants' country of birth and chargeability are also contained in the INS files. The country of chargeability—the immigrant's country of birth—is the independent country to which an immigrant entering under numerical limitations is accredited. Independent countries cannot exceed 20,000 immigrants in a fiscal year, and dependencies of independent countries cannot exceed 5,000 of the 20,000 limit. Exceptions under immigration law are permitted for family members when the limitation for the country has been met.

According to INS files, of the total number of African immigrants admitted between 1980 and 1993 (249,759), slightly over three-fourths came from nine countries. This study grouped the countries into two tiers. The first tier countries of chargeability were Egypt, Nigeria, Ethiopia, and South Africa, which accounted for over one-half (53 percent) of those admitted between 1980 and 1993. The second tier countries were Ghana, Cape Verde, Morocco, Kenya, and Liberia, accounting for about a quarter of those admitted. Approximately 60 percent of the African immigrants whose status was adjusted fell into the non-quota category, suggesting that they were not subject to numerical immigration quotas. Prospective immigrants not subject to numerical quotas are spouses, parents, children, and siblings of United States citizens, permanent resident aliens, and those with refugee or asylee status.

The majority of the African immigrants are from the former British-controlled territories of Nigeria, South Africa, Kenya, Egypt, and Ghana. Of the Africans from the former French colonies, immigrants from the Ivory Coast, Senegal, and the Democratic Republic of Congo form the dominant group. Linguistic culture is an important determinant of migrant destination.

The INS also collects data on immigrants' country of last permanent residence. The country of last permanent residence is the country in which the alien habitually resided immediately prior to entering the United States. Although the majority of the immigrants resided in Africa prior to their immigration to the United States, the INS data show that Africans are coming to the United States from all over the world. Four percent of the Africans whose statuses were adjusted for permanent residence between 1980 and 1993 came to America from the United Kingdom. This is the largest group not coming from Africa. Another 2 percent entered from Canada. Approximately 1 percent entered the United States from countries outside Africa, including France, Portugal, Latvia, India, Israel, and Saudi Arabia. Truly, this shows that the Africans are a transnational group. The survey confirmed the trans-global, multistage dimensions of African immigration to the United States (U.S. Immigration and Naturalization Service, Immigrant Tape Files, 1980–1993).

The INS data reveal that Africans enter the country through a number of ports. Seven ports of entry were used by 41 percent of the African immigrants who were admitted. Twenty percent of the immigrants entered through New York City alone. The remaining six major ports of entry were Los Angeles, Washington, D.C., Dallas, Houston, Newark, and San Francisco.

INS data also provided information about the intended place of residence of legal aliens in the United States and their distribution in the general population. Like many other immigrants, the African immigrant is a city dweller. The analysis of Africans who adjusted their status to become resident aliens between 1980 and 1993 showed the top five cities where the immigrants resided to be New York City, Los Angeles, Boston, Newark,

and Washington, D.C. The five cities with the next highest African immigrant populations were San Francisco, Atlanta, Chicago, Baltimore, and
New Orleans. Generally, immigrants choose to settle in relatively few
states and urban areas. For fiscal year 1996, the top five states of intended
residence for all immigrants were California, New York, Florida, New Jersey, and Illinois. The five leading metropolitan areas of intended residence
for all immigrants were New York City, Los Angeles–Long Beach, Miami,
Chicago, and the District of Columbia–Maryland–Virginia area.

The immigration laws under which immigrants are admitted are as varied as the immigrants to whom these laws apply. Immigrants may be admitted to the United States based on a specific immigration law. The
immigrant class of admission entitles the alien to become a permanent resident. Immigrants are admitted under a preference system that operates numerical limitations on immigration. Preferential status is determined either
by a family relationship with a U.S. citizen or by needed job skills. According to the INS, no more than twenty thousand immigrants may come from
any independent country and no more than five thousand from a dependent territory. Those who are admitted outside the numerical limitation include immediate relatives of U.S. citizens, refugees and asylees adjusting
their status, certain ministers of religion, and children born abroad to legal
permanent residents.

African immigrants are admitted as spouses, children, or parents of U.S.
citizens, permanent residents, refugees, or asylees. The largest group of Africans admitted for permanent residency were admitted as spouses, children, or parents of a U.S. citizen. Together, this group comprised 42 percent
of Africans admitted into the country. Those admitted as asylees or refugees and their dependents comprised another 15 percent. Those who entered on the basis of second preference provisions (spouses of lawful
permanent residents and their unmarried children) together formed about
8 percent of lawful admissions. Immigrants admitted in the third preference category (those with needed job skills) and their dependents made up
4 percent. Those who were admitted in the fifth preference category (brothers or sisters of U.S. citizens and their spouses) and their dependents accounted for 8 percent of those admitted.

As with other immigrant groups, family reunification is the main chan-
nel by which Africans become admitted as legal residents. During fiscal
year 1996, data from the INS showed that of the 52,889 Africans admitted,
5,153 came under family-sponsored preferences, 16,158 were admitted as
immediate relatives of U.S. citizens, and another 4,945 entered under em-
ployment-based preferences. Under the U.S. Immigration diversity program, 20,808 Africans were admitted. The number of African refugees
admitted during the same period was 5,464 (U.S. Immigration and Naturalization Service, 1996: Table 6).

Previous studies (Chiswick, 1986; Borjas, 1990; and Greenwood, 1983) have noted that the emphasis on family reunification as a basis of admission for legal permanent residency is affecting the overall quality of the immigrant cohorts admitted. Borjas (1990), for example, contends that new immigrants are less skilled than their predecessors. My study found limited support for this contention. In the case of African immigrants, the family members who are sponsored for reunification tend to have postsecondary credentials. Families tend to sponsor relatives who have the educational credentials to pursue advanced studies in the United States. The sponsorship is undertaken to improve upon the family's human capital. In the long run, those who are sponsored graduate and are able to find good employment.

## CHARACTERISTICS OF AFRICANS IN THE UNITED STATES CENSUS: 1970–1990

The 1990 census showed that a total of 363,819 Africans had been admitted to the United States. Of this number, 215,750 or 60 percent were admitted between 1980 and 1990. According to the census, four countries were the main sources of African immigrants to the United States: Nigeria (55,350 or 15 percent of all Africans admitted), Ethiopia (34,805 or 10 percent), South Africa (34,707 or 9 percent), and Ghana (20,889 or 6 percent). Together, these four countries supplied about 40 percent of the Africans admitted into the United States. In addition to these countries, there have been significant flows of Egyptians into the United States. Egypt's share of immigrants as of 1990 was 66,313, forming 18 percent of the total number of Africans who were admitted. The Egyptian presence is particularly felt in New York City. Between 1982 and 1989, of all the North African immigrants in that city, three-quarters were from Egypt (U.S. Bureau of the Census, 1990: Table 144).

Census figures also show that the Northeastern region of the United States has the highest concentration of African immigrants—123,760 or 34 percent of the total number of Africans admitted. This is followed by the Southern region (115,619 or 32 percent), and the Western region (82,902 or 23 percent). The Midwestern region of the country showed the lowest concentration, a total of 41, 538 or 11 percent (U.S. Bureau of the Census, 1990: Table 144).

Census data for 1990 also provides information about the foreign-born in the United States by their place of residence. This information can be used in identifying not only the residential or settlement patterns of Africans in the United States but also the changes in the foreign-born populations. The top eight states attracting African immigrants based on data from the 1990 Census were California (47,271 residents), New York (36,719), Texas (18,782), New Jersey (17,274), Maryland (14,029), Florida

(9,482), Virginia (8,590), and Illinois (8,380). Out of a total of 160,527 Africans in the top eight states, almost 30 percent were residents of California. New York State boasted the second largest percentage (23 percent). The African immigrants are thus concentrated in states with relatively large immigrant populations.

Since the 1960s, the nation's capital has witnessed an influx of immigrants from the African continent. Most of the immigrants in that city come from the Horn of Africa (Ethiopia, Somalia, Sudan, and Eritrea), Ghana, Liberia, Sierra Leone, South Africa, Kenya, and Nigeria. One of the primary reasons the immigrants choose to settle in the capital district is that their national embassies are located there. A second reason is the existence of a thriving community network of Afro-Caribbean immigrants who are bonded by a collective cultural experience. Religious organizations have been crucial in the establishment of African immigrant communities in the capital district. In Minneapolis–St. Paul, the Lutheran church has been pivotal in the relocation and settlement of victims of wars and natural disasters from the Horn. Aside from the Hmong from Asia, Somalis, Ethiopians, and Eritreans are the fastest-growing group of new immigrants to settle in Minnesota.

Census data also show that Africans are admitted for legal entry into the United States under various immigration categories. Of the 25,532 persons that the census reported as admitted, 10,743 or 42 percent were admitted as immediate relatives of U.S. citizens of African descent—spouses, children, and parents. Spouses and parents alone formed 87 percent of those admitted as immediate relatives. Similar findings were reported from the INS data.

Egypt, Ethiopia, Kenya, and South Africa sponsored the majority of relatives of African immigrants who were admitted. The 1965 law that established a preference order for prospective immigrants facilitated the process for Africans to become permanent residents and naturalized citizens. Under the 1965 act, immigrants gained entry into the United States under a preference system that favored close relatives of U.S. citizens and aliens with special skills. The law enabled citizens and permanent residents to sponsor their parents, unmarried children, and spouses for legal entry into the United States. As with other immigrants groups, the sponsorship of immediate relatives outside of the numerical quota restrictions added to the numbers of Africans in the United States.

As shown earlier, the passage of the IRCA by Congress in 1986 also enabled many Africans to become permanent residents of the United States. This legislation also allowed many Africans living in the United States to sponsor their spouses, children, or parents for legal residence in the United States. Between 1989 and 1993, about 2.7 million people had their status legally adjusted. Although the principal beneficiaries of the IRCA were Mexicans, the long-term impact of the reform was to dramatically increase the size of the African-born population living legally in the United States.

Census data for 1970, 1980, and 1990 provided additional information about occupational and labor force characteristics of Africans in the United States. Approximately one-third of those who were counted indicated a professional-technical occupation, 19 percent reported clerical and kindred occupations, and 12 percent were managers and officials. Seven percent were sales workers, another 9 percent were operatives, while 14 percent were in service-related occupations. When labor and occupational participation was broken down by industries, the data revealed that Africans were more likely to be working in the professional and related sectors (17 percent) and wholesale and retailing (12 percent). Compared with other immigrants in their class of work and employment status, census data show that Africans are more likely to be employed full-time and to work for someone else. Their rate of self-employment is lower than among other immigrant groups such as Asian-Americans.

The settlement patterns of the immigrants revealed by the INS data are confirmed by census data, which show that the largest proportion of African immigrants reside in major metropolitan areas such as the counties forming the Chicago and northwestern Indiana metropolitan area; the Dallas–Fort Worth and Arlington area; the District of Columbia–Maryland–Northern Virginia metropolitan area; the Philadelphia, Wilmington (Delaware), Trenton, Newark, and New York areas; Atlanta; the San Francisco–Oakland area; and the Boston region.

African immigrant settlement patterns in the United States are influenced by an immigrant's family relations in the place of intended destination, perceived economic opportunities, cultural or educational advantages, and climate. (Africans prefer warmer locations.) In addition, African immigrants choose cities and towns with racially diverse and minority populations, especially cities with a large African-American, Caribbean, and Hispanic presence.

The extent of internal migration among the immigrants is very low. The survey of African immigrants showed that only 7 percent of those surveyed had changed their residence within the past five years. For the few who do move, the movement is from relatively small towns with populations below five hundred thousand to more urban locations with population in excess of two million people. The primary reason for internal migration is the desire to pursue further education and to be closer to relatives and friends. Another motivation behind secondary migration is economic. Some of the Africans have migrated from other locations in the United States to the Minneapolis–St. Paul metropolitan area to join family members. Others moved to Minnesota to take advantage of job opportunities in food processing plants in the southern part of the state. The majority of those who moved within the past five years (56 percent) had completed a postsecondary education, usually a bachelor's or master's degree.

## RESULTS OF FIELD SURVEY

Demographic characteristics of African immigrants were also obtained from field surveys conducted in Charlotte, Atlanta, Washington, D.C., and Minneapolis–St. Paul. The survey showed that the majority of the immigrants (62 percent) had a spouse who was also from Africa. A common trend is for the men to emigrate first, secure their green card, save money, and then go home and marry or have family members find a spouse who is later sponsored to come to the United States. This practice cuts across educational and national lines. The women who come to America to unite with their spouses tend to be well-educated, most having postsecondary credentials.

A noticeable trend in family formation patterns among African immigrants is the growing number who marry American-born blacks (24 percent of the respondents). Responses from the survey revealed that African immigrant women form closer relationships with African-American women than African men do with African-American men. The African immigrants who are married to American-born spouses tend to have a higher education level than their counterparts whose spouses are from Africa. These immigrants have undertaken graduate level studies. Their family income ranges from $75,000 to $95,000 per year. They hold jobs in academe or some professional or technical occupation and easily become acculturated to middle-class American culture while remaining connected to African culture. Four percent of African immigrants responding to the survey are married to white spouses. Family income in this group is also high, almost $90,000 per year. This group's level of education is high, often including graduate or professional degrees.

A small but growing number of African immigrants marry immigrants from the Caribbean basin. Nearly 8 percent of the Africans have spouses from Trinidad and Tobago, Jamaica, the Bahamas, or Guyana. Another 2 percent were married to women from Puerto Rico, St. Thomas, or Grenada. A similar percentage had spouses from Asia, mainly South Korea and India. The African immigrants who marry outside of their national origin tend to be those who have engaged in multistage migration that took them to other parts of Africa, Asia, the Middle East, and central Europe.

In terms of age, African immigrants are young. The survey showed that approximately 25 percent of the immigrants were children under ten years old. Immigrants between 10 and 19 years old comprised 9 percent; 20 to 29 formed 18 percent, and 30 to 39 comprised another 20 percent. By far the largest number of the immigrants are in their twenties and thirties (38 percent). Those between 40 and 49 were 10 percent. Those in the age group of fifty and above were 18 percent.

The field survey results also show that African immigrants are distributed across various occupational categories. Employment in the service sector (mainly taxi driving, hospitality services, food and restaurant services, clerical services, and administrative services) is common, especially among those immigrants with less than a university or college education. This group formed about one-third of all the respondents. A majority of the immigrants employed in the service sectors indicated that they did not receive any medical, retirement, or tuition reimbursement benefits. In a few cases where employers offered health benefits, most of the respondents employed in the service sectors could not afford the insurance premiums.

Among those immigrants who hold baccalaureate degrees, employment in sales, clerical, administrative or managerial, and technical or administrative capacities is common. The professional class includes mainly teachers, college professors, accountants, chemists, social workers, and engineers. This group comprised approximately 15 percent of those who were surveyed. For immigrants with doctorates, a principal source of employment is in institutions of higher learning, especially historically black colleges and universities.

According to the survey, the percentage of immigrants employed in manufacturing and production was low, only 6 percent. Only 3 percent of the immigrants in the survey were self-employed. The majority of the self-employed specialized in the retail sale of imported African goods. Students formed 18 percent, and over 90 percent of them indicated that they worked regularly, averaging twenty-seven hours of work per week. The unemployed and those not looking for a job accounted for 6 percent of the respondents. Another 6 percent were retirees. Housewives made up 4 percent, and clergy under 1 percent.

An examination of the survey data on African immigrants in the United States shows that two institutional forces, educational attainment and family organization, have been pivotal in shaping their lives. The education the immigrants receive in their home countries, their continued education in the United States, and their strong family networks have significantly influenced their access to formal and informal labor markets. Among those who have completed professional graduate education, movement into primary and formal employment offering good pay and fringe benefits means living their American dream. Using education and their ability to speak English as their human-capital modes of incorporation into the primary labor market, these group of African immigrants have been able to obtain high-level professional jobs. Their successful economic adaptation also stems from the fact that the majority of them live in dual income households where both spouses work.

According to Speer (1995), nearly 88 percent of adults who immigrate from Africa to the United States have a high school education or higher. The national average for native-born adults is 77 percent. Only 76 percent of Asian immigrants and 46 percent of Central American immigrants are high school graduates. The average per capita income of the African immigrants is $20,000, much higher than the $16,700 for Asian immigrants, and $9,400 for Central American immigrants.

In 1990, the median family income for black Americans was $21,548, compared with almost $30,000 for African-born blacks. The African immigrants tend to be highly motivated to succeed. And America's black African immigrant population (15 percent of the foreign-born black population) form the most highly educated ethnic group in America. Three-quarters have some college education; one in four has an advanced degree ("Race in America," 1996: 27–28).

The immigrants do not all occupy a homogeneous niche in the labor force. There is a tier of African immigrants who are confined to nonprofessional, blue-collar occupations. For these immigrants, the principal modes of economic incorporation are ethnic enclave business formation or employment in the low-wage labor sector usually offering minimum or slightly higher wages without benefits. The structural constraints to their full incorporation into high-paying jobs stem from their relatively low levels of education (high school diploma or less) and language deficiencies. But the majority of these immigrants are able to develop strategies to minimize and in some cases overcome their structural limitations. Once again, using their strong family networks, these immigrants improve their family's income by using the unpaid services of matriarchs and extended family members residing in the home for services such as child care and cooking. This enables the women to find work outside of the home and contribute to household income. In some immigrant households, the strategy for increasing family income is to live in a multiple family dwelling where all the families make a financial contribution to the household budget. The majority of the immigrants with low educational attainment and poor language skills are not confined to the low end of the employment spectrum for long. To ensure further economic advancement, some African immigrant families engage in collective savings. These become the capital for the establishment of an ethnic business enterprise.

The main countries of African immigration to the United States are Nigeria, Cape Verde, Egypt, South Africa, Ghana, Liberia, Kenya, and, more recently, the Horn of Africa, including Ethiopia and Somalia. Many come to the United States to pursue postgraduate education and stay upon completion of their studies, later becoming permanent residents. Most have come to the United States since the 1970s and 1980s. Unlike other immigrant groups, their rate of acquisition of citizenship is very low. Intending to return and resettle in Africa once economic and political conditions improve, for most of them, their immigrant experience and sojourn in the United States is temporary. Finally, a majority of the African immigrants have only been in the United States during the last two decades. Those who were living in the country prior to 1982 were able to adjust their status when the Immigration Reform and Control Act was passed by Congress in 1986.

Seasoned transnational travelers who reach the United States in stepwise fashion, sometimes living in several other countries before managing to secure a visa for their ultimate destination, African immigrants in the United States are united by a collective dream to improve their lives and those of their relatives at home. Most of them are driven by a cultural orientation that stresses the importance of education, industry, and family bonding. For the majority who have used education as a means of social advancement and mobility, living standards in America are high. Among the professional class of African immigrants, employed in academe, research institutes, and business organizations, incomes and earnings have exceeded those of their African-American professional counterparts and have reached near parity with Asian-Americans. For those who do not follow an educational track, the collective use of capital and resources generated by extended family members is opening up opportunities in international retailing—the import and export marketing of goods and services catering to the growing African immigrant population in the United States, Canada, and Europe.

# Chapter 4

# From the Horn of Africa to the Northern Plains of Minnesota: The Case of the African Refugees

## EXPERIENCES OF AN ETHIOPIAN REFUGEE FAMILY

Abdullah and his family came to the United States in 1987 as refugees from Ethiopia. They fled from the terror, famine, violence, and persecution that was prevalent during the Ethiopian revolution. They first fled to the refugee camps in the Sudan. From there, members of the family went in different directions. One section of Abdullah's family found safe havens in Denmark and the Netherlands. The second group, Abdullah, his wife Habiba, four matriarchs, two patriarchs, and five children, found a safe haven in the United States.

In Ethiopia, the section of Abdullah's family that came to the United States owned and operated a successful grocery store near the capital city of Addis Ababa. Other members of the family were small-scale entrepreneurs, working in diverse areas such as baking, fish smoking, contracting, and hardware trading. The young women in the family were all "petty traders." The immediate family lived in a large house with seven rooms. Though the roof leaked during the rainy season, the house had electricity, indoor plumbing, and a living room with a television. After finishing their daily chores, Abdullah and his family retired to the living room where they watched television well into the night. For his part, Abdullah's father preferred listening to his short wave radio. Their standard of living was considered middle class by local standards. The family raised a small herd of cattle and sheep. During religious festivals, some of the animals were slaughtered, and extended family members gathered in the large compound to eat to their hearts' content.

The family was devout. Abdullah's father responded to the call for prayers every day. He went on the annual pilgrimage of Muslims to Mecca. At the end of the yearly fasting, he organized a party and invited every member of the family to his house. Abdullah's father made sure that all his children followed in the tradition of Islam.

Even though Abdullah's parents never received any formal education, they stressed the importance of education. Unlike others who discouraged the education of girls for a variety of cultural and religious reasons, Abdullah's parents did not prevent the girls in the family from becoming educated. At a minimum, the family believed that elementary education would provide the girls with better opportunities in the future. For Abdullah, there was no question that he was going to go beyond elementary education. Since Abdullah was the only son and sole heir of his parents, they made sure that his school work came first. His sisters had to help with household chores, which left little time for studying or playing. His father recruited the services of a part-time teacher to help Abdullah with difficult subjects. The teacher came to the house three times a week, and Abdullah was the sole beneficiary of the tutoring.

Abdullah entered a secondary school where he distinguished himself, and he was able to secure a place at a university. While there, he specialized in business administration with a minor concentration in accounting principles. After graduation, he was able to secure employment with the government as a cost accountant. He moved out of the family house to his own place, just a stone's throw from his father's house. By all accounts, he became successful. He bought two lorries and hired drivers to transport agricultural produce from nearby farms to the market for sale. The combined income from his civil service and transportation work was more than enough to enable Abdullah to provide for his parents and renovate the family house.

At this point in his life, Abdullah's parents began to pressure him to marry. Though he could have chosen his own bride, Abdullah deferred to his parents. The family concluded all the customary rituals for an arranged marriage. After their families had finalized the marriage arrangements, the newly married couple moved into a new house. Habiba, Abdullah's wife, had graduated from a secondary school after which she enrolled at a nearby business school to study secretarial science and office management. After her graduation, she taught typing at a private school near the capital city.

Habiba's work outside the home gave her an adequate income with which to care for herself and her parents. She took over the responsibilities of educating her younger brothers and sisters by sending them to a private school. Like Abdullah, she renovated her family home. The biggest changes to the house were the addition of indoor plumbing, electricity, and a new roof. According to Habiba, this gesture was very much appreciated by her family for several reasons. First, for the women of the household, having electricity meant that they no longer had to travel, sometimes five miles each way, to collect firewood for cooking. The same applied to the provision of pipe-borne water. The women and children no longer had to go to a public pipe-stand to fetch water for domestic use. Habiba bought a bicycle for her father. This bicycle, according to Habiba, became her father's joy. Among his peers, the bicycle gave him a new status. He rode the bicycle to visit his relatives who lived almost fifteen miles away. On his way back, he bought foodstuffs, which he carried on the back of the bicycle. Life became much better for everyone in the family. Habiba's father began to change his attitude about the education of girls. Given Habiba's success, it was possible, her father rationalized, that the other girls would follow in her footsteps if given an opportunity equal to that of the boys. He started encouraging the girls in the family to look beyond the household for ways to improve upon their quality of life.

But like many of her compatriots, Habiba found that her job was affected by the war. Safety became an issue. She cited reports of young girls disappearing, apparently abducted by rogues who demanded ransom from parents. In some instances, women were subjected to sexual abuse or taken to Kenya where they were forced into prostitution. At one point, according to Habiba, so many armed people roamed the streets that going out alone at night was unwise. Law and order had broken down. People no longer could tell who were, or were not, law enforcement personnel.

Even as the conflict intensified, Abdullah's family never imagined that they would have to flee. After all, Abdullah rationalized, the politicians would end their posturing and talk peace, and lives would be spared. Like his fellow citizens, he was also counting on the international community to broker a settlement. But the amount of fire-power that the various factions in the conflict had accumulated during the Cold War made it difficult to negotiate a settlement. Each faction felt its cause was just and victory was in sight.

The various factions committed atrocities against innocent civilians. According to Abdullah, the refugees who fled to the Sudan all told similar stories. In the refugee camps in the Sudan, Abdullah's family and the other refugees tried to rebuild their lives. Some were given employment by the Sudanese government. But for the majority of the refugees, life came to a halt. They had to depend on the Red Cross and the international community to provide food and medicine. The children and the elderly suffered the most. According to Abdullah, sanitary conditions in the refugee camps became so deplorable that some of the children became ill with cholera, diarrhea, fevers, and measles. Wailing in the dark shadows that engulfed the

refugee camps well into the night was a sure sign of death. The dawn revealed ghastly images of death overnight. The dead were buried every
morning in makeshift graves.

When news came to the Ethiopian refugees camped in the Sudan that
agreement had been reached on their resettlement in the United States and
in other Western nations, despair turned to hope. Their cramped life in the
tents was about to end. But confusion and anxiety about coming to the
United States lingered. Although at the mercy of the West and international
philanthropic organizations, including the United Nations, Abdullah and
his family had much to be grateful for. Abdullah knew that the rest of his
family was in another camp in the Sudan. They had kept in contact through
the social work volunteers who maintained a notice board in the camps for
the refugees to exchange information. Even more importantly, the notice
boards helped to ensure that family members, especially children and the
elderly, were accounted for after the hasty flight from Ethiopia to the Sudan. Abdullah's prayer was that the whole family would be given a safe haven together in the same country. But some of his relatives were resettled in
Holland and Denmark. Abdullah and the rest of the family were bound for
the United States for resettlement, they were told by refugee officials, some-
where in the American Midwest. Abdullah searched his memory to recall
his geography lessons about the northern plains. The picture that formed in
his mind was of the Great Lakes, shipping, grains, cold weather, and industrial production.

Upon the refugees' arrival in the United States, representatives of the Office of Refugee Resettlement (ORR), a division of the U.S. Department of
Health and Human Services, and private organizations welcomed them.
Funding to support the refugees for the first three years came principally
from a grant given by ORR to the states that received the refugees. Abdullah
and his family received cash advances, medical assistance, housing, English
language training, social security cards, and employment services.

For almost three years, Abdullah's family relied on services from public
and private organizations. Initially, the welfare assistance was sufficient for
the entire family. The food stamps alone provided more than enough food
for the entire family. The cash assistance even enabled members of the family to eat out occasionally. Abdullah, his father, and the one family patriarch
sometimes went out to eat and have a few drinks at the Blue Nile or the
Addis Ababa, two very popular Ethiopian restaurants in Minneapolis.
These restaurants became the point of convergence where members of the
Ethiopian diaspora gathered after work to socialize, affirm kinship and interpersonal bonds, and discuss politics and events at home. More significantly, it was at such places, according to Abdullah, that information about
job opportunities was exchanged.

To supplement the welfare assistance, Abdullah drove a taxi. For him,
this was downward mobility. But he liked his job and the income he re-

ceived. In a good week, he made about $250 working forty hours. According to Abdullah, some of his refugee friends, especially the men, had not been able to cope with the downward mobility they faced when they arrived. Some refused work that they considered beneath their educational level. Others were willing to work, according to Abdullah, but encountered administrative problems. A common problem was the nontransferability of credentials earned in Ethiopia to the United States. In Abdullah's estimation, the loss of their breadwinner status had a deleterious impact on the psychological well-being of the young men. In some refugee households, pride overcame hunger; some educated men with professional degrees from Ethiopia would not take a job in the service sector where jobs were plentiful in Minneapolis–St. Paul. But for the majority of the refugees who had once held professional positions in Ethiopia, continuous reassessment of their current conditions in America was the key to their survival in this country. The majority of them lost the power and prestige that came with their jobs in Ethiopia. But the loss of status was compensated for by the existence of strong kinship bonds. With time, they expected to regain social mobility, no matter the type of employment they were currently engaged in. Their downward mobility has been mitigated over time by the establishment of a strong ethnic community and a realistic assessment of the realities of labor market conditions in the United States. The presence of a strong refugee community can favorably influence the adjustment of its members by providing a comparison referent that will not diminish their sense of self-worth (Rogg, 1971; Portes, McLeod and Parker, 1978). For now, what is to be cherished, according to Abdullah, is the fact that economically, their lives are better in America; they are not starving. Politically, they remain free of the devastating impact of war and terror.

According to Abdullah, the psychological effects of the downward mobility experienced by some of the Ethiopian men are so grave that their situation has resulted in alcoholism and domestic violence. This, according to Abdullah, is more prevalent among the men who have tenaciously held on to their patriarchal beliefs that husbands and fathers must be the breadwinners. In some refugee households where the women are working and sometimes earning more money than their husbands, Abdullah believes that violence is especially prevalent. Most husbands who engage in wife-beating are not reported to the authorities. Family and clan elders intervene, often mediating in the dispute and offering counseling to the affected family.

To improve the economic fortunes of his family, Abdullah attended English language classes. He also took courses at a local college. His wife was able to find employment with a food processing establishment where she earns almost $7 per hour.

Initially, as mentioned earlier, the family was on welfare. To Abdullah and his family, welfare was humiliating. His family welcomed the initial assistance they received from social service agencies. But over time, the money they were receiving was reduced significantly while the amount of paper work increased. At that moment Abdullah and his wife decided to chart a different economic course. With both Abdullah and his wife's parents living at home with them and taking care of the children, Abdullah and his wife took second jobs. The family saved the income from the second jobs for a down payment on a house. They were also able to send their children to a private school. A long-term goal was to save enough money to start a business catering to the Ethiopian community. A short-term goal was to save enough money to sponsor Abdullah's sister-in-law to come to the United States.

Abdullah and his family expressed their profound gratitude to several charitable organizations and religious institutions, notably Lutheran Social Services and the Catholic Relief Organization, for the assistance they gave to all the refugee families. Upon hearing a local news account about the frustration that social service agencies in the city were encountering in delivering services to Ethiopian and Somali refugees, Abdullah and his wife became volunteers for a local chapter of the Meals on Wheels program. Abdullah's wife spends four hours a week assisting older refugee women with their banking transactions; she also accompanies them to the hospital where she serves as an interpreter.

In Abdullah's household, the dynamics of the gender role relationship have changed significantly. In Ethiopia, Abdullah never performed household chores. Patriarchal dominance of women is part of the fabric of Ethiopian society. Male clan elders make decisions that affect the lives of women. In Minnesota, things are different. Abdullah's relationship with his wife has become more egalitarian. Decisions affecting the household are made collectively with the other adults. In Abdullah's view, collective decision-making is the only way that his family can attain economic sufficiency and improve the living standard of its members. He decries the patriarchal domination of women in Ethiopian society and the structures that support the relegation of women to second-class status as inimical to economic development. This attitudinal change came about because of his encounter with American society.

Despite the progress they have made in Minnesota, the toll of the war is still fresh in Abdullah's mind. The economic cost is incalculable. Like many refugee families from Ethiopia who have now settled in Minnesota, Abdullah's family lost the modest assets they had acquired. The refugees had to leave with only the clothes on their backs, and most of them entered the United States with no money at all. Abdullah's wife recounted stories of the rape and brutalization of young women by Sudanese law enforcement personnel. Her sister was raped and killed by Sudanese army personnel. Some of the refugee women who were working as domestic servants for Sudanese families were raped by their male employers (Kebbede, 1992). Many of Abdullah's friends never made it to safety. People were ambushed and robbed as they attempted to flee. Relatives were killed or left behind. Fortunately, Abdullah has been able to sponsor some of his relatives to join him in the United States.

The family members who have been reunited with the rest of the family in Minnesota are not as well-educated as those who came in the first wave. The second wave of Ethiopian refugees tends to be from the rural areas, to be uneducated, and to have no understanding of English. According to Abdullah, the first group of family members who came with him were educated, professional, and considered middle class by Ethiopian standards. The first and second waves of refugees have both experienced culture shock. But in Abdullah's estimation, the first wave of refugee families has fared better than those who arrived later. Coming from the rural areas of Ethiopia, the members of the second wave have never been to school, are in poor health, and lived in homes without indoor plumbing. For those in poor health, the refugee experience is even more frightening. Area health service agencies have recruited interpreters and multi-lingual personnel to assist in the delivery of medical services to the refugee population. But an intense mistrust for the "white man's medicine," according to Abdullah, keeps many ailing refugees away from the clinics. For many of the refugee families, especially those who until the 1974 revolution lived in pastoral and agrarian communities, Abdullah does not expect assimilation to occur. Cultural and traditional persistence has thwarted their acculturation.

The living standard of Abdullah and his family has improved significantly. Abdullah and his wife gross $35,000 per year. This figure rises to $43,000 when the income of extended family members living in the household is included. Combining their resources has enabled the family to maintain a relatively comfortable lifestyle in Minneapolis. The family is, however, very concerned about the relatives they left behind, especially the aged and the children. Every month, a generous amount of $200 is sent home to support those left behind.

Abdullah cannot estimate the size of the Ethiopian community in Minneapolis–St. Paul. But by all accounts, it is growing, due mainly to the secondary migration of other Ethiopians to the twin cities of Minneapolis and St. Paul. The secondary migration to Minnesota, according to Abdullah, is coming from Ethiopians who had initially settled in Washington, D.C., Los Angeles, and New York City. Two factors are behind this secondary migration. First, Minnesota's unemployment rate is under 4 percent, and there is a demand for workers in the food processing plants in the southern parts of the state (Ronningen, 1996). A second factor is reunification with family members.

## BACKGROUND TO THE REFUGEE CRISIS IN THE HORN OF AFRICA

The crisis that brought Abdullah's family and thousands of other Ethiopian and Eritrean refugees to the United States started in 1974 with the overthrow of Emperor Haile Selassie. After his overthrow, a provisional revolutionary council (the Dergue) was formed to run the country. Like so many military regimes that have overthrown elected civilian governments in Africa, the Dergue was supposedly a transitional government, expected to return the country to civilian, democratic rule. For almost twenty years, however, Mengistu Haile Mariam and the Dergue held onto power. They introduced Marxist ideology and, following in the path of other military dictatorships in Sub-Saharan Africa, started a purge of Ethiopians who challenged the government's policies. International economic and military support for the Mengistu regime came principally from the Soviet Union, the Eastern European nations, and Cuba, thrusting Ethiopia into the throes of the Cold War. The Orthodox Church, a vibrant aspect of Ethiopian society for centuries, was stripped of its power and influence.

Internal strife prevented the Dergue from consolidating its power. Problems came from Eritrea, which had formed a federation with Ethiopia under United Nations auspices in 1952. But the federation was unstable because the government of Ethiopia replaced indigenous Eritrean institutions, stripping Eritreans of their autonomy. Internal resistance movements against the regime also came from the Oromos, Afars, and the people of Tigray. The external challenge to the Dergue came from Ethiopia's eastern neighbor, Somalia, over the ownership of the Ogaden region. Somalia attacked Ethiopia (Woldemikael, 1996). The Dergue now found itself embroiled in a conflict with Eritrea, anti-Dergue forces, and Somalia. The ensuing conflicts destroyed Ethiopia's infrastructure, ruining the economy and uprooting thousands. Ethiopians and Eritreans alike were forced to flee from their homelands. The conflict destabilized the entire Horn of Africa. Refugees fled not only from Ethiopia and Eritrea, but also from Somalia and the Sudan (U.S. Committee for Refugees, 1994). In May 1991, the Dergue reign of terror ended when the Eritrean People's Liberation Front (EPLF) and the Ethiopian People's Revolutionary Democratic Front (EPRDF) joined forces and liberated Ethiopia from military dictatorship.

The Refugee Act of 1980 paved the way for the United States to admit the refugees. From 1974 to 1994, a total of 33,195 Ethiopians and Eritreans gained entry. Of the 43,727 Africans allowed lawful entry between 1982 and 1994 as refugees, the majority, almost 70 percent, came from Ethiopia and Eritrea. In 1994, Somali refugees replaced Ethiopians and Eritreans as the major refugee group from Africa to settle in the United States (U.S. Committee for Refugees, 1994).

## SOCIAL AND ECONOMIC ADAPTATION OF AFRICAN REFUGEES

The number of African refugees living in the United States is small when compared with the number refugees and stateless people from Eastern Europe, Cuba, Haiti, Vietnam, Central America, and China. According to the census, 22,149 Africans were admitted as refugees between 1981 and 1999. During the same period, refugees from Asia admitted for permanent residence totaled 712,092. The number of refugees entering the United States from the Soviet Union between 1981 and 1990 was 72,306. In 1994, Africa's share of refugees admitted for permanent residency was still a small proportion of the total.

According to the census, in 1994, 6,078 African refugees were admitted. In the same year, 45,768 refugees were admitted from Asia, 50,756 from the Soviet Union, and 14,204 from North and Central America (Cuba, El Salvador, Guatemala, and Nicaragua). In 1995, African refugees who were admitted totaled 7,527 (while refugees admitted from Europe, Asia, and North America totaled 46,998, 43,314, and 16,265, respectively). Data for fiscal year 1996 from the Immigration and Naturalization Service show that a total of 128,565 persons was granted refugee and asylee status in the United States. Africa's share of the total was 5,464 or 4 percent (U. S. Immigration and Naturalization Service, 1996: Table 6). Africa's refugee population in that year came mainly from Ethiopia, Somalia, Sudan, Eritrea, Ghana, and Liberia.

Africa's refugees in the United States are concentrated in a handful of cities—Los Angeles, Washington, D.C., Minneapolis–St. Paul, and New York City. Some secondary migration and dispersion patterns are discernible. Some of the African refugees living in Minneapolis–St. Paul migrated to Minnesota from Washington, D.C., Chicago, New York, Miami, and Los Angeles. Frequently, the goal of secondary migration is, predictably, to reunite with family members, pursue education, or seek better economic opportunities.

Information gathered from the African refugee community in Minneapolis–St. Paul reveals that civil wars, political unrest, violence, and factional conflicts are at the core of Africa's refugee problems. The majority of the refugees indicated that the principal source of the political upheavals is greed, avarice, and the insatiable desire among Africa's ruling elites to hold on to power no matter the cost. The result is that political deals are brokered often to appease dominant ethnic groups. In the process, less dominant groups are excluded from political and economic decision-making and their communities denied government projects.

Once in the United States, some of the refugees find themselves confronted with cultural, psychological, and economic problems such as poverty, low educational attainment, linguistic barriers, isolation, depression, and confusion. For the majority of the refugees from the Horn of Africa living in the Minneapolis metropolitan area, the conflicts that redefined their lives left memories that time has not been able to eradicate. Although they are no longer confronted by the psychological impact of statelessness, the refugees find themselves living in a state of anxiety, uncertainty, and stress that often triggers mental illness and depression.

Refugees cite additional problems including financial hardship and the lack of economic opportunities and access to jobs that lead to social mobility and high social status. The majority of the refugees work, but most do not earn high wages with fringe benefits. Their incorporation into the labor economy of the Minneapolis metropolitan area has occurred at the lower economic levels and in jobs offering limited chances of upward mobility. More than 80 percent of the adult refugees living in Minneapolis–St. Paul are employed in the service sector where they earn on the average $10,500 per year. Food service, hospitality management, driving cabs, attending parking ramps, and staffing private security services are the main employment options available to most of the refugees. Older women (aged fifty years and above) who once operated very profitable businesses selling foodstuffs and consumer items find themselves without any niche at all in the labor market. Only 2 percent of the refugees are employed in professional and managerial capacities. The economic challenges facing the refugees who held professional jobs in healthcare, education, and business prior to coming to America are even more acute. For this group, economic participation and integration have been very difficult to achieve due to cultural differences and professional licensing procedures. Degrees and professional credentials earned in Ethiopia and Somalia have not been easily transferred to the United States. Most of the refugees with professional skills in the arts, business, and sciences have not been able to incorporate their skills into the U.S. labor market. Because some of the refugees have no choice but to accept jobs below their educational levels, underemployment is common. This downward mobility has brought about frustration, depression, and anger among refugees with high credentials. Repatriation features very prominently in the minds of those who once held professional jobs. Only 7 percent have gone back to school and retrained.

For some of the young men and women whose education was terminated as a result of the Ethiopian and Eritrean crisis, continuing their education has been one of the most difficult transitions. Most reported a lack of interest in completing their education after they arrived in the United States. Because their education had been disrupted, many entered the United States with no credentials to show. Often, when they attempted to continue their education in the United States, they encountered humiliating difficulties. Some were placed in classes with much younger students. With limited skills in English, some of the refugees felt alienated in the public school system. Their peers often teased and ridiculed them. The refugee students, therefore, had no choice but to limit their interactions to other refugee students. This thwarted their successful integration into the educational system, causing a lack of interest in school and sometimes causing them to drop out. The lack of desire to complete their schooling has been replaced by the desire to work, even if the work is menial and the pay is low.

Some of the African refugees whose education was terminated during the crisis have gone back to continue their education. A growing number of African refugees are realizing the importance of education as a means of social mobility and advancement in the United States. Increasingly, young refugee women are attending trade and vocational schools in Minneapolis–St. Paul. Education had not previously been a priority for these young girls due to the patriarchal systems that dominated their lives. In Africa, limited family resources meant that the boys would be the first to be educated.

Now, in the United States, young Ethiopian and Somali girls are redefining their social identities although family pressures are put on them to retain African cultural roles. Refugee youth are torn between maintaining African or adopting American cultural identities. Some of them are resisting the wholesale adoption of African culture by claiming their right to define and interpret the world from their own perspective and the new choices that America offers. Among young refugees, the expression of identity in the refugee community is seen in clothing, hair styles, and language patterns. Social identity among these young people is formed by two factors: class and education. Refugees' class background and educational status in the country of origin play significant roles in shaping cultural identity. Ethiopian and Somali teenagers whose parents held professional, managerial, or white-collar jobs prior to their arrival in the United States tend to adopt an American cultural orientation. In some instances, to facilitate their assimilation and integration, families convert from Islam to a new religious faith. From the perspective of these refugees, being successful in America is articulated in terms of individual accomplishments, independence, and autonomy rather than the fulfillment of collective family goals and obligations.

For the children of refugee families, adopting an American orientation is facilitated by continuing contacts with the families and religious organizations that have sponsored them. For refugees who were living in rural areas prior to coming to the United States, contacts with members of the host society are often limited. Strong contacts are fostered with kin group relations. These refugees tend to be traditional, limited in their social outlook, and bound by a rigid system of social control whose goal is to maintain conformity to religious values. Some refugee parents encounter role strain as they attempt to shape the cultural identity of their children. Refugee matriarchs and patriarchs strictly enforce discipline, but often, their strict and swift approach collides with the need to protect children from physical harm. In two refugee families, patriarchs came into conflict with child protective services for their physical disciplinary approach. In Africa, using corporal punishment to discipline children is not considered abuse. This practice, however, conflicts with American child-rearing values. Refugee and social service agencies in the Minneapolis–St. Paul metropolitan area confirmed the growing value conflicts between some of the refugee children born in this country and their elders and parents.

Religion permeates all of social life among the refugees from the Horn of Africa. A rather mixed group in terms of faiths (primarily Muslim, Orthodox, or other Christian), they have been served by religion, which has fostered unity and cultural identity among people who are divided by class and language. Religious ties tend to be much stronger than the bonds fostered by national identity. The refugees create American versions of their various religious practices, often in the form of festivals or ceremonies that bring African clerics from all over the world to the refugee communities. Through the religious rites and cultural ceremonies that serve to define their cultural presence, the refugees show the non-refugee community in Minneapolis–St. Paul that they are part of a social fabric with a proud cultural heritage.

The disruptive impact of the flight from the dangers of war in Africa can be seen in the eyes of the Ethiopian and Somali women. Some of the women spoke about the violent sexual abuse that they encountered in refugee camps in the Sudan. The psychological effect of the victimization has not eased. Women commonly feel anger, self-blame, mistrust, low self-worth, and social alienation. For the majority of the refugee women, the rebuilding of their lives in the United States involves a search for and construction of new meanings, experiences, concepts, values, and support systems. However, the social spheres that define the world of the refugee women in America are very limited. Their relationships are confined to other refugee women from the Horn of Africa. The result is that they lack access to the social capital necessary to engage in the formation of the community networks, alliances, and coalitions that are vital for economic and political empowerment. For the refugee communities to survive, it is imperative that they (including their women members) form economic and political networks that transcend the boundaries of their communities. By so doing, they will be in a better position to negotiate inclusion in the affairs of the host society.

Some refugee women spoke about the cultural inhibitions that restrict their involvement in work outside the home. When they work outside the home, some of them (mainly Muslim women) prefer to work in establishments where they will have minimal contacts with men. This restricts their employment opportunities. In other spheres of their lives, the dominant influences of the patriarchal structures are also evident. The women are tied culturally to their traditional roles of motherhood and care-giving. Religious and normative standards dictate that Muslim women dress according to their traditions. However, despite the structured gender roles dominating the lives of the refugee women, work outside the home is not seen as a rejection of traditional Ethiopian and Somalian cultural values regarding women and work. Instead, it is seen as necessary for the economic survival of the entire family.

At home, strong kin group relations are fostered by ritual activities that recognize reverence for elderly matriarchs and patriarchs. But power inequalities in these kin groups can be discerned in the relationships that the women form within the nexus of patriarchal-centered relations. Education, however, has enabled some of the women to free themselves from the traditional power structures maintained by husbands and fathers. Combined with the availability of opportunities for gainful employment in the United States, education has enabled some of the women to negotiate more equal relationships with their husbands and with patriarchal elders. From the perspective of the refugee women, education and gainful labor force participation have diminished the psychological and physical violence that dominated their lives prior to their migration. But remnants of such abuse still persist. When abuse occurs, these women are usually torn between resolving the conflicts using informal family arbitration or reporting the abuses to law enforcement agents.

Cultural, economic, and social factors prevent the complete integration of the refugees from the Horn of Africa into mainstream American society. Differences in customs between them and the members of the host society bar successful integration. Refugees in Minneapolis–St. Paul say that while the churches, charitable organizations, and social service agencies have played critical roles in attempting to integrate the refugees into the community, strong resistance, hostility, and fear have come from segments of the community that are concerned about minority encroachment. The refugees' encounter with racial discrimination is painful, stifling, and cumulative. To cope, the refugees tend to segregate themselves by living in close proximity to other refugees from the same national or ethnic group. The collective celebration of their cooperative and spiritual values has aided in sustaining their culture and community.

The cultural capital that the refugees brought to the United States included their strong, close-knit family relationships. The refugees derive emotional, economic, and social security from the community of extended family members who have come to live in the United States. Through extended family networks, the refugees are able to structure household relationships whose primary goal is to facilitate the adjustment process and provide economic support to household members.

This theme emerges constantly in the conversations with Ethiopian and Somalian refugee communities: the vitality of the extended family structure has been pivotal to their survival in Minnesota. Among the refugee families experiencing downward mobility as a result of the devastating impact of the war and the loss of their property when they fled, the rebuilding of family wealth is undertaken in a collective spirit. Family members combine resources to provide economic assistance to vulnerable members, especially the elderly and the children. This form of cooperative economic assistance has worked well in refugee families in which the majority of the household members hold regular jobs, even if these jobs pay minimum wages.

In some African refugee households, however, entire families are sometimes dependent on a single wage-earner. Households with multiple wage-earners have fared better. Conversely, in almost all the households where entire families are dependent on one or two wage-earners, the amount of income available to support extended family members is meager. My survey confirmed what other studies of refugee populations have persistently found. That is, in refugee households with multiple wage-earners, the level of economic well-being and personal satisfaction is higher than in those households where several family members are dependent on a sole wage-earner for sustenance.

The experiences of African refugees are similar to those of refugees who came to the United States during the 1980s and 1990s. Like the Haitian and Hmong refugees who have settled in the United States, the African refugees tend to be young (average age thirty years), predominantly male, unskilled, possessing reading and writing skills in English, and occupationally limited to low-paid service sector jobs. Substandard housing, downward mobility, underemployment, poor health, economic dependency, clinical depression, and racism are problems commonly encountered by America's refugee populations. Despite the problems they encounter in their new home, however, refugees in general are united by a strong work ethic, entrepreneurial skills, and a desire to become successful in America. In addition, close-knit familial relationships and a group, as opposed to individual, approach to life has made it possible for a growing number of refugees to achieve economic mobility, in some instances in less than a generation (Haines, 1996). The refugees show a strong motivation to work. But low pay is a major drawback.

## THE DECISION TO REPATRIATE TO AFRICA

Refugee families in Minneapolis–St. Paul indicated a desire to return home when political and economic conditions improve. Sixty percent of the refugees cited economic reasons as the major consideration in deciding to return. Political reasons to repatriate were cited by only 43 percent of the refugees. The desire to repatriate is often punctuated with feelings of nostalgia about home. They would like to return, but this is an unlikely possibility. The economic and political problems that led to the flight out of Africa persist: clan feuds, erosion of political civilities, economic deterioration, and resurgence of warlords. The Sudan, where some of the refugees initially went, is embroiled in a war between that country's Muslim and Christian populations. Libya maintains its support for the Muslim faction. This crisis has the potential to spill eastward, engulfing Ethiopia and Somalia.

The number of family members who have settled in the United States also influences the decision to repatriate. In general, large refugee households, many of whose family members have been able to settle in the United States and other Western countries, showed a reluctance to repatriate now or in the future. For these families, repatriation becomes difficult considering its cost. In addition, large refugee families have an economic advantage over small refugee households—the ability to combine their economic resources more efficiently, especially where there are multiple wage-earners.

Further variations can be found among the refugees concerning the decision to repatriate. Occupational and educational status at the time of flight are equally important considerations. Those refugees who once held professional jobs and who have experienced downward mobility after resettling in the United States are eager to return home. Yet, they remain ambivalent about repatriation because memories of the crisis still loom large in their minds. I sensed a genuine interest on the part of the professional class to return home and to assist in the task of nation-building. But these refugees decry current living conditions in their home countries. Some even want guarantees from the governments that the return home will be safe and that economic and political measures will be implemented to ensure their successful re-incorporation into society. This will require financial commitments on the part of the governments. I doubt such a commitment (political or economic) will be forthcoming from the regimes currently in power in the countries of the Horn of Africa from which the bulk of African refugees in the United States have come. Limited economic resources and the fragility of current political coalitions will pose major barriers to governmental assistance in repatriating. Cooperation from both sides is needed. At present, such cooperation is absent.

For most of the refugees with limited occupational and educational opportunities before resettling in Minnesota, no compelling economic or political reasons to return home exist. Life in America is better than it was in Ethiopia or Somalia. These refugees have greater freedom in charting their destinies in America. The general perception is that it is better to endure the drudgery of being locked into low-paying jobs and to endure racism and discrimination than to repatriate. Even if conditions improve at home, the desire to return home is simply not there. Some refugees make occasional visits home to attend funerals and to see elderly relatives who were left behind.

In this respect, the orientation of some African refugees regarding future repatriation differs significantly from that of the African immigrants who came to the United States voluntarily. First, the African immigrants who came to this country of their own volition tend to view their stay as temporary. Once conditions improve, they will return home. Second, the African immigrants who came voluntarily make more frequent visits home. During these visits, businesses are set up, savings invested, houses bought, or

plans made for houses to be constructed. Such preparations make repatriation less traumatic. Refugees send remittances home for various entrepreneurial ventures, but it is highly improbable that positive returns will
accrue from their investments, due to the volatility of political and economic conditions. Most of the refugees lost all their assets during their
flight, and bitterness about the loss still remains.

Moving from the things they left behind to the people they left behind,
the refugees in Minneapolis–St. Paul expressed concern for their family
members still in Africa. Strong family ties, whether in Africa or in the
United States, are pivotal for individual and collective achievement. But
the loss of ties to extended family members left behind is not a major motivation to repatriate. The majority of the refugees prefer to stay in the United
States and use current immigration laws on family unification to sponsor
relatives to come to America. In addition, the economic benefits of having
relatives living in the United States outweigh the imperative of repatriation
to Africa for the sole purpose of restoring kinship ties. The economic benefits of life in America are usually shared with other family members back
home. As already stated, African families with relatives residing in the
United States have money remitted to them periodically. Such remittances
go a long way toward easing the economic burden on the family at home.

The dynamics of repatriation become complex for refugees with young
children who were born since resettlement in the United States. As would
be expected, these families prefer to raise their children in the United States
because of better economic and cultural opportunities here.

Refugee families teach their children about the culture of Africa and the
circumstances surrounding their settlement in the United States. In teaching
the refugee children about their African roots, the parents seek to foster in
their children the understanding that, refugees or not, they come from a rich
traditional system dating back centuries, an older culture than America's.

The future of African refugees will be determined by their degree of economic and cultural participation in American society. Presently, for the African refugee population in Minneapolis–St. Paul, the acculturative stress
associated with the flight from Africa has necessitated the strong family ties
that refugee families foster among themselves. Laudable though these ties
might be, because they are so close, they also have the potential to impede
structural and cultural assimilation. The ability of the refugees to merge
their cultural patterns with those of American core society will depend on
whether they continue to rely exclusively on family institutions or form
new ties. Next, full participation will also be contingent upon the degree to
which social service agencies are able to meet the language, educational,
healthcare, counseling, and economic needs of the refugee population. The
refugees will follow different paths in defining the forms of inclusion that
they intend to seek in the dominant society. Refugees' class status prior to
departure, their age, their individual motivation, and educational attain-

ment after resettlement will ultimately determine the extent of incorporation into the core society. Sustained employment will be equally significant
in predicting the future of the refugees. Currently, refugee employment is
in the service sector where there is competition for low-paying jobs with
other immigrant groups whose members often have better educational and
linguistic skills. In addition, the refugees' positive outlook regarding education will be pivotal in mapping a future direction. As a group, African
refugees have already enriched the landscape of Minneapolis and St. Paul
with their cultural uniqueness, family collectivism, strong work ethic, and
desire to become successful in the United States.

# Chapter 5

# African Immigrant Social Networks, Race Relations, and Social Integration

The social and cultural processes involved in immigrant assimilation or acculturation are complex and sociologically interesting. Assimilation is a process whereby groups that are culturally distinct and separate come to create and share a common culture. Sometimes, the term assimilation "is expressed in the metaphor of the melting pot, a process in which different groups come together and contribute in roughly equal amounts to create a common culture and a new, unique society" (Healey, 1998: 36). Acculturation (sometimes referred to as cultural assimilation) describes the process by which one group, usually a minority or immigrant group, learns the culture of the dominant group.

Assimilation and acculturation are particularly complex in a society like the United States that is characterized by internal diversity and variety in its material and non-material cultures. Immigrants who want to become integrated into the affairs of the host society must learn the behavioral norms and expected roles. The learning process entails socialization and a commitment on the part of the immigrants to incorporate elements of the culture of the host society into their normative system.

The history of immigrant adjustments in the United States shows that the pace of assimilation and integration into the affairs of the host society varies significantly among immigrants. A number of factors affect immigrant adjustment and integration patterns. These include age at immigration, country of origin, racial and ethnic identification, immigrant normative and cultural values, and the presence of relatives already settled in the United States. Other factors are immigrant socioeconomic status and educational attainment before and after entry, and the extent to which the inclusion of immigrants is encouraged by the host society. Immigrant incorporation into the host society is a function of the values and expectations that the immigrants hold and the degree of openness of the host society.

For immigrants, building social ties and networks of friendship is crucial for social, cultural, and economic survival. The formation of cultural attitudes, identities, values, and expectations is actualized in group settings, especially in those settings that encourage immigrants to internalize normative standards designed to ensure their inclusion and full participation in all spheres of social activities.

African immigrants are confronted with the problems of all new settlers—how to transform their status as aliens and peripheral members of society into a status of inclusion and participation. Two choices become apparent to the African immigrants—either to exclude themselves by design or to vigorously pursue inclusion. The purpose of this chapter is to identify both the social processes whereby African immigrants establish their cultural identities and the types of the relationships that the immigrants forge with members of the new society. Immigrant social networks, race and ethnic relations, institutional bonding and status integration, and social and political participation and confidence in social institutions will be stressed.

## AFRICAN IMMIGRANT NETWORKS

For African immigrants in the United States, the establishment of a cultural community begins with the formation of intra-immigrant relationships. With the increase in the African immigrant population in the United States since the 1970s has come a growth in African immigrant associational networks. African immigrants from Ghana residing in Washington, D.C., and Atlanta have formed mutual aid associations. They form these associations to represent their ethnic, clan, religious, village, alumni, and national affiliations. In Atlanta, these associations include the Ashanti, Ewe, Akwapim, Kwahu, Okuapemman, Asanteman, and Ga-Adangbe Associations. There are also mutual aid societies representing alumni from the three main universities in Ghana—Legon, Cape Coast, and Kwame Nkrumah University of Science and Technology (KNUST). There is also a national association of Ghanaians living in Atlanta. Similar associations have been established by Nigerian and Ethiopian immigrants in the District of Columbia, Minneapolis–St. Paul, and Charlotte.

The associations serve a number of functions. They provide economic, psychological, cultural, and political support. They assist immigrants during periods of crisis such as illness or death and payment of legal expenses. These associations adapt traditional African institutions to urban life

(Mabogunje, 1972). In addition, they provide socialization for new immigrants, teaching the mores and culture of the host society. The African immigrant associations disseminate information about job prospects and access to capital for setting up businesses. Such associations perform the same functions for Africans who move from the rural to the urban centers of Africa in search of better economic opportunities (Little, 1965, 1974).

As secondary groups, the African immigrant associations have become a vital part of the networks of associative relationships. Immigrants have always established such associations in host societies to forge closer ties among themselves, with the members of the host society, and with their places of birth. The African immigrant associations are the building blocks for the creation of African cultural communities in the United States. Immigrants who are involved in the associations are able to tap into a wealth of ideas and strategies to minimize individual and collective apprehension. It is within these associations that problems emanating from the immigrant experience are defined and solutions sought. According to Attah-Poku (1996: 63), the African immigrant organizations stress the fostering of unity among members, protecting and projecting ancestral cultures, providing support to members in times of need, and connecting them with development projects at home. In short, the African immigrant associations have become symbolic representations and re-creations of the African presence in America, a way for the immigrants to affirm their individual beliefs and, at the same time, affirm group cohesiveness.

The interpersonal bonds that the immigrants foster among themselves within these associations are crucial to how they define and express their cultural distinctiveness and identity as Africans. Diverse in their composition and structure, the ethnic associations maintain boundaries that are loose enough to allow members to link up with other immigrants from different ethnic areas within the same country or from the African continent as a whole to express a national or continental identity. The bonds of ethnicity form the nucleus of a larger transnational continental affiliation that brings all the immigrants together. Although the immigrants recognize diversity in their ethnic or national identities, such differences have not prevented them from recognizing the necessity of pursuing a pan-African identity. The immigrants believe that they have a role to play by promoting the overall development of the continent and by improving upon the quality of life of every African. This is a mutual responsibility that transcends ethnicity and national identity.

Once in the United States, many of the immigrants have little in common except for their geographical affiliation with the continent of Africa. Difficulties often arise when an attempt is made to generalize and connect the immigrants to a common tie of Africanness. Even within the same national group of immigrants in the United States, one can discern significant differences in culture and social organization. These differences, whether based on language, ethnicity, culture, or economic and social status at home, are crucial in explaining variations in African immigrant adaptability, adjustment, and cultural patterns in the United States (Attah-Poku, 1996).

The importance of the immigrant associations in fostering interpersonal bonds among the immigrants was emphasized by a Nigerian immigrant living in Atlanta, Georgia. "The immigrant associations," he stressed, "are formed to remind us of our African culture. The enclaves and pan-ethnic ties we form culturally sustain us in America. [The ties emanating from the immigrant associations anchor] us to our roots in Africa while we are here, ever reminding us of possibilities, opportunities, and the dreams of what the future holds."

An immigrant from Sierra Leone in Washington, D.C. indicated that "the interpersonal bonding fostered by the immigrant associations provides the main base for organizing resources in the pursuit of collective economic and cultural advancements. The interactions with immigrants from my home town and country [have] been pivotal for my success in America. I came to America with three clothes and $25 on me. Today, I earn $1,000 a month. The immigrant associations assisted me in finding a job and a place to stay."

The internal dynamics that these associations create are intended to define mechanisms through which the immigrants relate to the host society. This relationship to the host society occurs mainly when aliens are able to establish their own sense of community with its own normative and institutional systems and then use these communities to negotiate entrance into the affairs of the host society. The ethnic community created by the African immigrants is like a family, which, like every immigrant community, facilitates the adjustment of newcomers, furnishing them with a variety of support while guiding them toward the services they need or the opportunities they desire (Haines, 1985).

## NEGOTIATING THE CONTOURS OF RACE AND ETHNIC RELATIONS IN AMERICA

A major aspect of immigrant adjustment in the United States is the relationships that immigrants establish with the members of the host society. Throughout the history of the making of American society, racial status and identity have been the most socially visible elements. Ideological racism, the normative cultural system asserting that particular racial groups are inferior, is an enduring legacy of American race relations. It defines the cognitive and affective contents of racial minority and majority group relationships. It structures the system of stratification, while also influencing access to wealth, power, and economic opportunities. The contents of racial relations and dominant-minority group interactions have been shaped by economic, legal, cultural, and political forces. Legal and institutional discrimination have also affected the lives of present-day immigrants to the United States. Modern institutional discrimination helps to perpetuate systems of inequality that are just as pervasive and stifling as were those of the past. Past-in-present institutional discrimination involves practices in the present that have discriminatory consequences because of some pattern of discrimination or exclusion in the past (Feagin and Feagin, 1986).

In 1968, the Kerner Report of the National Advisory Commission on Civil Disorders concluded that the United States was "moving toward two societies, one black, one white—separate and unequal." Today, these words have never been truer, with blacks and whites living in different worlds separated not only by race but also in many cases by class.

In terms of race, what types of relationships do African immigrants form with members of the host society? As a group, African immigrants in the United States have had varying racial experiences. With the exception of the African immigrants from South Africa who suffered from an apartheid system of racial exclusion until a few years ago, Africans in the United States came from countries where blacks are in the majority and have responsibility for shaping their own social, cultural, political, and economic destinies. As a result, the majority of Africans come to the United States with little or no understanding of the dynamics of discrimination against black Americans and people of color in general.

Among the African immigrants studied, a central theme emerged in relation to the economic opportunities offered by the United States. The immigrants were unanimous in their belief that migration to the United States has had a positive impact on their lives. Their standard of living has improved significantly since they left Africa. The lives of their immediate relatives in Africa have also improved due to the financial support they give to family members. For African immigrants, economic factors seem to dominate their perception of race relations and racial encounters with the core society. But most of them are troubled by the black-white racial polarization and the pervasiveness of institutionalized discrimination. A major theme running through the African immigrants' experiences in the United States is that immigrants and peoples of black African ancestry often become targets of discriminatory practices designed to exclude them from mainstream society. A common perception among the immigrants is that issues pertaining to peoples of African ancestry are generally considered peripheral and unimportant by members of the dominant culture. African immigrants find this puzzling when almost 13 percent of the total population traces its origin to Africa.

When Africa's existence is acknowledged, its importance and impact on the world scene are usually overlooked. The peoples of the region gain visibility among Americans only when there is a crisis, like the Rwandan and

Zairean crises of the early 1990s, or while communist countries such as Cuba, China, and the Soviet Union maintained influence in the region from the 1960s until the collapse of the Soviet empire.

In their interactions with Americans, the immigrants portray an American society that holds little or no respect for people of color, particularly blacks. Cast in peripheral and marginalized status, many of the immigrants believe that the structural barriers associated with racial inequality must be removed before racial harmony can be promoted. The cultural images that Americans have associated with Africa and blacks, they maintain, is usually dominated with negative stereotypes in areas of crime, violence, drugs, laziness, welfare, and the formation of subcultures.

Immigrants of the African diaspora in the United States find themselves caught in the complex web of race relations in America. The relationship between African immigrants and the dominant society is characterized by racial exclusion, de facto segregation, prejudice, racism, and discrimination. The control of minority groups and immigrants has usually involved the creation of exclusive group relations by the dominant group. The immigrants perceive that they are held in low esteem by the dominant society. Many of them believe that even if they achieve the highest social mobility in the United States, they will continue to experience problems with integration simply because of their skin color. In fact, according to some of the immigrants, one cannot hide one's blackness in an American society that is filled with race consciousness. Being black in a dominant white society, the immigrants noted, will continue to be a major impediment to full integration. The predicament of blacks living in a dominantly white culture is that no matter what people of color accomplish, their lives will continue to be characterized by the inequalities of power, prestige, and class.

Racism and discrimination against blacks and other minorities still abound in America. African immigrants see the perniciousness and insidiousness of racism against peoples of African ancestry (whether they are born in Africa or the United States). But while the African immigrants are cognizant of deep-seated racism and discrimination in America and experience it, they seem not to be as preoccupied with the social, cultural, and political entanglements of racism and discrimination as are native-born blacks. This sentiment is reflected in a statement by an Ethiopian immigrant living in Charlotte, North Carolina, who said, "Most African immigrants perceive that their status as foreigners makes it difficult, if not impossible, for them to understand the historical contents of the black-white divide in the United States." A similar theme is echoed by a Ghanaian immigrant in Minneapolis–St. Paul. She stressed that "cultural barriers and the historical void in the knowledge base of Africans about race relations in America has had a deleterious impact on how Africans relate to both black and white Americans alike." "In America," according to another immigrant, "you are reminded constantly of your racial identity; in

Africa, you didn't have to worry about [being] racialized. Consequently, [in Africa] you feel freer to engage society without agonizing about being discriminated against on account of skin color."

Prior to their emigration, many of the immigrants identified America as a land of opportunity and were eager to travel to this promised land. Now that they have had the opportunity to engage in the affairs of American society, the majority of them are convinced that the racial polarization and the institutionalized patterns of discrimination in America are antithetical to what American stands for: freedom, equality, and justice for all. Over time, the African immigrants adjust their attitudes about race relations. The adjustment process takes into account the reality that the immigrants are powerless to alter the balance of racial relations in their favor. Their integration into the dominant culture is hindered by racial separation based on jobs and housing. It is also hindered by fear stemming from the perception of many native-born Americans that immigrants are a threat to the economic and cultural standards of living of the native population (Bach, 1993).

Most of the immigrants indicated having experienced discrimination, prejudice, and racism. Some mentioned that they had been victims of hate crimes on account of their race, accent, or national origin. But generally, the immigrants tend not to allow racial conflicts to dominate their social consciousness. Why is this so? First, their sojourner status seems to influence their attitudes. From the perspective of the immigrants, the race crisis is between American blacks and the dominant white culture. One respondent said "The black-white racial divide is not our fight, neither is it our struggle. We Africans are here temporarily. One day, we will engage in our own struggles to free ourselves from poverty and economic miseries. Our struggle is to find ways to confront our leaders back home who have brought miseries and woes to so many of our people." Second, as already indicated, the expected economic returns and benefits to be gained in America overshadow African immigrants' objective perceptions of the insidiousness of racism. Coupled with this is the fact that the majority of the African immigrants came from countries where blacks are in charge of all aspects of administration and have the responsibility for making decisions that affect the citizenry. This may be politically and economically empowering even if such empowerment cannot be translated into meaningful social change because of Africa's corrupt, undemocratic, and inept political system. Nevertheless, the empowerment contrasts with the plight of American blacks in the United States who have been politically marginalized and sometimes completely left out of political and social discourse.

The problems of racial inequality and the legacies of slavery and the Jim Crow laws are all etched on the minds of the immigrants, making it possible for them to form a mental map of life in America. The immigrants recognize the racial politics of the United States as a major source of potential cultural conflicts. But most are not sure how to confront the black-white polarization. The source of their ambivalence can be traced, in part, to African cultural norms regarding stranger-host relations (Shack, 1978). One of the fundamental aspects of African culture is the recognition that in stranger-host dynamics, rights, obligations, and privileges are the prerogatives of the host society and that strangers or temporary sojourners are allowed to stay due to the benevolence of the host society. In Africa, strangers or aliens must pay homage to the host society by offering gifts and often casting themselves in a role subservient to the host. Strangers do not question, challenge, or meddle in the affairs of the host society. The balance of power is tilted to the interest of the host. The submissiveness of the strangers to the host is rewarded by the host society in permitting the strangers to stay as long as they wish. In all social and cultural interactions between hosts and stranger societies, Africans believe that the superordinate status of the host must be revered and that stranger societies must not ally themselves with members of the host society to cause shame and dishonor to the host. The host is always right. But a source of solace for the African immigrants living in the United States is that one day they will go home, their legal status in the United States notwithstanding.

It is conceivable, therefore, that cultural factors and economic benefits converge to influence and explain how the African immigrants negotiate the complex terrain of race relations in the United States. Generally, as people of low visibility, Africans are not meddlers. They will participate in the affairs of their host societies only to achieve culturally predetermined goals, mainly economic and educational. Their individual and migratory activities in the United States, according to one immigrant, are constructed to "keep one foot in the United States. The other foot mediates the connection and ties with Africa, the ultimate place of return." Describing how the African immigrant confronts the racial polarization, another immigrant summarized her feelings by using an African adage:

The African immigrant in the United States reminds me of the story of the little boy who tried to peep inside a bottle with both eyes opened. The little boy's parents, watching the futile efforts of their son, advised him to close one eye and then peep inside the bottle with the other eye. The African immigrant must always keep one eye opened to appreciate the realities of being an immigrant. Meanwhile, the other eye is left free to focus on the realities of life at home in Africa.

Thus, while the immigrants actively agitate for political and economic reforms at home, they remain virtually silent on the matter of race relations in the United States. However, the lingering racism in America is the single most important worry for them (African Profiles International, 1996: 13). They express great concern at the media portrayal of young black men as menacing, threatening, and violent. In addition, very troubling to the immigrants are the economic dislocations and deterioration in the quality of living standards in predominantly black urban communities across the nation at a time when the rest of the nation is enjoying an economic boom. Pressured by the dominant society to identify as "American blacks," the African immigrants prefer to identify as "African blacks," sometimes accentuating those cultural traits (for example accent and dress patterns) that are uniquely African. From the perspective of the immigrants, the need to identify themselves as "African blacks" stems from the negative images the dominant society associates with native-born blacks—poverty, crime, violence, and exclusion from mainstream society (images often associated with downward mobility). The African immigrants' perception of the importance of race and class in the definition of the minority underclass has been crucial in their definition of their own racial identity. The racial status that the immigrants attempt to present to the larger society is that of "foreign-born black," a status that the immigrants perceive to be higher than the status of "American black" (Waters, 1994: 2).

## AFRICAN IMMIGRANTS AND RELATIONS WITH NATIVE-BORN BLACKS

For most American-born blacks, Africa is the ancestral motherland, the place of their origin. Spiritually and culturally, identification with the continent of Africa is what the majority of black Americans have always sought to establish. Culturally, an ever-growing number of black Americans are embracing the material (inventions, creations) and non-material cultures (symbols, philosophies, conventions, ideas, values, beliefs, and institutions) of Africa.

A growing number of African-Americans are searching for their roots in Africa by visiting the coast of West Africa to experience its culture. Sometimes, the trip to Africa is characterized by visits to historically significant places such as the forts and dark dungeons that held captured slaves prior to their shipment to the New World. To those who have been to historical sites such as Goree in Senegal or Cape Coast Castle in Ghana, this has been a journey of renewal and self-discovery, a spiritual pilgrimage to connect with their ancestral home and at the same time confront the source of past and present servitude.

The responses I obtained from the African immigrants indicate that the cultural, political, and economic affinity between African immigrants and their black American counterparts is not as strong as it should be considering the historical cord that ties them together. A wide gap exists between the two groups. What are the tensions that have brought about this rift? What are the consequences of it? The cultural barriers and the social and economic differences separating the Africans and the African-Americans is sometimes the cause of a simmering hostility and misunderstanding between them. Sharing the common physical characteristic of skin color has not ensured cultural and economic unity between African immigrants and American-born blacks.

There are feelings of distrust, a lack of understanding, and a cultural and economic gap between the two groups (Asika, 1997). Mary Waters (1994) describes the relationship between Afro- Caribbean blacks and their native-born counterparts. She noted the tension between them in terms of family life, education, and commitment to work. Black immigrants, according to Waters and Kasinitz (1992), see black Americans as lazy, disorganized, obsessed with racial images, and having a laissez-faire attitude toward family life and child raising. On their part, native-born American blacks view black immigrants as arrogant and oblivious to the racial tensions between blacks and whites. Indeed, as Simon R. Bryce-Laporte (1973) and David Lowenthal (1972) have argued, black immigrants, in general, perceive that in America, mobility, thrift, achievement, and success are a function of ability, assiduousness, and motivation. These qualities made it possible for other immigrants (for example, Jews and Japanese) to achieve mobility.

As I probed into the attitudes of the immigrants toward American-born blacks, I found that some of them seem to believe, a belief similar to that of dominate white society, that many native-born blacks (especially the black underclass living in the inner-cities) have yet to take full advantage of the educational and economic opportunities America offers. Their statements depicted an urban black America in which the scourge of poverty has been compounded by joblessness, school drop out, crime, drug use, teenage pregnancy, low self-concept, and despair. When I indicated to some of the immigrants that the present conditions of native-born blacks have been caused, in part, by their colonized status, by centuries of de jure segregation, and subtle forms of institutionalized discrimination that has kept blacks from the mainstream economy, one immigrant from Sierra Leone said "In spite of past discriminatory practices, I know many native-born blacks who have quit trying. Some have consciously decided not to empower themselves by committing to education. You cannot always blame the white man." Another immigrant from Liberia painted an image of a segment of black America that ostracizes those who overcome the perils of discrimination and racism through education and entrepreneurial initiatives to become successful. "Even when you succeed," she went on to say, "you are still considered a failure because you left the ghetto and became too white."

In a comparative study of black immigrants living in New York City and in London, Nancy Foner (1985: 717) found that foreign-born blacks tend to stress their distinctiveness from American-born blacks, setting themselves apart by emphasizing their ethnic pride and culture. The black immigrants, Foner found, view themselves "as more ambitious, harder workers, less likely to be on welfare, less hostile to whites, and [they] feel more dignified and self-assured in their dealings with the white majority" (Foner, 1985:

717; Foner 1979). Like African immigrants, black immigrants from the Caribbean empathize with the mistreatment American blacks endure as a result of discrimination and racism in America. But they perceive that as immigrants, they themselves need to direct their energies toward economic advancement.

As a minority group whose presence in the United States has been shaped by the forces of international migration and not by enslavement, African immigrants believe that they do not have to be burdened by the injustices of racism and discrimination in America. Neither do they feel compelled to fight the results of racial injustice. But one fact remains clear for both African immigrants and American-born blacks: their access to economic opportunities and political power have been influenced, in part, by their perceived low racial status relative to whites. Both groups (African immigrants and native-born blacks) have been relegated to a subordinate position in the American stratification system.

Culturally and normatively, however, the two groups are very different. The patterns of socialization and cultural identification are different. Sometimes, the cultural gap and differences in value orientation become sites of conflict and tension between the two groups. To the majority of African immigrants, the key to social mobility in the United States is education and human capital as broadly defined in terms of strong family relationships, foresight, frugality, pursuit of educational goals, and cultural value based on entrepreneurship. Racism and discrimination serve as structural constraints to full participation in society. And African immigrants and native-born blacks both experience its harmful consequences. But African immigrants and native-born blacks differ in terms of the relative value that they attach to race as affecting advancement in the United States. African immigrants see high levels of investment in human capital as crucial to economic advancement. The African immigrants who were surveyed spoke about the economic opportunities in this country. They made references to the educational and cultural opportunities America offers and generally concluded that racism and discrimination notwithstanding, those who apply themselves usually succeed in America. This finding is consistent with Sowell's (1983) observations on the value of human capital and the importance of education as determinants of economic mobility. Differences in human capital produce large differences in mobility and standards of living. Applying Sowell's model, African immigrant success in America is attributable to the investment that Africans make in education, economic persistence, and entrepreneurial motivation. Race, the immigrants perceive, is crucial for status attainment in a color conscious society, but it alone does not explain performance. The black immigrants are sensitive about their racial identities, but as Waters found, they are not as sensitive to race as are native-born American blacks. An extreme sensitivity to issues of race on the part of native-born American blacks is, after all, to be expected consid-

ering the racial violence, the lynchings, and the vigorous enforcement of
Jim Crow laws that denied them civil rights. As Vander Zanden said, "slavery so completely disrupted black institutions, culture, and communication that it was virtually impossible for blacks to mount a serious challenge
to their subjugation" (1983: 150). And to deny or minimize that aspect of
black history in America is to deny the history of enslavement, the human
denigration that African-Americans experienced, and the remaining racial
stratification. Racial classification with its stratificatory appendages "has
implications for a person's life chances because racial stratification is a social hierarchy" (McDaniel, 1995; Bashi and McDaniel, 1997).

In examining how racial identity has influenced the conditions of racial
minorities in America, one must also consider the intersections of class,
family structure, gender, and labor force participation. The status of African-Americans in the United States has been influenced, in large part, by
family structure, urban poverty, and persistent discrimination in wages between men and women (Wilson, 1980). Previous and current institutional
policies have made this inequality difficult to eradicate. The continuation
of black-white inequality in other spheres of life—housing, education,
health, and criminal justice administration—further erodes the cultural basis of the relationship among the peoples of the black diaspora. "One must
always be conscious of the forces causing this inequality and at the same
time work within these structures to overcome the inherent racism and discrimination," one African immigrant concluded.

The survey data reveal that although African immigrants in the United
States have much to offer and gain from interactions with American-born
blacks and whites, the social world of the immigrants is largely limited to
intra-African immigrant circles. African immigrants tend to form much
closer relationships with black immigrants of the African diaspora (mainly
from other developing nations such as Jamaica, Trinidad, the Bahamas,
Guyana, and Haiti) than they establish with the native-born black American population. Generally, native-born blacks do not feature prominently
in the African immigrants' webs of associative relationships. Similarly, African immigrants are not featured prominently in African-Americans' web
of relationships. Some African immigrant women, however, form closer relationships with African-American women. In addition, second generation
African immigrant youths associate with inner-city youths representing diverse cultural and ethnic backgrounds.

Three factors undergird the close relationships between African immigrants and their Caribbean counterparts. First, African and Caribbean immigrants share a common experience as immigrants in the United States.
Both African and Caribbean immigrants are risk takers, motivated by a
common economic goal, to become successful and then leave and go home.
Second, most of them share a colonial history of Western European domination (especially those from the British Commonwealth). The two groups

discuss the impact of colonization on their lives and relate to each others' cultural and political experiences. Third, coming from less developed regions of the world, both groups approach their presence in America with a sense of urgency, believing that as immigrants, time is not on their side, thus necessitating a focus on a particular goal, usually economic or educational. This may explain the entrepreneurial activities and educational accomplishments among some African and Caribbean immigrants. A common denominator is that like their African immigrant counterparts, Caribbean-American blacks (especially those from the former British Caribbean) are doing better economically than their African-American black counterparts. The same, however, cannot be said for Spanish- and French-speaking Caribbean blacks, who are doing worse economically than African-American blacks (Kalmijn, 1996: 927; Dodoo, 1991a/b/c).

Among African immigrants, stratification along ethnic lines is more important than race in determining access or lack of access to institutional resources and opportunity. (In the recent history of Africa, divisions along ethnic lines are at the core of civil wars, genocide, and national fragmentation.) A persistent theme emerging from discussions with African immigrants on their relationship with black Americans is that both sides perceive the other as culturally ethnocentric. In the African immigrant community, there is a perception that the cultural images native-born blacks associate with the peoples of Africa are usually no different from the stereotypical and prejudicial views held by white Americans. The social stereotypes and images associated with "black" and "African" are cultural and economic backwardness, degradation, and even savagery. The result, according to one survey respondent, is that "African-Americans have become ashamed of their African heritage; this shamefulness is accompanied by a sense of cultural inferiority and, thus, the need to limit or sever their African cultural ties. The racial kinship that should exist among peoples of the African diaspora is lacking."

An African immigrant from Senegal who has lived in the United States for about thirty years stated that "African students are taught about slavery, about African history and culture. But native-born black Americans are rarely taught African history. The result is that native-born blacks know little about their African heritage. Few native-born blacks have taken it upon themselves to learn about African culture. We are a house divided." African-born and American blacks are divided by history, and by a lack of understanding and appreciation of the historical forces that have shaped each other's cultural heritage and experiences. African immigrants believe that native-born blacks have shown no sustained understanding of African history and culture, or of the impact of foreign domination and colonization on the lives of Africans. Native-born blacks react to African immigrants' allegations mainly by highlighting the immigrants' lack of knowledge of the historical conditions (discrimination, exclusion, and violence) associated with being black in America.

In addition, cultural differences can be discerned in patterns of educational attainment and family structure between the two groups. The immigrants and their children recognize the necessity of education as a facilitator of advancement in America. The immigrant families encourage their children not to regard the completion of high school as the end of their educational pursuits. The majority of the immigrant families organize their resources to support children who show the potential for higher education. In addition, the majority of immigrant households are engaged in income-generating activity. Work is a major component of African culture. The extended family as a unit of production relies on the economic contributions of its able-bodied members to provide economic sustenance and raise the living standard of the family as a whole. Immigrant family members often rely on each other for the rotation of capital to start businesses. The benefits accruing from such business activities are shared by the entire family. Entire families live frugal lives to save money to sponsor other family members who come to the United States for education. The opportunity to assist in the education of family members eventually pays off when these family members themselves become employed. The cultural capital of the African immigrant families can be found in the stability of members' relationships. Single parenthood is not the norm. In cases of father-absence, maternal and paternal extended family members step in to assume the responsibilities of fatherhood. The ties emanating from strong kinship bonds enable African children to benefit from the collective economic contributions of both close and distant relatives. In some cases, single-parent households send children back home to Africa to be raised by relatives. While in Africa, the children receive quality education. They attend private schools paid for by financial remittances.

In addition, there is a strong motivation among the immigrants to succeed by taking advantage of the educational and economic opportunities offered in the United States. As a group, immigrants take risks (such as undertaking transnational migration in search of better opportunities) to maximize whatever human capital they possess. The result is that African immigrants are enjoying rising household incomes and economic opportunities stemming from their educational accomplishments, their strong commitment to self-empowerment, and a stable family unit in which husbands and wives both work. The collective experience of the African immigrants in their relationships with native-born blacks is that the immigrants perceive that they are not responsible for the social, cultural, and economic problems of the urban underclass in America.

Thus, in the course of delineating the sources of the apparent tension and uneasiness between African and American-born blacks, economic and cultural reasons come to the fore. An Ethiopian immigrant, reflecting on his experiences with American blacks, said, "They [African-Americans] tell us [Africans] that we come to their country and take their jobs." Africans are gradually beginning to overshadow Asian traders in major cities like New York City, where Africans peddle anything from jewelry to electronic items. Senegalese immigrants in New York are now operating their own bank, offering mortgages, business loans, and wire transfers to Africa. Joel Millman's study describes the Senegalese social structure in New York and notes the economic and political contributions that Senegalese-based institutions are making to the cultural plurality and economic progress of minority districts in that city.

My study reveals that with the penetration of African-owned businesses into minority communities (especially native-born black American communities) have come murmurs of discontent among native-born blacks. The owners of the African-owned stores in my study expressed collective concern that American-born blacks believe the Africans are milking the poor and not investing in the communities where they operate their stores. The hostilities, one store owner indicated, come from a few wayward youths who, in his estimation, have little or no understanding of the collective history and common destiny of the peoples of the African diaspora. According to this immigrant,

The minority community is a gold mine for business. Past immigrants (Jews, Italians, and Anglos) all set up businesses there. Now, new immigrants from Asia, Africa, and the Caribbean have set up their businesses in black communities. Some businesses are pulling out, leaving these communities, in some cases, without banks, grocery stores, or laundry services. Some of us are filling the niche. It's unfortunate we get blamed for milking these communities. We do not make enough money on our capital to permit a sustained investment in the economic development of the African-American communities where we draw the bulk of our clients.

Sometimes this uneasiness is given a political dimension in the form of statements, allegedly made to African blacks by black American youths, that the Africans did nothing to stop the slave trade and that the Africans are partly to blame for selling the African-Americans' ancestors to the white man hundreds of years ago. Such pronouncements, another store owner reflected, do not advance "the mutual cause of economic and political determinism that we are trying to foster among the peoples of the black diaspora."

Culturally, the two groups can learn much from each other. Building bridges and coalitions to close this gap is the key to achieving unity among the peoples of the African diaspora. Both sides would have to foster closer economic, political, and cultural ties for the mutual benefit of their peoples. Such ties would bring about a common determination to contend with the economic problems with which African blacks and their American counterparts are faced. The African-American business community must become an active participant in economic and industrial development. The goal is to invest in economic and social programs to raise the living standards of Africans just as immigrants of European ancestry in America have assisted in the development of Europe.

The role that Africa would have to play in forming an unshakable alliance between the two groups is described by an immigrant from Sierra Leone who acknowledges that

Africans have failed to educate their counterparts in the United States about the aspects of African culture that have brought misery and violence to most of the peoples of Africa, especially blacks in Sub-Saharan Africa. It is very difficult to agree on how to forge alliances and unity among peoples of the African diaspora when African leaders institutionalize violence by victimizing their own people.

In their efforts to bridge the cultural divide that exists between African and American-born blacks, the immigrants in my survey cited examples of social and economic activities in which they are involved to bring the two groups closer. One mini-mart owner said the merchants in his area, mainly Africans, have set up a scholarship fund to assist two local minority students to go to college. Another mentioned supporting the United Way in the community as well as donating food during holidays. Symposia, lectures, and cultural events designed to portray African culture are among the community-based cultural activities that the immigrants organize in their localities. Some immigrants give lectures at area high schools on topics related to African history and culture during Black History Month. These cultural exchanges, the immigrants confirmed, are vital to promoting community social and cultural development. The professional class of immigrants is also contributing its share to the cultural, social, and economic development of its communities. One Nigerian immigrant, a certified accountant, mentioned a program in his community involving African- and American-born black accountants and lawyers visiting churches and mosques to provide basic education about personal finances, investment in stocks, home ownership, living wills and trusts.

The achievement of racial justice and equality for the peoples of the African diaspora in America and in other parts of the world is a collective cause that must be championed and embraced not only by American-born blacks but also by black Africans irrespective of their countries of origin or nationality. While most of the immigrants had favorable perceptions of race relations in America prior to their arrival in the United States, encounters with racism and discrimination have made them change their attitudes. The African immigrants agreed that irrespective of where the peoples of the African diaspora have settled, they have to confront not only racism and discrimination but also in many cases economic deprivation and poverty. African immigrants in the United States are not immune from the economic and cultural segregation encountered by American-born blacks. African immigrants confront racism and discrimination in their daily lives. To deal with discrimination and exclusion from mainstream society, like any other marginalized group, they tend to form African-based immigrant clusters, a form of voluntary segregation. In their social relations with the dominant culture, they create zones of comfort for themselves. These provide mutual assurances, collective security, and buffers against a race and class conscious American society.

The degree of residential and economic segregation facing minorities, especially American blacks in the United States, is no different, according to the immigrants, from what they themselves are confronted with. They reject suggestions that peoples of the African diaspora have unlimited access to abundant opportunities to pursue their life dreams. But on the whole, in comparison with their home situation, they remain fully aware that their lives have improved significantly, and racism and discrimination notwithstanding, they are confident that when their children reach adulthood, their lives will be even better.

The economic survival and political destiny of the black African immigrant in the United States is invariably tied to black-white racial polarization and marginalization in America. Even though they come to America with a solid educational background, and thus they are more likely than American-born blacks to enroll in institutions of higher learning, African immigrants face another problem. They are foreign and black, with distinctive accents and different cultures from that of the dominant group. These cultural differences about which the dominant culture in America knows very little, have produced mistrust, alienation, and exclusion from dominant spheres of social interaction.

Stereotypical media representations of the peoples and cultures of Africa have not helped advance the cause of Africa and Africans in the United States. While the immigrants might have a sense of powerlessness, marginalization, and alienation from mainstream American society, they, nonetheless, are clear about their economic participation in America; even those who are unskilled and subject to fluctuations in the labor market as well as exploitation by unscrupulous employers and who seek to accomplish very modest economic goals. African immigrants perceive that they do not have to be formally involved with conventional society to realize those goals. In spite of their problems, the African immigrants are responding to the economic benefits to be had in America while recognizing that the social forces that have driven them out from their home country are only temporary.

One area of complete unanimity among Africans in the United States concerns the way that news and events in Africa are portrayed. In concert, the survey respondents indicated an intense and fierce concern for the lack of understanding of Africa. One immigrant expressed his sentiments thus:

White-controlled television networks have brought into America's homes the wild-life and the safaris, given exhilarating accounts of the African elephants, the political economy of ivory, the social structure of . . . lions, mountain gorillas, and other wildlife species unique to the continent. Knowledge about the African wildlife is cast with intensity to television viewers. Usually, the tapestries and cameo of human cultures of the people in the immediate areas surrounding the wildlife parks are left out or given peripheral focus. The view of Africa etched in the minds of Americans about Africa, therefore, is antiquated, a continent where the worst in humanity, misery, abject poverty, and hopelessness come to the fore.

Concerns about race relations with the dominant society feature very prominently in the social world of the African immigrants. The majority of them indicated their concern for the anti-immigrant campaign waged by former California Governor Pete Wilson to deny benefits to illegal aliens and their children. Their fear is based on the belief that this anti-immigrant sentiment is going to spread to the rest of the country. But even though they show concern when politicians advocate strict, closed door immigration policies and the withdrawal of social services from undocumented aliens, the results of the survey showed that more than sixty percent of the African immigrants are themselves in favor of such strict immigration requirements, even if this means that children of illegal aliens who are born in the United States will also be denied access to education or healthcare. This is the immigrants' contradiction. The African immigrants believe in the economic possibilities offered to immigrants by American society, but they perceive that when illegal aliens violate United States immigration laws, they cast a shadow of doubt on legal residents and thereby cause an intensification of "immigrant-bashing" in general.

## AFRICAN IMMIGRANT INSTITUTIONAL BONDING AND STATUS INTEGRATION

Education, proficiency in English, occupation, and ethnicity have shaped the status integration of African immigrants living in the United States. Education has allowed those immigrants with postgraduate credentials to obtain high-paying professional jobs and provided some immigrants with social mobility. But generally, one finds that among African immigrants, the possession of advanced degrees, professional employment, and proficiency in English have not translated into high status and social acceptance in mainstream society.

Primary bonding relationships, such as those that are established within family networks, are an important aspect of status integration and social bonding. The secondary institutions and structures through which individuals establish a sense of integration and affiliation with society are also important. Whether the bonding and integration into society is through primary or secondary social groups, an essential element of any bonding process is adherence to a set of predetermined roles, norms, values, expectations, and statuses.

In a culturally heterogeneous and complex society like the United States, much of the behavior exhibited by individuals and groups is institutionalized and governed by common, taken-for-granted expectations associated with various social roles. When social bonding and integration are weak, commitment to institutions and social affiliations is also likely to be weak. As strangers in a highly diverse cultural system, immigrants as a social group are expected to become acculturated and, if possible, assimilated into the dominant culture. The expectations of assimilation theorists (notably Milton Gordon and Robert Park) is that new immigrants will adopt and embrace the values and beliefs of the host society, especially Anglo-Protestant conformity. An alternative view is that immigrants will retain their separate cultures, forming an enclave whose beliefs and norms may or may not be contradicted by the norms of members of the dominant culture.

For most immigrants, Africans included, the preferred approach to the resolution of this apparent conflict is the blending of immigrant expectations and values with those of the host or dominant society. Over time, immigrants interact with various social institutions including legal and political systems. In the course of their interactions, immigrants learn about institutional expectations and adapt or modify their views, opinions, and attitudes accordingly, either moving toward conformity or toward a rejection of the status quo. Impressions of how a particular institution functions will invariably determine confidence, or lack thereof, in the institution in question. The participation or non-participation of immigrants in the political and social affairs of the host society offers a gauge of the extent of immigrant integration, affiliation, and commitment to the values espoused by the members of the host society. In aspiring to become part of the host society, the immigrants must show a clear understanding of the processes involved in establishing a civil society. The study of how immigrants see institutions as functioning is crucial to our understanding of immigrants' levels of confidence in social or public institutions.

Social, cultural, and economic factors account for a lack of social integration among immigrants. African immigrants tend to restrict their social networks to other immigrants. They consider a strong reliance on associations formed with other Africans and other immigrants of the black diaspora as vital to their economic and psychological security. Through these associations, the immigrants are able to hold on tenaciously to their cultural institutions, thereby avoiding assimilation and full participation in American society. Within their ethnic affiliations, the immigrants are able to create enclaves whose relationships with the outside community are defined solely in economic terms. As already shown, even when African immigrants form secondary associations outside of their immigrant enclave groups, these relationships are usually not as close-knit as those that are formed along ethnic lines. In general, these secondary groups confer little or no status on the immigrants; neither are they important in facilitating immigrants' integration into American society. Moreover, the strong intra-ethnic ties that immigrants forge among themselves serve to impede social integration, leading to further isolation and disengagement from wider social discourse.

Integration is resisted by older and first-generation immigrants and even by those who stand to gain most from integration—well-educated immigrants holding professional jobs. Among the older and first-generation immigrants, integration is problematic due to linguistic barriers, strong intra-ethnic ties, cultural isolation, and particularly the perception of sojourner status in the United States. For the majority of immigrants who as a result of low educational attainments are compelled to settle for low-paying jobs in the service sector of the economy, integration is unlikely to occur. Given their low status in the economic hierarchy, African immigrants with poor educational credentials are even more culturally isolated than their counterparts with undergraduate and postgraduate education.

For African immigrants in the United States, the negotiation of a status other than "foreign" or "alien" is based on beliefs that America is both a closed and an open society. First, this belief system recognizes that immigrant status implies a limit to social, cultural, and economic participation. Second, it recognizes that people seek certain degrees of material comfort and economic prosperity for their advancement, empowerment, and general well-being. The status that the African immigrants seek is not defined or articulated in terms of the American class dynamic with its structured ethos of individual material comfort as opposed to group or community well-being. For the African immigrant, the social derivation of status and its accompanying structures are relatively constructed and determined. The immigrants do not articulate or negotiate a status or role using standards determined by American cultural values and belief systems. Instead, the immigrants engage in comparative status negotiation in which statuses and roles are determined by the material and non-material levels of status-identity relative to the status identity they were culturally accustomed to while living in Africa. African immigrants realize that they do not have to engage the entire society to derive a sense of status and fulfillment. Actually, the sense of status that they seek is informed by the need to improve the lot of their family members at home. Status fulfillment and role recognition are derived from the financial remittances that are sent home to family members. Denial of status in the affairs of the host society is compensated for by the status that is derived from meeting culturally defined expectations.

## POLITICAL PARTICIPATION AND SOCIAL ACTIVISM

The political opinions of the African immigrants have been particularly influenced by their experiences with the political systems of Africa. The majority of the immigrants noted that they have had limited opportunities to participate in the political decision-making process. Only one-third of the immigrants indicated that they participated in politics at home in Africa by voting in elections. Those who were registered to vote participated in other ways: registering people to vote, canvassing, marching, attending political rallies, making donations, following politics in the news, writing letters, and distributing literature. Overall, the immigrants expressed a very negative perception of the political process in Africa. This is due to political corruption, cronyism, lack of commitment by African governments to nurture democratic institutions, political exclusion, and violence against political opponents. In addition, the lack of political accountability is a major obstacle to democratic reform (Nickel, 1990: A18).

A Senegalese immigrant living in Charlotte, North Carolina, while treasuring the political calm in his country, nonetheless felt that

Africa's political maturity [will] arrive when democratically elected lawmakers learn a basic lesson in human political organization: that in the fullness of time, the politically oppressed will shake off their yoke of oppression and demand social justice and human dignity. The politics of combativeness and the divide and rule practiced by most African leaders cannot work in perpetuity. After all, divide and rule was a colonial legacy inherited from the British and French. The African electorate is becoming better educated with each passing year. Television and mass communication are exposing Africans to other viable political alternatives.

An immigrant from Ghana, residing in Atlanta, who was a victim of General Acheampong's reign of terror against university students in the 1970s, stated that "the lesson is there for future African leaders to see; that African leaders who gain and hold on to power by stealth and by the barrel of the gun eventually fall by the same tactic. When military officials usurp power using violence to overthrow other military or civilian regimes, they also become vulnerable to insurrections and violence when future government takeovers occur." In the atmosphere of continued political violence and erosion of political order in most parts of Africa today, according to one immigrant, "It is the poor mass of Africans who suffer as political violence becomes legitimized as a tool of waging conflict. The principal beneficiaries of political disorder have been Africa's leaders."

A Nigerian immigrant, showing his frustration while reacting to the political problems in his country, said contemplatively that "African leaders are making a laughing stock of the true meaning of our political independence, further confirming stereotypes about Africa that it is a continent gone awry; that Africans are incapable of self-governance and self-determination. Maybe, the colonialists should have stayed a bit longer for political and democratic institutions to become nurtured before departure." While this last sentiment does not reflect the prevailing view of how to steer Africa politically, it nonetheless reveals the sense of political despair and the abyss into which political organization in Africa has fallen.

The immigrants are unequivocally opposed to military dictatorships and to African leaders who have anointed themselves as life-long presidents; they characterized most of these leaders as despotic and tyrannical. They talked openly about their admiration for the American political system and, while not attempting to compare it with the system in Africa, they remain certain that Africa is ripe for political change. When that change comes, the immigrants seem to be confident that their experiences with the American political system will prove beneficial. One Ethiopian immigrant, a medical officer in his home country, who came to the United States as a refugee and now lives in Minneapolis–St. Paul said that

[t]he difference between African and American leaders is that politicians in America provide for their constituencies. They provide them roads, hospitals, schools, and industries. In Africa, the politicians are not only corrupt, but they go one step further. They take the clothing off the backs of the poor; they take away food from the mouths of infants and feed it to their military comrades and their accomplices because they will be there to protect them. They negotiate international aid deals and siphon the money to foreign banks and meanwhile keep telling the rest of their citizens to tighten their belts for further economic austerities. Meanwhile, they, the politicians, are living very lavishly while the masses perish. There is something immoral about this.

"Africa is a rich continent," he went on to say, "but the lack of political accountability, suppression and stifling of ideas, and the political aloofness and haughtiness of the leaders will eventually spell the continent's doom. Meanwhile, the poverty, ignorance, disease, and suffering continues unabated. Despair is the number one enemy in Africa today."

From America, the immigrants watch with keen interest the political developments in their home countries. A quarter of the immigrants indicated they follow political events in Africa by listening to the British or French broadcasting stations that cover Africa in depth. Half of the survey respondents rely on newspapers from Africa, which can be bought at African ethnic stores. The rest obtain news from Africa through correspondence and American television coverage.

In terms of political participation in the American political system, a majority of the immigrants follow politics in the news, but they are less likely to participate. Many are constrained by their ineligibility as permanent residents to vote in American elections. But even among those who are citizens and who are registered to vote, few actually vote or participate in politics. Those who do vote tend to favor centrist democrats. Those voting in the 1992 and 1996 presidential elections favored Clinton over Bush and Dole. While they do not constitute a voting bloc at the national level yet, they definitely have a voice in local politics. The immigrant associations organize political activities for those of their members who are eligible to vote. They organize political events that bring in candidates for school board, city council, and mayoral elections. Citizens and non-citizens alike are coming to recognize the importance of participation in local politics, especially if they perceive that they can increase their political base by joining with other immigrant groups, notably Hispanic and Caribbean groups, to define a common agenda for collective political action.

Political and social participation at the national and local levels among the immigrants is influenced by cultural forces. As would be expected, educational attainment, class, income level, size of the community, size of the minority population, length of stay in the United States, and citizenship status are the major determinants of social and political activism. Participation is also determined by how far the immigrant chooses to integrate into society. The degree of participation in social and political activism is matched by the extent to which the immigrant identifies with the American social and political systems. African immigrant incursions into the political affairs of the host society may be limited. Politically, immigrant mobilization at the community level is usually defined around core issues such as quality education for children, support for healthcare and health initiatives, and access to affordable housing.

Despite their interest in political inclusion, political incorporation in America will remain elusive for African immigrants as long as they hold on to their sojourner status. For the majority of the immigrants, social and political activism will continue to be confined to Africa. Even though they are away from Africa, the immigrants maintain close connections with social and political issues at home. Immigrant newspapers highlight these issues. Fund-raising to support political and social causes at home is common. They lobby political leaders at home through letter writing and sponsorship of political activities in the host society. These forums are intended to call attention to particular issues at home and to formulate and coordinate action. The immigrant groups are a force to be reckoned with in African internal politics—a special constituency of relatively well-off people in America whose voices are having an impact on African social and political policies.

As African immigrants involve themselves in the social, economic, cultural, and political systems of the United States, they form perceptions and attitudes about the major social institutions. Coming from countries where major social institutions have failed to meet expectations, the immigrants view themselves as very fortunate to be in America. But as they negotiate the contours of life in their new home and interact with people, they begin to perceive the cracks in the system. An aspect of American social structure that the immigrants perceive as problematic is the interface between police and minorities or immigrants. Dominating the consciousness of the immigrants is the general perception that the police tend to be disrespectful, abrasive, and uncivil in their dealings with immigrant and minority populations. Among immigrants residing in large urban areas, perceptions of the police are even more negative. A twenty-one-year-old immigrant employed as a cab driver living in Minneapolis–St. Paul, expressed the view that

[t]he police are very aggressive with our type, people of color, people with accents, and, moreover, those of us who are non citizens. I have been stopped at night, had lights flashed in my face, and been questioned by them sometimes just because I happen to be a black man in an all-white community. This experience is not an individual one; it is a shared experience. Go to the West Bank of Minneapolis near the university and talk to Ethiopians and Somalis, and they will corroborate what I am saying.

Among those immigrants earning under $20,000 per year, confidence in and support for the police as expressed in the survey were very low. About 60 percent stated that they had been stopped and questioned by their local police for no apparent reason. Favorable comments on the police came only from immigrants who live in the suburbs, with college educations and household incomes above $50,000.

The fear of crime is also a major concern to the immigrants. Since the majority of them live in large urban areas, they are confronted with crime and its toll on inner-city minorities. Over 90 percent of the immigrants believe that crime is out of control in their communities. They attribute crime to family breakup, minority unemployment, the lack of affordable housing, and economic deterioration. A quarter of the immigrants indicated that they knew of an immigrant neighbor, friend, co-worker, or relative who was a victim of a violent or property-related crime. But generally, the forms of personal victimization commonly experienced by the immigrants were robbery and burglary. Fewer than 5 percent indicated that they owned a gun. The most common reason given for owning a gun was to protect family members. The level of confidence of the immigrants in the criminal sanctions imposed by the judicial system also revealed their perception of and level of confidence in social institutions. Like most Americans, the majority of the immigrants thought the courts were too lenient and needed to be more punitive. They would also favor laws that would restrict handgun purchases in their communities. This was certainly the case among those immigrants who had been victims of crime. Immigrant women were more in favor of gun restrictions than immigrant men.

In sum, an understanding of the cultural and ethnic identity of African immigrants is central to the economic, political, and cultural progress of the members of the African diaspora in the United States. The processes involved in the formation of cultural and ethnic identities are immensely complicated. A standard notion undergirding African immigrants' negotiation of racial identity and status integration involves the reaffirmation of the determination to become economically successful in the United States while socially and culturally remaining noninterventionist. African immigrants are yet to become fully integrated into mainstream American society. The ethnic associations that they form are not set up to enable the immigrants to put down roots in America. They are designed for the preservation of immigrant ethnic enclaves. Immigrants' strong ethnic and cultural identities serve to confine their social and cultural activities to carefully chosen aspects of the host society. Their intra-immigrant group structures have yet to foster closer relationships with the host society. The continued cultural isolation and alienation of the immigrants preserve their cultural heritage and ethnic identities. By relying on their strong networks of kin group associations, the immigrants are able to deal with problems arising from their experiences.

The African immigrants' survival in the United States has not been achieved by reaching out and establishing social and economic connections with the host society. Cultural and economic survival has come through the immigrants' ability to expand their contacts and connections with other immigrants of the African diaspora. Using the social capital of trust, kin bonding, belief in group as opposed to individual fulfillment, and a strong tradition of ethnic pride, the majority of the immigrants has been able to carve an immigrant identity. This identity is based, in part, on the cultural expectation of becoming economically successful in the United States.

The patterns of cultural and ethnic identity formation discerned among the immigrants are certainly under stress. Whether future generations of immigrant children will be able to maintain these patterns cannot be predicted. Suggestions can, however, be made. In the future, the vitality of the African immigrant networks will influence the degree of social integration into American society. In the dynamics of cultural integration and African immigrant lifestyles in the United States, economic and educational forces are bound to converge to determine the type of inclusion that the immigrants can negotiate with the host society.

# Chapter 6

# Family, Household Structure, Educational Attainment, and Business Formation

This chapter uses data from the INS, the census, and the survey of African immigrants in four American cities to describe family structure, educational attainment, and business formation among African immigrants. Family structure, educational attainment, and entrepreneurial participation help shape and define the contents of the relationships that the immigrants forge with the members of the host society as well as among themselves. Furthermore, the dynamics of immigrant family structure, educational pursuits, and entrepreneurial activities indicate the immigrants' expectations and undergird the various strategies that immigrants adopt to ensure their survival in the United States. In delineating immigrant participation in the affairs of the host society, a consideration of these forces becomes important for two main reasons. First, it defines the character of the immigrants and helps emphasize the motivations behind their desire to become successful in the United States. Second, it defines the social, economic, and cultural openness of the host society, its intergroup relationships, and the extent of its willingness to incorporate diversity into all its affairs.

INS data on family and household composition of immigrants are confined to basic demographic information such as age, marital status, and gender. One has to rely on the census for detailed information on the structure, composition, and internal dynamics of households and families of African immigrants. Household and family composition information found in the census includes number of children, number of older and younger children (siblings), family size or unit, total family or household income, number of families residing in the household unit, and number of fathers, mothers, and couples present. Other household characteristics included in the census are age composition, relationship of the head of the household to the rest, age at marriage, number of marriages, and ownership of the household's dwelling.

## FAMILY COMPOSITION AND HOUSEHOLD STRUCTURE

To most Africans, the family is a community of people related by blood and marriage. The maternal and paternal ancestry of the family members together determine the spirit and personality of the individual. Families have a governing structure whose responsibility is the management of family resources, assets, and conflicts. Families are extended, even though the forces of social change such as increased geographic mobility, ascendancy of achieved as opposed to ascribed status, divorce, and rising levels of industrialization and economic development are weakening the extended family structure. In spite of the impact of these forces, the African family generally remains extended.

The strong networks and kinship bonds that the Africans have brought with them to the United States ensure the vitality of the immigrant family. The African immigrant family is more than a social unit. It is also a unit of production, harnessing the contributions of its members to help raise their standard of living. Economic cooperation among extended family members makes possible the realization of group goals. Group goals and collective needs tend to be emphasized over individual needs and expectations. Conformity to the goals of the extended family unit is vital if members are to achieve a sense of collective economic security. To the majority of African immigrants, the journey to America is a family's investment in its future. It is hoped that those who are sponsored to come to the United States will one day assist other relatives as well.

Information from the census revealed that nearly 70 percent of African immigrant households had no children living at home. Another 11 percent reported one child at home. Households with two or three children at home formed another 12 percent. The survey that was administered to the immigrants in the four research sites showed that, on average, three children resided in households surveyed. The immigrant survey revealed a pattern in which some immigrants send their children home to Africa to be raised by extended family members. Fifteen percent of the respondents indicated that they have children who were born in the United States but are now living at home in Africa with relatives. According to the survey responses, while families would prefer to raise the children themselves, economic factors (high cost of child care, coupled with employment and educational demands) have compelled some to send their children home. The delays encountered in applying for a visa for extended family matriarchs or immediate relatives to come to the United States to assist in the rearing of children were also cited as reasons for sending children home.

The majority of the children residing in the African immigrant family household were born in the United States. Fifteen percent of the respondents reported households in which the children were born outside the United States and in places other than Africa. This finding offers additional support for the trans-global experience of labor leaving Africa in search of better economic opportunities in foreign lands.

The census revealed that the African immigrant's household is dynamic. Ninety-five percent of immigrant households comprise one family unit. Households with two or more families form 5 percent of households in the census. Information was also available on the number of mothers and fathers present in the household. Sixty-five percent of the households reported one father present. Those reporting two fathers in the household formed slightly over 2 percent of the sample, and those reporting no father at all formed nearly 33 percent. More than two-thirds of the Africans reported only one mother present. Households with two or more mothers present formed 5 percent of the total, with slightly over 25 percent reporting no mother present.

Another sociologically interesting variable in family and household structure is the number of siblings. According to census data, a majority of the households (nearly 65 percent) did not report the presence of any siblings. A quarter of the immigrant households had one or two siblings living at home. Immigrant households with three or more siblings present comprised approximately 10 percent of the total. The results of my field survey of the African immigrants revealed that about 11 percent of the households reported a sibling residing in another location. There is considerable secondary migration among household and family members within the United States. Students form the bulk of the siblings currently not residing at home.

Almost half of the African immigrant families (47 percent) included in the census had a total family income of under $20,000. Those with total family income between $20,000 to $39,999 formed 27 percent, with another 12 percent earning between $40,000 to $59,999. Those with a total family income of $60,000 or more comprised 14 percent. Included in this last group were households with a total family income in excess of $100,000, which comprised nearly 5 percent of the total. Census figures also indicate that as a group, African and Caribbean immigrant families had higher incomes than their African-American counterparts. The median family income for the African immigrants was about $32,000 per year, $10,000 more than the median earnings of African-American families (Census of the United States, 1970–90). The differential in income is accounted for by higher levels of education among Africans, white employers' preference for black immigrants rather than native-born blacks, and multiple wage-earning in African immigrant households (Waters, 1994).

Variations were noticeable in total family income by type of economic activity. Survey responses showed that total family income among self-employed immigrants ranged from a low of $21,000 to a high of $80,500. The highest group of earners were families operating immigrant stores. Their average total earnings were $60,000 per annum. Taxi drivers came in next with an average income of approximately $52,000 per year. In nearly eight out of ten immigrant households, spouses, siblings, and in-laws all worked and made contributions to household expenditures.

Information about immigrant home ownership was also available in the census. Slightly over one-half (52.4 percent) did not report the value of their home. For those who reported the value of their home, 30 percent of them owned or were buying their home. Those who owned their homes free and clear formed less than 3 percent of the African immigrant population. Twenty percent of the African immigrants were paying a monthly mortgage, and 43 percent were paying a cash rent. Under 3 percent were not making any rent or mortgage payment. Among those who stated that they owned a home, nearly 30 percent reported the value of the home as $109,999. Nearly 19 percent reported the value of the home at $110,000 or more.

Often, African immigrants prefer to rent rather than to buy a home. Evidence from my survey shows that the decision to rent and not buy is influenced by a number of factors. Size of household and family composition, occupational status, length of stay in the United States, and perceived time-table for returning home to Africa affect housing decisions. In general, the survey revealed that home ownership is the norm in immigrant households with multiple extended family members in residence. Home ownership is common among professional, as opposed to blue-collar, immigrant households. In addition, the average length of stay in the United States was eighteen years for immigrants who owned their homes. As expected, home ownership is low among those immigrant households whose members expected to return to Africa to resettle in less than five years. Among immigrants who were renting, a major barrier to home ownership cited in the responses to the survey was an inability to come up with a down payment and a lack of credit.

A cultural aspect of the immigrant household is the language used in communicating at home. Responses from the survey show that families communicate in English, French, or various African languages and dialects. In immigrant households with young children, English is the preferred language of communication even if the immigrants come from Francophone Africa. Immigrant parents who speak French also teach their children how to speak French to ensure that the children are exposed to their linguistic and cultural heritage. The immigrant children learn and play together in a multi-lingual environment. But generally, in the long term and for the sake of their education in the United States, the children of both French- and English-speaking African immigrants are encouraged by their parents to communicate in English.

Young men, fathers, grandfathers, and uncles dominate everyday family social life and interactions. Adult women and young females are relegated to attending to household responsibilities. During social events involving other immigrant families, the men and boys often socialize together in the living room while the girls serve food and drinks. The women foster their own interactions in the kitchen area.

In immigrant households with grandparents and in-laws, the young boys are accorded special treatment because they are the ones to continue the family's patrilineal line. Sometimes they are sent to private schools while the girls attend public schools. The expectations that fathers have for their sons are different than the expectations for daughters. The boys are expected to model themselves after their fathers. They are allowed to "hang out" with paternal relatives. The young boys are given more autonomy than their sisters. Both boys and girls receive an allowance from their parents, but boys are allowed to keep their money in a piggy bank. The girls usually give their allowance to their mothers for safe keeping and request the money when needed. In matrilineal immigrant households, the expectations that mothers have for their sons and daughters are similar. The equal treatment of children, irrespective of gender, is the norm. Household responsibilities involving children are assigned without regard for gender. Age has a greater influence in determining children's responsibilities than gender.

In the survey, the immigrant families stressed the need to guard and protect their daughters. A common perception is that daughters should not be exposed to sex and violence on television. The immigrants decry the pervasiveness of sex and violence on American television and feel that exposing children, especially girls, to television at an early age is the main cause of sexual and moral degeneration. In line with African traditional values, immigrant families with young daughters insist on their chastity until they are married. A daughter who becomes pregnant prior to marriage brings the whole family into disrepute.

When the family is visited by other immigrant families, the females' domain is restricted to the kitchen and bedroom area where cooking or clothing displays take place. Often on summer weekends, fathers and sons may go out to soccer fields, malls, auto shows, or the homes of other immigrant families. Grandfathers and fathers-in-law sometimes accompany them. But wives and daughters usually perform household chores, go to the supermarket, wash clothes, or visit other immigrant women. Even in households where a wife works forty or more hours a week, her weekend is taken up with household work—mainly cooking, sewing, and washing clothes. Usually, wives are assisted by their daughters and their mothers. The level of intimacy and emotional attachment among mothers and daughters is much warmer and more intimate than that among males.

## IMMIGRANT EDUCATIONAL ATTAINMENT

The importance of education in the migratory decision-making process has long been recognized by scholars. Educational attainment, especially in developing countries, is a major determinant of rural-to-urban migration among primary and secondary school leavers. In the developing areas of the world, completion of secondary school education has been linked to rural out-migration, especially from agricultural communities.

The reason for this is not hard to trace. After completing secondary education, graduates form aspirations that cannot be fulfilled in the rural setting. With the exception of jobs related to agriculture, producing and marketing, not many employment opportunities exist in Africa's rural areas. Cultural, recreational, and healthcare opportunities are located in the urban centers. The cities are the centers of political activity. Those leaving rural schools find that the rural economy does not offer the economic, political, and cultural advantages available to urban dwellers. The expected income is much higher in the urban sector, even though the costs of living are usually much higher. Over time, the net benefits of potential earnings in the urban labor market outweigh potential savings in a rural area.

Prospective African immigrants to the United States have already acquired significant experience as migrants in Africa, where they are likely to have traveled to distant places to attend secondary school or to unite with relatives. Nearly 80 percent of the survey respondents indicated that they had engaged in some form of migration for the purposes of education or work. People choose schools or employment possibilities in destinations where they can derive the greatest benefit.

For most African immigrants, links with the United States are first established through educational sponsorships provided by family members and government funding. Of the two sponsoring sources, family sponsorship to the West has become common due to the inability of many African countries to raise enough foreign reserves to pay for the cost of sponsoring students to go abroad. Deteriorating economic conditions have meant that many of the Africans countries are sponsoring fewer students for studies abroad.

Both the census and the survey data on immigrant education showed that 16 percent of the immigrants indicated they had completed high school. Those who had completed one to three years of college education comprised another 18 percent. Those with four or more years of college education formed 24 percent of the census total. In addition, 32 percent of Africans who have become naturalized citizens of the United States have a postgraduate education.

To many African immigrant families, education is an investment in human capital, the key to status and mobility in the United States. The gradual rise of African immigrant intellectuals testifies to the central role that education plays in the lives of Africans. For the immigrants who have had access to education in America, it is the confluence of their class status in Africa and America's tremendous educational opportunities that has propelled many to respectable jobs in this country. African values that are favorable and conducive to academic accomplishments are serving the immigrants very well.

Black African migration to the United States for educational pursuits provides major insights into the continuity of the African diaspora. Education is the major conduit by which Africans establish contact with the United States: first, as nonimmigrants on student visas and later as prospective immigrants and naturalized citizens. The expansion in primary, secondary, and postsecondary education in Africa following independence has produced educated Africans who cannot find jobs in their own countries because their economies have not expanded fast enough to absorb them. The result is that some African countries are confronted with the same problems that Ireland and Scotland experienced earlier—slow expansion in employment opportunities and oversupply of educated labor. This compelled thousands of Scottish and Irish people to search for jobs in other parts of the world, especially in the United States. The Africans coming to the United States are, therefore, not unique in this regard.

In general, the African immigrants represented in the survey reported having baccalaureate degrees in the arts and sciences prior to coming to America. The survey showed that many of the respondents had come to the United States as nonimmigrants on student visas to pursue higher education. Approximately 40 percent of the respondents had completed university-level training in Africa prior to coming to the United States. Once in the United States, the majority (80 percent) of those who had completed university education have acquired another degree at the master's or doctorate level. This high educational attainment cuts across gender lines, with about the same percentage of females as males pursuing advanced degrees.

Family-sponsored education was found to be very important among the immigrants. Ninety percent of the survey respondents cited family-sponsored education as the primary reason for coming to the United States. Government- and interagency-sponsored students formed a small percentage of the respondents who were studied. Among this group, the possibility of remaining in the United States after completing their studies is limited due to stringent visa restrictions and contracts requiring that they return home to serve in a predetermined role or risk legal problems.

The survey revealed that those Africans who entered the United States with a university degree were more likely than those without degrees to pursue advanced studies and thus they have higher prospects of social and economic mobility. Among this group were African immigrants who gained employment in professional and managerial positions. Among those immigrants who had completed only their secondary education prior to coming to America to pursue further studies, educational attainment in the United States was lower. This group was more likely to have completed an associate's degree.

Self-improvement and empowerment through continuing education is very common among those who did not come to the United States with a college or university degree in hand. This group shows a noteworthy resourcefulness and commitment to educational pursuits. Many of them, especially in the large urban centers, are combining full-time work with evening and weekend classes. Even among those who came to the United States illegally and later had their status adjusted to permanent residence (by marriage, immigration lottery drawing, or amnesty), it is common to enroll at a college or university immediately upon receiving a green card. According to a Ghanaian immigrant residing in the Washington, D.C. area, "Education is the key to social mobility for minorities, especially for immigrants in America today; it is the proven means for immigrant black social mobility."

Another immigrant residing in Charlotte, North Carolina, stated:

I see the connection between higher education and high status. I will do everything in my power to teach my children to see this connection. For without it, they will automatically disqualify themselves from a labor market that is very credentialized and competitive. To me, the lack of education is the missing link in the inability of blacks and other minorities to empower themselves. Good quality education is the key to advancement and personal empowerment everywhere you go.

The increasing success of the immigrants in reaching their educational goals is no surprise. African immigrants come to the United States with a rich tradition of commitment to education. Children are often sent to boarding schools or to distant locations to live with extended family relatives while they attend school. Limited space in African institutions of higher learning makes the system of education highly selective and fiercely competitive. The number of universities is rising but so is the demand for higher education. University entrance exams at both the "Ordinary" and "Advanced" levels are very competitive.

Access to higher education in America provides the African student with many opportunities for self-empowerment. An overwhelming majority (97 percent) of the survey respondents strongly agreed with the statement that "to become highly marketable, immigrants should pursue advanced degrees in the arts and sciences." A similar percentage of the respondents also agreed that to remain competitive on the labor market, immigrants should attain educational levels higher than those of the general population. The immigrants, thus, see the connection between higher education and the opportunity to attain positions with high salaries and fringe benefits. Seventy-five percent of the immigrants said they had taken advantage of tuition reimbursement programs offered by their employers. Even where tuition reimbursements were not offered by employers, more than 85 percent of the immigrants reported full participation in employers' on-the-job training programs. Participation in employers' on-the-job training program is seen as a way to gain advancements and a high salary. Like other Americans, however, the immigrants are concerned that the high-paying jobs in manufacturing and industrial work that used to provide opportunities for middle-class families are being replaced by low-paying jobs in the service sector.

Today, education continues to fulfill the function of introducing African immigrants to American values and culture. It provides access to social mobility and entrance into middle-class lifestyles while, at the same time, assisting in cultural integration. The majority of the immigrants who were surveyed viewed education as the only route to pursue to avoid being caught in the web of underclass status in the United States. Since the 1960s, large numbers of highly educated Africans have been arriving in the United States to pursue advanced learning. But also coming to the United States or already residing here is a growing number of Africans in their twenties who have yet to achieve educational credentials sufficient to provide them with access to quality jobs. For this group, the survey revealed, employment opportunities are limited. Though many are able to secure jobs in the service sector, increasingly, the seasonal nature of these jobs means that they face frequent layoffs. In addition, institutional discrimination rooted in color coding has restricted access to relatively high wages for African immigrants with minimal education.

Structural changes in the American economy have contributed to the employment problems of the African immigrants who do not possess educational credentials. The decline in inner-city manufacturing and production in the cities of the eastern United States has had a deleterious impact on the number of high-paying jobs available to immigrants with a low level of education. To stay employed, some engage in circular migration, moving from one city to another in search of jobs that pay above the minimum wage. This circular migration exacerbates their plight, sometimes preventing the continuation of their education. In addition, for those with families, circular migration disrupts family life, including the education of children. Eventually, however, some are able to increase their earnings by working multiple jobs, pursuing further education, or saving enough money to start their own business.

The employment picture is grim for those immigrants with low educational levels living in single-parent households. Responses from the survey reveal that African immigrant families headed by single, separated, or divorced mothers with limited educational qualifications tend to be poorer than those with both parents present. Even though the majority of these women are working multiple jobs, the total income from all employment sources is still below that of dual-income immigrant families. The lack of continuous gainful employment offering fringe benefits is a major hindrance to the economic mobility of female-headed African immigrant households.

Gender discrimination in the workplace aggravates the economic conditions of these immigrants. Accounts of African immigrant women working in a poultry industry near Charlotte testify to the discrimination these women sometimes encounter. Three African women who have worked for seven years at this plant earn, on the average, 20 percent less than their male counterparts in the same plant with fewer years of working experience. Locked into an employment condition offering little or no chance for mobility, female immigrants with limited educational skills find themselves in the ranks of the underclass. But not all the immigrant women who earn low wages are poor. Some of them adopt strategies to lessen the impact of the economic conditions associated with their low status. Using a system of cooperative economics, some of the women often join their resources by living together in the same household, taking turns baby-sitting, and sharing household expenditures.

In general, African immigrants' commitment to education in the United States has been facilitated by two main factors: first, the emphasis that African culture attaches to education; second, the immigrants' proficiency and fluency in English. Whether they come from Anglophone or Francophone Africa, the immigrants demonstrate sufficient knowledge of spoken and written English to enable them to pursue their education or engage in economic activities.

## AFRICAN IMMIGRANT BUSINESS FORMATION AND SELF-EMPLOYMENT

African immigrant business formation and self-employment are directly linked to family composition, family human capital, and intra-ethnic resources. The African immigrant family is the main provider of social capital for the fulfillment of economic goals (Portes and Bach, 1985). Immigrant family social networks can be effectively harnessed to provide comfortable incomes for their members (Kibria, 1994; Portes and Zhou, 1996). Self-employment entails entrepreneurial acumen and resource mobilization, and it provides an outlet for economic participation.

Survey responses show that business formation and self-employment among African immigrants are influenced by family size, gender roles, marital status, length of stay, ability to speak English, and educational attainment prior to immigration. The Business formation is more common among large immigrant households with multiple families in residence, households with three or more teenagers present, and households headed by a matriarch. The larger households rely on family labor. Teenagers contribute to family social capital through work. In addition, self-employed African immigrants have a longer duration of stay in the United States, averaging five years longer than those who are not self-employed. Their level of educational attainment at the time of immigration is completion of grade school. They are, therefore, less likely to continue their education upon entering the United States. In Africa, the majority of them were self-employed in some capacity, working with family members in the retailing business and utilizing family capital to facilitate business start-ups. Many newcomers to the United States bring human capital resources (multiple families, kinship, and strong interpersonal bonds) that promote self-employment. By forming immigrant ethnic enclaves, newcomers are able to mobilize economic resources.

As the African immigrant population in the United States has risen, so have the business enterprises owned and operated by Africans catering to other immigrants. As with other immigrant groups (Koreans, Chinese, and West Indians), family- and ethnic-based resources have facilitated business and self-employment activities among Africa's immigrants in the large metropolitan centers. Importing from Africa the consumer goods that the immigrants desire, immigrant retailers have managed to fill a void in their communities by serving as the sources of African foods, clothing, jewelry, newspapers, magazines, videos, and cultural artifacts. Bonacich's theory of middleman minorities (1973) fits the business formation and self-employment practices of African immigrants. At the Gold Coast Market Store in Atlanta, Georgia, a Ghanaian couple exemplifies how ambition and the drive to succeed have culminated in the establishment of a highly profitable African ethnic store. This store is oriented toward immigrants from Africa and the Caribbean. The owners have relied on family labor and on ethnic and family credit sources to fund the business. The success of this enterprise stems from the diversity of products and services that they provide. Originally, the Gold Coast Market Store sold Afro-Caribbean foodstuffs. Later, its owners began to promote African tourism and started offering their customers electronic message services.

The Gold Coast Market Store has become an information center where flyers announcing births, deaths, marriages, and the latest news from Ghana are exchanged by Ghanaians. There is also another ethnic store catering to the increasing immigrant African population in Atlanta. Here, traditional African medicinal herbs and root fibers for the treatment of all kinds of ailments can be purchased. The owners of these two stores have managed to eliminate brokers by going to Africa and buying these items directly. Their reliance on family labor works to their advantage because it reduces costs.

The growth of African ethnic markets in major cities across the country is assisting the rise of affluent middle-class African immigrants. The business enclaves that the immigrants form provide contacts among the immigrants and enable them to pool resources to meet common economic challenges. This economic base strengthens ethnic bonds and power, which can be translated into a political voting bloc. And, considering that the majority of the families said in the survey that they had no business experience in Africa prior to coming to the United States, their success is testimony to the human spirit fueled by the strong desire for success.

The survey respondents cited many reasons for the success of African-owned ethnic businesses in their communities including strong family units, collective resources, eagerness for self-employment, and the emphasis on hard work and trust. The businesses also fill an economic void in African-American and minority communities often ignored by large businesses due to redlining, racism, and the claim that business costs are high in crime-prone environments.

Gaining access to capital from banks and other financial institutions is the major problem encountered by immigrant store owners. In the survey, almost all of them said they are aware of the Small Business Administration and other state and federal agencies for assisting minority-owned small businesses. But only 15 percent of the store owners have utilized the services of these agencies. A general complaint is that the process of applying for a loan is tedious, and, more specifically, most of the store owners do not have the resources to hire a financial expert to prepare the detailed accounting report that is required.

Due to their location in predominantly minority communities, these businesses have difficulty securing loans from banks even though their owners can prove that they are capable of paying back the loan. Their location in predominantly minority and crime-prone areas is a major drawback. Most are located in minority districts not served by financial institutions. These businesses use other sources of capital. The major source is family/individual savings. One-third of the immigrant store owners indicated that the primary source of capital for their business has been credit card advances with very high interest rates. A common practice is for two or three immigrants to combine the credit on their cards. Capital is also raised from savings accumulated from other employment such as taxi driving.

A quarter of the store owners indicated that they received contributions from family members in the United States and Europe, which, when added to their own resources, enabled them to get started. The contributions from family members were usually paid back without any interest when the business began to make a profit. When the cash flow becomes stable, the business may assist other immigrants in the same extended family with capital to start up a business elsewhere. The African immigrant ethnic stores in the United States are examples of an adaptive role that the immigrants brought with them from Africa. This role is played by enterprising middlemen in almost all the major urban centers of Africa. Families and friends come together to form petty trading organizations selling everything from batteries to watches at traffic intersections or in small kiosks. Even when they engage in intra-African migration, the preferred forms of economic activity include retail and operating hardware and clothing stores catering to the needs of other immigrants from the home country. Capital is raised from extended family members, and young children are recruited from the pool of urban child labor to sell all kinds of consumer items.

This kind of cooperative economic spirit has worked very well for African immigrant business enterprises operating taxis, parking lots, clothing stores, and restaurants and selling hair products. The cooperative economic spirit is illustrated by three African restaurants in the Minneapolis–St. Paul metropolitan area. The proprietors of these restaurants all cited the importance of family resources and cooperative capital. Motivation to succeed is also crucial to the vitality of the immigrant ethnic stores.

By many measures, African-owned businesses are doing well, most deriving moderate-to-significant returns on their investment. Their mode of economic incorporation into the mainstream society is through economic self-reliance and internally generated capital. African immigrant business formation and entrepreneurial engagement is an adaptive mechanism designed, in part, to serve three goals—the formation of an ethnic economy, the generation of income, and the provision of steady employment.

Strong kinship bonds sustained by and anchored in traditional African values have been pivotal in the immigrants' adjustment to life in America. The majority of African immigrants have been able to preserve their traditional cultures. They have managed to retain their languages, value and normative systems, and socialization patterns. For example, they use their traditional African languages as a means of strengthening ethnic and clan affiliation and, at the same time, creating trust. The emphasis on family as opposed to individual dynamics has served the immigrants well in America. And, although they bring differing educational, family, and occupational backgrounds to their new country, for most of them, the collective familial recognition of the value of education has worked well to incorporate them into the fabric of American society. The stress on education, strong family bonding, hard work, and labor force participation have facilitated their incorporation.

# Chapter 7

# The Lives of the Immigrant Women and Their Children

Migration in Africa is highly selective by gender, age, birth order, and educational attainment. Physical and economic correlates, including distance, geographical barriers, and cost also influence the migratory process. In Africa, male migration is encouraged. When migrants travel to the large cities, the experience raises their social status and prestige, especially when they return home with consumable items, money, and gifts for extended family members and friends. For rural young men, traveling, working, and living in the major cities are considered part of the rites of passage from youth to adulthood. Celebrations and elaborate rituals await those who successfully make the trip to urban Africa. Rapid urbanization and population growth have made Africa's major cities the centers of business, commerce, arts, culture, and recreation. Cities such as Accra, Lagos, Nairobi, Johannesburg, Abidjan, and Kampala are examples of this.

Historically, women usually stayed behind to raise children, operate cottage industries, farm the land, and sell goods. When young women have been sponsored by family members to migrate to urban employment centers, they have usually been sent to married women living in the urban centers to serve as helpers or maidservants. In exchange for their domestic functions, the young women are often given economic and cultural sustenance, including education. By sending daughters away, parents are able to avoid the cost of educating them. These young women also make financial contributions to their family's budget.

Education, employment in the formal sector, and removal of cultural barriers have affected the migration of women. The introduction of compulsory primary education following decolonization has significantly altered the expectations and roles of women and children. Through education, women have come to recognize the enormous benefits to be gained by migrating to areas of economic and industrial concentrations. While some women migrate to the urban centers to continue their education, others leave the rural areas in search of jobs. Urban employment opportunities in the civil service, in petty trading, and in domestic work have brought African women into contact with the world outside the rural areas. The cultural barriers that prevented women (especially single women) from migrating to the large urban centers have weakened. African women are, therefore, not strangers to the complexities and uncertainties of the urban system, and, by extension, of international migration.

When they migrate, African women use various adaptive techniques to ensure their survival in the sometimes anonymous and impersonal urban system. In urban Africa, women migrants create and tap into networks of social and cultural associations formed to replicate the customs and traditions they left behind in their villages. Frequent contacts are also made with extended family members in the village. These help to sustain the migrants and provide emotional support.

African women also are bringing their migratory experiences to the United States. Young women and their children undertake the journey to America, usually unaccompanied, to seek the same economic and educational benefits as their male counterparts. African women provide an opportunity to understand the interactive significance and dynamics of gender in the international migratory process.

## FAMILY RELATIONS AND GENDER ROLES

To what extent have African immigrants replicated the structure of the African family in the United States? What are the statuses and roles of women and children in relation to male immigrants? What factors have shaped or defined how the African family functions in America? What are the patterns of kinship bonds, descent, and marriage? And how are these patterns forged in the host society? Are there any sources of cultural tension and conflict, and how are these resolved within the nexus of gender and sex roles in Africa and the United States? Are there any discernible child-rearing patterns among immigrant families? What means of social control are exercised by immigrant families, and how effective are these in promoting conformity and membership in the community? The answers to the above questions are central in revealing the structure of African immigrant family life in the United States.

In Africa, family relationships are usually extended as opposed to nuclear, even though cultural and technological changes are threatening age-old traditional beliefs about marriage and the family. Bonds of kinship are very strong. They stress the strength of the relationship among relatives of the husband and the wife. Every Ghanaian, for example, belongs to two families, patrilineal and the matrilineal, and every child is an amalgam of the blood (*mogya*) of the mother and the spirit (*ntoro*) of the father. The husband's blood maintains the well-being of the body and determines the male personality that transforms boys to men.

Expectations of family life and marriage are defined according to the laws and customs governing matrilineal and patrilineal relationships. Women's and children's roles are defined according to gender and age expectations. Families have a hierarchy or a governance structure that functions to arbitrate conflicts, ensure the economic viability of the family, and promote psychological well-being. Rules of inheritance and succession rights are also determined by the family council or elders. Socialization and social control are exercised by the collective, and decisions are binding and enforceable. Families always have the experience of elders to depend on for the transmission of norms, mores, and culture to the young. For this reason, the absence of a father or mother does not have the same deleterious impact on children as it does in the United States and other industrialized societies.

Children, especially sons, form the center of immigrant women's lives. For these women, the challenge of child-rearing and socialization is a daunting one. They must raise children in a foreign culture and, at the same time, inculcate in their children African cultural values and norms.

A common practice among the immigrants is sponsoring a family matriarch to come to the United States to assist in child-rearing and socialization. Reliance on matriarchs is a central feature of socialization and child-rearing patterns in Africa. Weeks before they give birth, women living away from home take up temporary residence with relatives until the child is born. Some women stay for long periods in their maternal or paternal family homes where they benefit from matriarchal skills in child-rearing. Other women stay at home until weaning is well advanced. Family members often live in the same household with their daughter and son-in-law, assisting in the rearing of children.

As children grow, they become anchored in the traditions and culture of the community. The vitality of African immigrant families originates in the kinship bonds, cultural ethos, and resiliency of the extended family. The sense of the family as a community and the relations that are forged among its members are the main source of adaptability of African immigrant women and their children. Actual and fictive kin provide economic, social, psychological, and cultural support, thereby lessening the pressures of child nurturing. By forging relationships based on reciprocity and inclusiveness, the women are able to expand the boundaries of their social lives in America without increasing the structural barriers they have to overcome as immigrants and minorities.

The immigrant families replicate African kinship structures that are central to their survival in the United States. They tend to cluster in particular neighborhoods for collective security in dealing with the problems of daily living. Bonds are fostered, friendships renewed, and goals and values reaffirmed. For the women, traditional roles and expectations defining how children are to be raised are predetermined and deviations from those roles are rare.

A common practice is to arrange for a wife to come from home. Alternatively, an immigrant returns home and, assisted by extended family members, selects a wife.

The immigrant woman is confronted with several problems in her role as mother-wife in a different cultural system. The process of integrating her new role as immigrant and mother with her minority status is complex and filled with stress. Immigrant women identify and construct their roles primarily in terms of safeguarding their families' interest and inculcating in their children a sense of hard work, self-reliance, perseverance, and service to family and community. To cope with the uncertainties and hardships of living in a foreign country, immigrant women form surrogate family circles. Over time, the networks of friendship are transformed into permanent relationships.

In America, however, the women redefine their roles to assert a measure of autonomy and independence from their husbands. The women avail themselves of the wide range of opportunities that America offers. Work outside the home, a major way to seek autonomy, is undertaken to supplement family income. Another source of independence is decision-making on family size. Women's preference is for a small family, usually two children. The taboos and cultural perceptions that the women may have associated with contraceptive devices while in Africa have disappeared. The women in the survey noted that being in the United States has considerably lessened the social pressure on them from extended family members urging them to have many children. It has also eased the pressure on them to produce male offspring. No longer do the women define their marital roles exclusively in terms of providing maximum satisfaction and happiness to their husbands. A sense of collective egalitarianism enters the world of the women, especially in their relationships with their husbands. The dominance of husbands and brothers is considerably diminished. The majority of the women no longer allow their husbands to claim the rights of dominance that the patriarchal system confers on males in Africa.

Some men, however, try to retain this dominance through physical and psychological abuse. Although the extent of this problem is difficult to assess, some of the women I interviewed, especially well-educated, financially secure women, were willing to volunteer information about their relationship with a current or former spouse. From the perspectives of the women, the strain resulting from changing gender roles is the root cause of spousal abuse. According to one female immigrant residing in Washington, D.C., "Some of the African men cannot deal with African women who become too Americanized. The men become insecure when you get a good job and start earning some money. They want you to stay at home and become a housewife. If you challenge them, they threaten you with divorce and remind you that they made it possible for you to come to America."

An immigrant woman living in the Atlanta metropolitan area was faced with a similar situation. Her ex-husband was finishing his doctorate when he came home to Nigeria and they got married. After completing his studies, he secured a job and a green card. He sponsored his wife to come to the United States. They had two children. Initially, the husband was supportive and encouraged his wife to go back to school. A few weeks before she was due to earn her nursing diploma, however, he started abusing her and the children on the grounds that her education was wasteful and incompatible with her status as wife and mother. On two occasions, he violently attacked his wife, who had to be hospitalized. A neighbor called the police and reported both incidents. Six months later, the woman filed for divorce and custody of the two children. For other women, male abuse includes threats of deportation, monitoring of phone calls, cancellation of joint banking accounts, restriction of contacts with other women, and even confiscation of passports and other travel documents.

## EXPECTATIONS OF CHILDREN AND INTERGENERATIONAL CONFLICTS

Expectations regarding the role of children in African societies are structured within the context of close-knit familial interaction. Parents stress to their children the importance of education, social responsibility, respect for authority, hard work, and service. African immigrant parents recognize potential problems in replicating African-based expectations in the United States. They can no longer rely on a collective system of socialization and social control. Their unfamiliarity with the American cultural terrain makes women become extremely protective of their children, often shielding them from overexposure to American culture. While parents try to replicate African socialization, however, their teenage children tend to adopt American cultural images and identities. This can be seen in clothing styles, language, food, music, dating, and sexual behavior. The parents stress the necessity of preserving their African heritage and culture among the second generation. They all believe that, in an increasingly diverse society like

America, the adoption of an African ethnic role is vital for the cultural survival of their children.

Immigrant parents expressed particular concern about children who adopt American culture and lifestyles. Parents tend to be very restrictive of their children's associates and the settings in which interactions with other children take place. This is because parents are not sure of what to expect from the non-Africans who interact with their children. Even when they know what to expect, they still attempt to restrict the frequency of their children's interaction with others, especially with non-African children.

The parents believe that the way their children define themselves in terms of cultural affinity and identification will eventually determine whether they will adopt African culture or the culture of the host society. A primary goal of many parents is to preserve African institutions of kinship and ethnic bonds among future generations while at the same time reinforcing the culture upon which these institutions and bonds rest. But as will be demonstrated later, parental insistence that children adopt African roles and conform to the same expectations as their parents often leads to family schisms.

Immigrant parents strongly desire to preserve their African cultural and ethnic identity. But by restricting the cultural interactions their children have with non-African immigrant families, these parents are also limiting the world view of their children and alienating them. The immigrant parents are adopting a viewpoint about urban native-born minority children that is based on the negative media portrayal of urban black and Hispanic families. The immigrant parents associate urban native-born minority youngsters with crime, gang subcultures, dropping out of school, drug use, lack of respect for parents and authority figures, and teen pregnancies. African parents see the social, cultural, and economic conditions associated with American-born urban minority populations as inimical to the values that African parents try to teach their children. Real or imagined, the immigrant parents' concerns about the influence of the urban minority culture on the lives of their children are fundamental to the flight of middle-class African immigrant families to the suburbs.

Length of stay in the United States does not seem to influence the social interactions of immigrant parents and their children. Irrespective of how long they have been living in the United States, immigrant families tend to confine their relationships and those of their children to other African immigrant families. The results of the survey indicate that for immigrant parents who have not been in the United States for long (under ten years), their second-generation children association with other parents and children from Africa is common. Their social network is confined to other African families who are also recent immigrants. The longer immigrant families have stayed in the United States (ten or more years), the less concern they tend to express about their children's associations.

The African immigrant community in the United States is not a self-sufficient, social, and economic unit. The immigrants, therefore, perceive the need to seek inclusion in the wider social polity. But they remain cautious about the pace of inclusion and integration that they should forge with the wider society because they do not want to lose their African cultural heritage. The intra-cultural security that the immigrants derive from their close-knit relationships is pivotal to the enclave communities that they form. The majority of the immigrants share the view that though their culture is undergoing stresses and strains, their survival in the United States is linked to their ability to preserve their institutions and pass on their African heritage to their children.

An investigation of subjective parental perceptions of the cultural affinity and identity of their children yields rather interesting responses. The majority of the parents in the survey (75 percent) believe that their children define their cultural identity as Americans. This is the case even for those parents whose children were born in Africa and immigrated at a very young age to the United States. In general, however, immigrant parents would prefer that their children identify with and adopt black African ethnic role models, not black American ethnic roles.

Immigrants are unanimous in their opinion that many aspects (for example, music, language, and clothing) of the urban hip-hop minority (mainly African-American and Hispanic) culture clash with African cultural expectations of children and adolescents. Immigrant parents expressed concern about gangsta rap musical lyrics' condescending manner and demeaning portrayal of women as sexual objects. Parents decried the declining significance of family life and the erosion of moral values. The majority of them indicated that they do not allow their children to listen to rap music at home. Often, this restriction causes a clash between teenagers and their parents. This clash, according to one immigrant, is a cause among immigrant teenagers of dropping out of school, early pregnancies, the questioning of parental authority, and the formation of subcultural values that contradict the values of responsibility, assiduousness, deferred gratification, and reverence for elders and authority figures.

An immigrant woman with a family in Charlotte, North Carolina, stated that "the values we brought from Africa are our anchor of survivability in America. Our kids who are copying the fads of the urban culture, especially their choice of music and clothes, are going to estrange themselves from us, their family, as well as the rest of America. This is of great concern to me." An immigrant parent who is raising a teenage daughter alone in northern Minneapolis said her daughter "was a stellar student in Africa before coming to America. In her junior year in high school, her grades went down, culminating in disciplinary problems at home. To avoid household chores, she registered for every after-school program. She spends her allowance on

*Vibe* magazine and gangsta CDs. Those gangsta rap musicians have stolen the mind and innocence of my child."

Although the world view of the African immigrant child is seen through the prism of American-ness as opposed to black African-ness or African-American-ness, immigrant parents perceive that assimilation and Americanization, while laudable, is acceptable only if their children emulate mainstream American values and not the values of urban minority groups who are becoming increasingly culturally marginalized. The following comment by a Nigerian immigrant (with an expression of frustration written all over his face) illustrates how immigrant parents' feelings about the cultural absorption of their children into the urban adolescent lifestyle:

My son now tells me that college is not for everyone; this coming from someone who while back home in Nigeria was living with my parents in a village setting where he completed secondary school obtaining a grade one in the General Certificate of Education examinations. He convinced me about the need to pursue college-level studies here, and I yielded to his request and brought him here just two years ago. Today, he is on the verge of dropping out because he hangs out with the wrong crowd, always talking about Tupac Shakur, Ice Cube, tire rims on a car he doesn't yet own, money out there to be made, and the latest musical video on Black Entertainment Television.

Another immigrant parent, obviously very concerned about the future well-being of her daughter who was born in this country, stated that "African immigrant children are redefining what roles and cultural identities they want to establish in America. As youths, most are beginning to adopt the garb and linguistic patterns of the inner cities to the dismay of their parents. Baggy pants, hooded or large athletic clothing [are] replacing the traditional African garb." According to this immigrant, there is nothing inherently wrong with urban minority cultural expressions. Her main concern, though, is that children do not become totally immersed in that culture. Children, according to her, must be guided by parents to recognize also the value of education, for without it, they will lose their economic competitiveness.

Certainly, the stress of the urban culture is felt by the second generation. Role strains and expectations are becoming a major source of intergenerational conflicts and rifts. While the cultural expressions and the identities of the second generation find expression in fads and artifacts that the parents deem to be a rejection of the values they brought with them from Africa, this growing intergenerational rift will persist. A major problem confronting the African immigrant parent is how to come to deal with the ethnic and cultural diversity of America, particularly the intra-cultural and intercultural fusion and mutual adaptation that is currently taking place among ethnic groups of different backgrounds. The group in the forefront of this cultural fusion and adaptation is the youth, whether of African, Hispanic, or Asian ancestry.

Parents fear that the values that they brought with them to America and that have sustained them thus far are being weakened and devalued by the second generation. For this second generation, their survival in America will be influenced in large part by how they define their ethnicity and the relationships that they are able to establish with the dominant society or with other minorities in the United States.

## WORK, HOUSEHOLD, AND LIFESTYLE DYNAMICS

Active participation in the labor force is common among African immigrant women both before and after immigration. In Africa, balancing work outside the home with housework is not uncommon for women. However, the stress associated with this duality of roles impacts the poor, rural, and uneducated woman more than her urban, educated counterpart. Women produce the bulk of food in Africa and their labor does not end on the farm. Some must travel great distances to fetch water, gather firewood for cooking, and take care of children.

African women are legendary in their entrepreneurial acumen. In Africa, women often dominate the marketing and distribution system, filling a void in a growing consumer-oriented population. Women serve as an essential link in wholesale and retail business by marketing the essential commodities consumed by the urban population. The financial and political independence that some African women have gained (for example, the Makola women of Ghana) as a result of their business and marketing skills is helping to redefine the role of women in African politics. Usually working with very limited capital, some women hawkers and petty traders have managed to transform themselves into forces to be reckoned with in African politics.

The immigration experiences of African women have not altered their traditional commitment to and involvement in work. The women immigrants are active participants in the labor force in this country, although most are confined to the service sector where wages are low and fringe benefits are few. They work primarily because working provides them with a sense of strong identity, reasonable financial independence, and a belief that they are contributing to household expenditures. By working, the women boost family income in immigrant households to levels that exceed the earnings of many native minority members, especially American-born blacks.

Female labor force participation at all ages in Africa is one of the forces that has led to an increase in the financial independence of African women from their husbands. In Africa, the majority of the women were self-employed, working in the wholesale and retail sectors of the economy where profit margins are very respectable. In the United States, whether they are self-employed or work for others, their entry into the labor market is facilitated by their fluency in English, a good work ethic, and their education.

The women accommodate one another's economic and social needs using a system of bartering that enables them to baby-sit children of other immigrant parents, cook, or sew, with little or no money changing hands. They also pass used children's clothing from family to family. The sharing of used children's clothing is indicative of their strong bonds of kinship rather than an inability to afford new clothes for their children. When no longer needed, children's clothes are shipped to relatives in Africa. Nothing is wasted.

Three recently divorced immigrant women and their six children living in suburban Atlanta exemplify this support system. The women encountered financial difficulties when they tried to move their families out of a high-crime neighborhood in Atlanta. They devised a plan whereby they saved enough money from their wage-based income to assist the family with the best credit rating to purchase a multi-level family house in a neighborhood with excellent schools and better quality living. For eighteen months, according to the oldest of the three women, they were each required to set aside $55 every two weeks. Angela, the youngest of the three, kept the money in a certificate of deposit at her credit union. After saving enough for a down payment, they approached a real estate agent. Once the house was purchased, the three families moved in together, and they shared the mortgage, cost of utilities, cooking responsibilities, child care, and parenting. This collective enterprise was dictated by one common goal—to pool resources to confront issues of daily living with an indomitable will to succeed. The three families plan to use the same cooperative spirit to fund a retirement plan and the college education of their children. The three women are bonded by a shared immigrant experience: the desire to achieve economic security and independence in a spirit of cooperation.

Continuing education is a major component of the experience of immigrant women. The survey found that the percentage of immigrant women who are employed and at the same time continuing their education exceeds that of males. Even though they are literate, the women perceive that the education they received in Africa prepared them for subservient roles that offered little monetary benefit. One female immigrant stated that the educational opportunities available in America have provided women with the chance to work and at the same time attend school. By combining work and education, the women are able to prepare themselves for lucrative positions. Like their male counterparts, these women see the link between quality higher education and well-compensated jobs.

The women have rejected wholesale assimilation into the dominant culture. They are fiercely traditional and deeply committed to African values when it comes to household organization, child raising, styles of dress, and expectations about children. Holding advanced degrees and well-compensated jobs has not altered the commitment of the women to African ideals. These women engage in a variety of social, economic, cultural, and political activities in their local communities. They join organizations like Parent Teacher Associations and Mothers Against Drunk Driving; they support the United Way; they volunteer at women's shelters and food banks; they fund-raise for charitable organizations; and they take turns hosting book club meetings. In these multiple roles, they could easily facilitate the assimilation process into mainstream society and become Americanized. But they do not.

The study found a growing trend among some women immigrants to send their first-born children home to be raised by maternal and paternal relatives. The biological parents in the United States send remittances home to support the child(ren). This practice is common among well-educated immigrants. The children are sent home not because the parents cannot afford the cost of providing child care in America, but because they want to expose the children to proven methods of family socialization and child-rearing in Africa. The children do not come back to the United States until they have completed the rigorous secondary-school curriculum. They return to the United States to attend college.

While immigrant women often defer to their husbands in decision-making affecting the household, this is only because husbands have usually been living in the United States much longer than their wives. The relationship that the women have with their husbands is generally more egalitarian than it would be in Africa. And although the majority of the women are involved in relationships that are structured according to patriarchal beliefs, they have redefined the boundaries of the patriarchal relationships. In redefining the boundaries of their patriarchal subordination, immigrant women rely on the experiences of American women, often alerting their husbands to the protections the law provides for women in areas such as property rights, inheritance, and obligations to children.

At gatherings involving other immigrant families, the women often discuss child care, fashion, cooking, hairstyles, and household management. The husbands usually chat about employment and job-related issues, education, the latest immigrant or nonimmigrant arrivals, preparations for weekend parties, naming ceremonies for the newly born, or marriages and funerals. Cooking is one way the women get to interact and exchange services or gifts. When people prepare it for other families, whether on a festive occasion or not, the cultural belief is that time spent on food preparation is inherently valuable and worth much more than a monetary gift.

Not many differences can be discerned between the types of foods the women cook in their households in America and the foods they cooked at home in Africa. The ingredients used in preparing common African dishes (*fufu, fanti kenkey, eba,* chicken or okra stew, peanut butter or palm nut soup) are readily available to them, especially in big cities. At the Weyone Enterprise store in Alexandria, Virginia, which specializes in the marketing of African foods, African immigrant women have access to a variety of African foods. They can also purchase clothing, the latest compact disks from Africa, jewelry, traditional footwear, and newspapers where they can read announcements of marriages, births, and deaths. Owned and managed by African immigrants, this store is truly international, attracting immigrants from the Caribbean and from other African diaspora communities. The Gold Coast Market, located near the Atlanta airport, is one of several African ethnic stores that cater to the culinary needs of the African immigrant community in that city. The Lagos African Market, located on Bloomington Avenue in Minneapolis, provides similar services for African immigrants.

The women play a major role in the celebration of annual religious festivals, as they do at home in Africa. Immigrant families from the same ethnic area come together to plan these annual festivities. Women buy and cook the food while men perform purification rites and ask their ancestors for protection from misfortune.

The women shape and define the dynamics of relationships inside and outside the household. The egalitarian relationships that they nurture between themselves and their husbands, as well as with their children, form the centerpiece of their roles as women and mothers. And when the balance of power between them and their husband's relatives tilts against them, they are very quick to respond and seek a remedy, first for themselves, and more importantly, for their children. A female immigrant from Nigeria gave an example:

Once I realized that my husband was sending the largest share of our collective funds to his relatives at home and sending only a fraction to my relatives, I became furious. I established my own banking account and started to withhold my personal contributions from his relatives. I made him account for the difference which I subsequently sent home to my mother. In Africa, I would not have had the courage to do this.

Of particular interest to the women is the decision whether to stay in the United States or go back to Africa upon retirement. The preference among the immigrants is to retire in Africa. But the women and the men often disagree on the time-table for retirement, and on whether it should be taken before or after the children are grown and have left home or after the husband reaches the age of eligibility to collect social security.

As a group, male African immigrants tend to confine their social networks to African and Caribbean immigrants. Their ties with American-born blacks are limited. The women, however, forge closer ties with American-born black females. The majority of the African women interviewed indicated that they interact frequently with black American women, often sharing ideas about African culture, especially cuisine, dress, linguistic patterns, and hairstyles. The relationship between the two

groups of women also centers on family life and techniques of child socialization in Africa. The purpose of this relationship, according to a Senegalese mother of three children living in Charlotte, is that black women feel
the need to give African cultural identities to their children. "It is through
intergroup interactions among the women of the African diaspora that we
can teach our rich cultural heritage to our children, nurturing in them values that recognize reverence for authority, meaning of work, and responsibilities of family life. This is the only way we can create and sustain African
communities that are self-sufficient."

The ties and bonds immigrant women attempt to forge with American
blacks are based on the common recognition that it is within the normative
ideals of African culture that the women can communicate to their children
the values, beliefs, religious practices, and legacies that form the foundation of African family, community, and social life. These bonds are vital if
the peoples of the African diaspora are to assert their cultural heritage in
white-dominated America.

As the number of black African immigrant women who sponsor aging
parents to come to the United States rises, so do concerns about the health
and welfare of these parents in the United States. In the survey, 20 percent of
the immigrant women reported that they live with an elderly parent. In Africa, aging parents are taken care of by the extended family, and the idea of
nursing homes and institutionalized care for the elderly is culturally anath-
ema. Children are expected to take care of their elderly parents. Coming
from societies in Africa where the system of national social security is not
well-developed, many families have invested in their children in the hope
that one day the children, in turn, will take care of them. Elderly parents
benefit from quality healthcare and better living conditions in the United
States. But the cost of providing healthcare and social services to aging parents is becoming stressful for many immigrant families.

The immigrants acknowledge the problems caused by depression and
ill-health among their aging parents but at the same time argue that they,
the immigrants, are unable to assist because of limited resources. But as one
immigrant woman indicated, though the elderly parents are faced with
many health problems, "they are surrounded by extended kin relatives and
grandchildren who interact with them and assist them with problems of
daily living." It is very difficult for the elderly parents to interact with the
larger society since most of them speak little or no English. Although this
limits their integration into mainstream American society, at least they can
interact with family members. From the women's perspective, the presence
of elderly parents in their households has not caused intra-family role conflicts. The elderly parents are respected for their age and wisdom. Their
presence has also eased considerably the younger women's child-rearing
burdens.

A transformation has occurred in the gender role self-definition of African immigrant women. In the United States, the majority of them have re-negotiated the patriarchal domination of their lives. The African woman is generally expected to be conformist, affectionate, and sensitive. Power, prestige, and status are often lacking in their relationships with male part-ners. Exposure to American culture is changing the routine interactions be-tween African women and their husbands. Their expressive and nurturing roles have been combined with instrumental and decision-making roles, thus lessening the unequal kinship structures that characterized their rela-tionships with men in Africa.

The majority of the women are enjoying the benefits of work outside the home. But at the same time, they are struggling to reconcile the demands of work, children, and social relationships. In the end, decisions about the res-olution and reconciliation of work and family relationships are made from the position of financial independence that the women have achieved in the United States. In their relationships with their spouses, the women seek personal development and autonomy to deal with the uncertainties of life in a foreign society. The majority of them recognize that they no longer have to accept the pressures and burdens placed on them by patriarchal struc-tures. An emerging pattern among the women is a willingness to experi-ment with alternate lifestyles that complement African culture. In this way, the women are able to maintain their African identities and cultures and at the same time embrace new roles and lifestyles. The power and authority in decision-making once held by their husbands have considerably dimin-ished in the United States.

Changes in gender roles are also affecting the lives of the immigrant chil-dren, who are becoming Americanized. In the multiple roles that they play at home and in public, these children are under extreme pressure from parents, especially from fathers, to pattern their lives after African cultural expecta-tions and role models. A bipolar pattern is emerging among the children. In the first group, which includes the majority of adolescent second generation immigrant children, there is cultural pluralism involving a blend of various racial and ethnic cultures. This group associates with youths of diverse cul-tures, native-born American blacks, Hispanics, white ethnic youth, and in-ner-city immigrant youth. These children coexist with various cultural groups and traditions and at the same time exhibit loyalty to a broader American cultural unity. The second group consists of adolescent immigrant children whose identities have mostly been influenced by strong ties to and identification with traditional African immigrant values and roles. Few in number, but fiercely loyal to their African heritage, these children tend to iso-late themselves from contacts with minority or majority youths. Most of them are fluent in at least one African language and have close-knit family relationships. Like their parents, these children have retained very strong Af-rican traditions, thus making their assimilation difficult.

## DEFINING NEW SOCIAL ROLES AND EXPECTATIONS

In the final analysis, issues pertaining to women and children cannot be overlooked when examining the broader context of international migration. Changes in women's roles in spheres such as labor force participation, education, fertility behavior, and child-rearing have consequences for the dynamics of gender role relationships in any society. In the case of African women immigrants, these changes assume an even more important dimension. As they attempt to forge or negotiate entrance into mainstream society, African female immigrants find themselves in a double bind. First, there is pressure to play new roles, become acculturated, or accept assimilation into the broader patterns of social roles in the host society. Second, they are faced with the traditional gender roles that they have brought with them from Africa. Third, they have to confront gender discrimination and sexism as they seek incorporation into the work place. The resolution of these role conflicts ultimately determines which roles they will validate and which they will redefine.

The African women immigrants have definitely undergone a cultural transformation as a result of their presence in the United States. They have, to some extent, maintained the social roles that they brought with them from Africa, but they have renegotiated them to achieve a more egalitarian relationship with their spouses. By not simply casting aside the traditional roles that they brought with them from Africa, but instead adapting these roles to meet new problems in a foreign environment, the immigrant women have demonstrated fortitude, resilience, and cultural continuity. By hard work, they have sought and obtained, individually and collectively, from their spouses, a clarification of the ambiguities in their traditional roles in relation to their new roles in American society. They have adapted their roles to reflect the cultural fluidity of American life. As the principal transmitters of African values and as care givers nurturing young and old alike, the women are the ones who define the parameters of African cultural identity for their children. In filtering out what they see as American cultural excesses and the shortcomings of African child-rearing ideals, the women are, in effect, providing guidance and direction to enable their children to negotiate the complex cultural maze of adolescent life in America. The sexism and discrimination confronting them in this country test their resolve to become economically independent of the dominating structures inherent in patriarchal relationships. Whether they are employed in the service sector where wages are low and benefits are hard to come by, or whether they are educated and occupy a professional niche, or whether they are housewives, one thing remains clear about the African immigrant women—they have evolved economic and cultural strategies to ensure the continuity of the rich cultural heritage that they brought with them from Africa. They strive relentlessly to pass on to their children this African heritage and its proven strategies for overcoming adversity. In Africa, a premium is placed on kinship and intra-family bonding. Children are an important aspect of family and kinship relationships. Age-graded expectations for children are incorporated into their socialization and control. Formal and informal systems of social control reinforce these values to ensure cultural continuity and preservation of the social and moral order.

# Chapter 8

# Pathways to Naturalization, Repatriation, and Future Goals

Citizenship is both a process and a destination. It directly affects immigrants' potential political influence and their social mobility in the host country (Portes and Curtis, 1987). In the world view of the African immigrant, becoming an American citizen is a long process beginning at the moment of entry into the United States and culminating in naturalization. The process has lifetime consequences for those who become naturalized citizens. Acquiring citizenship through naturalization involves a socialization process. Immigrants must learn the roles, mores, norms, beliefs, and values of the society in which they seek membership. With citizenship comes the recognition that one's belief and thought systems will be shaped by and conform to the core beliefs of the host society.

Naturalization is also a transformation of one's national identity, from being a "foreigner" to being an "American." The dynamics of the citizenship process involve role-taking. One of the outcomes of naturalization is the ability of the candidate to shape his or her behavioral patterns, assuming the roles and responsibilities of American society and seeing the world and oneself from the perspective of an American citizen. Naturalization is an act that fundamentally affects one's identity and, thus, it is emotionally and psychologically stressful (Pachon and DeSipio, 1994).

Are there discernible pathways that African immigrants follow to become United States citizens? What are the cultural meanings that African immigrants associate with citizenship, and how are these meanings constructed? The answers to these questions are important because they define the cultural dynamics within which images of American citizenship come to acquire symbolic meanings and social representation. In addition, an analysis of the naturalization process among African immigrants leads to an understanding of the choices confronting them as they reflect on the merits of naturalization. It also defines how the immigrants conceive of themselves and their status in the United States, and how they link their individual and collective identities with the community of which they seek to become citizens.

Several distinctive pathways to citizenship characterize the various African immigrant groups. For those who are undocumented, the process may begin with seeking legal adjustment of status as a permanent resident through channels such as marriage to a permanent resident or an American citizen, the immigration lottery, or the amnesty for illegal and undocumented aliens under the Immigration Reform and Control Act of 1986. For nonimmigrants such as students who have specialized in subject areas in high demand, the process may begin with practical training and proceed through labor certification and permanent resident status. Once permanent resident status is attained, immigrants have to wait from three to five years before they can apply for naturalization.

There are certain requirements for citizenship. These include meeting English language proficiency, learning about American history and civic and social responsibilities (including obeying the laws of the United States), paying taxes, and taking an oath of allegiance. The transformation from immigrant to citizen is thus accomplished through socialization.

For the immigrant seeking citizenship, there are not only requirements, but also costs. A major cost is having to give up the citizenship of one's birthplace. Having to give up one's national identity and take on that of another nation is a psychologically challenging endeavor, especially for those immigrants whose countries do not recognize dual citizenship. Candidates have to deal with notions of betraying the motherland. Giving up one's citizenship of birth is fraught with intellectual and emotional costs. In the end, no matter what decision is made, the goal is the maximization of the best interest of the immigrant. And this can be decided only when the immigrant has weighed the cost factors and weighed the perceived advantages and disadvantages of American citizenship.

What are the key factors in deciding whether to become American citizens or to retain the citizenship of national origin? Although many African immigrants seriously consider the advantages of seeking a naturalized status, a large number believe that citizenship does not erase the "alien" status imposed by their race. According to one immigrant, "Discounting the economic benefits that we enjoy in this country, there is no cultural benefit of naturalization. In America, my skin color marks me, defines who I am, and, more than likely, I will never achieve full integration in the affairs of this country even with the right to vote. So why should I give up my national origin only to become a peripheral and marginalized outsider in the United States?"

Another immigrant expressed his conflicts and ambivalence thus:

As long as African immigrants living in the United States continue to gravitate toward other Africans and persistently exclude others in their social relationships, citizenship will be meaningless. Full citizenship means being free to participate in the affairs of this country. It means [having] a committed interest in the larger issues promoting the betterment of all Americans. My sentiment is that the African immigrant, by choice, has yet to conceptualize the connections between citizenship and full social, cultural, and political participation. The economic participation through work they always cherish because it accords them positive self-worth and sustenance. Beyond that, aloofness dominates.

For most African immigrants, the possession of a legal status is sufficient, especially among those who do not intend to retire here in America. Most of them prefer to renew their alien registration certificate every ten years even though they are qualified to become naturalized citizens. In this respect, Africans are different from Hispanic and Asian immigrants who vigorously pursue citizenship. The Africans come to America seeking to negotiate a sojourner status, a temporary legal status that enables them to educate themselves, to work, and to save enough money to provide the capital needed to establish a business at home. Most African immigrants expect to return to Africa to live there permanently.

A number of factors undergird this decision to return home. First, rising levels of economic activities and industrialization in Africa (following almost three decades of economic stagnation) are creating opportunities for Africans who are living in the United States and in Western Europe. Growing numbers of businesses are forming in Africa, spearheaded by Africans abroad who are able to raise capital from overseas. They use the capital they raise from overseas to establish import-export businesses. These businesses make it possible for Africans to have access to imported consumer goods that are always in short supply. A majority of the African governments have not been able to meet the basic consumer needs of their populations due to a lack of foreign exchange and capital to buy goods from abroad. For economic reasons, therefore, most immigrants perceive that they stand to gain by operating a business in Africa. A statement from a Ghanaian immigrant reflects this sentiment:

As you know, the dollar and British pound go a long way in Africa. My goal is to save enough money to buy buses and operate a transportation service between Kumasi and Accra. With my green card, I can still have access to auto parts in the West because I can travel with minimal restrictions. One does not have to be a citizen of the United States to do the things that I want to do. The only thing that will compel me to apply for American citizenship is the passage of legislation that will deny or reduce social security payments to permanent residents because they are not citizens. Right now, there are people in Ghana who have permanent resident status in the United States and are collecting social security checks. To most of them, I think the economic benefits derived from the social security checks far exceed the opportunity to vote.

Although the decision not to naturalize may be influenced by rising aspirations and economic expansion in Africa, the decision to naturalize and remain in America permanently is sometimes influenced by non-economic forces, especially the precarious political conditions prevailing in Africa and what one immigrant referred to as the "resurgence of factional cleavages based on ethnicity that are causing political unrest and disorder." In more general terms, the naturalization decision is contingent upon whether conditions at home improve to the point at which the governments of Africa can assure their citizens human rights, freedom, and democracy. The immigrants and their families are going to choose to live in countries where they will be free to live unhindered by regimes that are corrupt and abusive of their citizens.

Another immigrant with permanent resident status who is planning to return home to Africa to take advantage of increasing business opportunities in his home country echoed the same economic theme:

Why should I spend over $100,000 for a house in the United States paying an interest of about 8 percent for thirty years when with only $20,000 I could build a nice two-story building or purchase one in [one] of the exclusive communities in the Accra-Tema area, or in Kumasi? The nice thing is that once I become eligible for social security, all I have to do is have the Social Security Administration direct-deposit my monthly check. We have banks in Ghana now that will allow you to draw your money in dollars once you have a foreign account. Life doesn't get better than this.

The African immigrant is a sojourner and a stranger in America and often does not aspire to naturalize or assimilate. Becoming culturally and economically integrated is not a major goal. Most African immigrants have one goal in mind, and this they pursue with relentless vigor—the goal of achieving economic independence and self-sufficiency and funneling their assets to Africa to start a business or retire. They realize their expertise and access to capital are needed in developing Africa. African governments are also liberalizing their industrial and commercial policies to make it easier for their nationals residing abroad to transfer capital home. The adversarial climate that was characteristic of relationships between African governments and their nationals abroad is being eased considerably.

During the economically turbulent years that Ghana experienced from the late 1960s to the early 1980s, stringent, though unenforceable, laws were passed to restrict the purchase and the exchange of foreign currencies, especially the American dollar and the pound sterling, except through a banking or other financial institution. However, Ghana's dependence on foreign currency brought in by citizens living abroad has now been recognized as crucial in the economic development process and has, therefore, legitimized these transactions.

The perception of African governments is that although the brain drain has had deleterious consequences in the process of national development, eventually the governments stand to gain when reverse migration occurs or nationals abroad send remittances home. These remittances are playing a vital role in business formation and entrepreneurial activities among returnees or, in their absence, among their family members or business associates. Three out of every five immigrants in the survey indicated that they are in the process of setting up a business back home or have already set one up. One immigrant said: "How can one not take advantage of the strong dollar at home in Africa to set up a small business enterprise? There is money to be made in Africa's expanding economies. There is a high demand for Western consumer goods, and some of us are going to establish businesses to meet that demand before American retail giants like Wal-Mart go there to dominate the retail market."

Immigrant economic culture in the United States is underpinned by the recognition that material prosperity, no matter how it is measured, assumes meaning only in terms of the fulfillment of specific economic goals. Most African immigrants structure their economic decision-making by focusing on the long-term economic potential of their homelands. Participation in the economic development of their countries of origin is paramount. The opportunity to be in America and the migratory process are tools that facilitate the accomplishment of economic goals. And for the immigrants, America provides ample opportunities for the fulfillment of these goals.

The degree of cultural, social, political, and economic integration into the daily activities of the host society has an influence in determining whether or not African immigrants decide to become naturalized citizens of the United States. Survey respondents' social class—measured by educational attainment, income, age, home ownership, and membership in professional associations—is strongly related to the probability of naturalization. In the main, the African immigrants who classify themselves as middle and upper class tend to apply for naturalization more often than immigrants who are lower in social class. The probability of becoming a citizen also varies by income. Generally, higher-level income earners, those with household incomes in excess of $50,000, are more likely to file for citizenship than those whose combined family income is under $30,000.

Educational attainment levels also influence the naturalization process. Higher levels of education were found to be associated with a higher frequency of applying for citizenship. Immigrants with degrees and postgraduate education or training tended to apply for citizenship more frequently than those immigrants with associate degrees or high school diplomas. In addition, those immigrants with educational backgrounds in technical and vocational areas applied for naturalization and citizenship at a higher rate than those with only secondary school education. Overall, naturalization was found to be common for those African immigrants who had completed a bachelor's degree at an African university prior to coming to the United States. The high frequency of naturalization among well-educated and professional African immigrants supports the "socio-economic-determinants" model in immigrant naturalization research literature (Bernard, 1936; Beijbom, 1971).

In addition, it was found that African immigrants married to American citizens tended to apply for citizenship status more frequently than those married to permanent residents. The number of children in an immigrant household, as well as their age, also determined whether or not citizenship would be sought. Immigrant families with three or more children at home under ten years old tended to apply for naturalization at a higher rate than immigrant households with fewer than two children under ten years of age. The reason for naturalization among the immigrants with children is clear: to ensure the best for their children. In addition, there is parental concern that their children will encounter discrimination and mistreatment on account of their race (Portes, 1994).

Status integration as determined by membership in professional organizations, age, and home ownership facilitates easier assimilation and increases the likelihood of naturalization. Citizenship was found to be higher among those immigrants who reported having memberships in professional associations. Significant variations were also found in terms of age and the probability of becoming a naturalized citizen. The relationship is inverse, meaning the rate of naturalization rises among all age groups before declining as age increases. In general, immigrants in the age category 20 to 40 have a higher frequency of applying for citizenship than any other age group. Home ownership also increases the probability of naturalization. The results of the survey indicate that those immigrants who made monthly mortgage payments as well as those who owned their homes free and clear of any mortgage payments were more likely to become United States citizens. A higher degree of immigrant integration and assimilation into mainstream American society is more likely to lead to citizenship (Guest, 1980; Evans, 1988; and Garcia, 1981).

Variations in naturalization are evident when nationality and place of birth are considered. First, immigrants from Anglophone Africa were found to have a higher rate of naturalization than those from Francophone Africa. Second, Nigerians and Liberians had a higher rate of citizenship than other immigrants from Sub-Saharan Africa. They were followed by immigrants from South Africa and Ghana. The lower rate of naturalization among Francophone immigrants can be attributed to two reasons. First, the emigration of Africans from French-speaking Africa to the United States is a fairly recent phenomenon. Second, many of them go to France, Belgium, or Canada for their education because of the strong cultural ties that they share with these countries. The linguistic division of Africa into Francophone and Anglophone has implications in terms of African immigration patterns to the West.

## PERCEIVED ADVANTAGES OF NATURALIZATION AND CITIZENSHIP

Immigrants who become United States citizens acquire rights, privileges, and benefits including the right to vote, to carry an American passport, and to sponsor immediate relatives to come to the United States. According to one recently naturalized immigrant, "American citizenship has enabled me to obtain [an] American passport. So far, I have used it for travel in Africa and Asia. Since becoming a citizen, I am accorded some degree of respect which I did not have previously when I traveled with my Nigerian passport. Almost all international ports of entry scrutinize Nigerians because of our complicity in international drug trafficking."

The survey results revealed that the most important determinant of naturalization is educational achievement. University degrees and professional credentials go hand in hand with higher rates of naturalization. The opportunity of access to high-paying public service jobs, state or federal, provides the primary motivation for becoming naturalized. Included in this group are Africans who hold master's and doctoral degrees in areas such as accounting, engineering, and computer science. By acquiring citizenship, highly educated immigrants become eligible to compete for jobs in sectors of the economy that require applicants to be citizens. In addition, the desire to compete for bilateral and multilateral scholarships and professional exchange programs between the United States and other major industrialized countries influences naturalization among African immigrants with advanced degrees. The purpose of citizenship for this group of Africans is to gain full participation in the affairs of this country. An ethnomusicologist from Ghana who migrated to this country and recently applied for naturalization illustrates this position. Commenting on what he perceives as the advantages of naturalization, he stated: "I want exposure to other countries to show my skills. I realized that there are several opportunities for American citizens to travel and live abroad under international agreements between the United States and other countries. Having a green card is great, but it limits your competitive edge in the global academic community. Once I get my citizenship, I will apply for the Fulbright Scholars Program."

The opportunity to vote, to participate in the political process, or to run for political office at the local level also ranked very high among the reasons offered for becoming a citizen. Engaging in the political affairs of the United States was seen as a way for African immigrants with citizenship status to shape and influence decisions at the national level on immigration and on political and economic issues affecting Africa. The immigrants noted that previous immigrants of European ancestry, upon becoming citizens of the United States, ran for political office at the local and national level. Over time, as one immigrant pointed out, "Every immigrant group—Irish, Italian, or German—has contested for a presence on the corridors of political power even if only to use that power to safeguard the economic and political interests of Europe. African immigrants who become citizens must do the same for Africa." However, the African immigrant political presence has not yet become a dominant feature of social and political organization in the United States. Neither has it become a comprehensive organizer of African immigrant social and political life. For now, other dimensions, especially the economic dimension, are far more powerful factors shaping daily life and expectations among African immigrants.

The effects on politics in the home country were also cited as a motivation to naturalize. Some of the immigrants naturalized so that they could become advocates of political change and reform in their home country. According to one Nigerian immigrant,

I naturalized so that I can get the protection of American citizenship to enable me to express my views about political corruption in my country, mobilize people for change, and fight for democracy. Without American citizenship, I can still work as an agent of political change in Nigeria. But I will fear for my safety and that of my family. I can be killed. Citizenship in this country gives me some political legitimacy and cover to actively engage the political system of my country with minimal repercussions.

A similar sentiment was expressed by a Liberian immigrant who is now a naturalized citizen. According to this immigrant, becoming a U.S. citizen has given him the courage to speak out about the political illegitimacy of African leaders. Having the status of a citizen has meant that "I can educate my fellow politicians in my country about something they have failed to understand—that it is all right to be in political opposition and still pursue democracy. Currently, several of our African leaders are yet to recognize political opposition as a form of legitimate representation."

African immigrants often view citizenship as crucial for the future prosperity of their children and their immediate relatives. "The best opportunity I can offer my children," according to one resident alien in the nation's capital whose children are currently citizens of Ghana, "is to apply for naturalization so that they can be reunited with me. Once here, they will have access to grants and scholarships to help pay for their college expenses, better healthcare, and an improved quality of life. If citizenship would ease their plight and guarantee them a better chance in life, then that's what I will do."

The possibility of reuniting with family members is a major reason for acquiring American citizenship. Citizenship also carries with it status and prestige among extended family members in the country of origin. Immigrants who have naturalized tell stories about how parents and relatives at home in Africa boast about their accomplishments. Praise and accolades are given to those who have become citizens. One immigrant summarized the collective views of his family in Africa about his naturalization. To his family, the symbolic meaning of becoming a naturalized citizen of the United States is a "cherished privilege, a blessing and the beginning of a brighter future. There are psychological benefits for being a citizen. The benefits are not always economic or political. The direct rewards of citizenship have far greater meaning for my extended family at home than for me. My mother tells her friends that her son went far away to *abrochi* and became a citizen." Another respondent indicated that becoming an American citizen is a status symbol not only for himself but, more importantly, for his extended family at home.

My citizenship has far greater consumption value back home. To my home folks, I have arrived, I have made it in the white man's land. You see it in people's eyes when you go home for a visit, when family and friends alike introduce you to others; the introduction is never complete unless reference is made about the fact that I am now an American citizen. Everyone, young and old, and especially those with aspirations to go abroad in the future want to see [me].

Immigrants who visit home regularly upon becoming U.S. citizens are hailed and often fed lavishly. Maternal and paternal relatives may travel considerable distances to pay homage and exchange greetings. There are celebrations, and everyone gets in a festive mood. On occasions when a visit home coincides with a religious celebration, the atmosphere becomes even merrier. From their meager resources, family members contribute money to organize a welcome party. A sheep or goat may be slaughtered. In return, family members expect the immigrant to open his wallet and liberally distribute money and consumer goods. The social and economic capital that comes with citizenship is highly valued. Furthermore, for those immigrants who are not married, citizenship enhances their prospects for marriage.

But with citizenship also come greater financial obligations. Extended family members expect remittances to increase. There is an expectation that the material rewards of citizenship will be shared with relatives at home, for example, by building a family house. In addition, annual visits to see relatives and visits during religious celebrations and funerals are expected. The majority of those in the survey with citizenship status agreed that while extended family members are willing to give them time to become permanent residents, when they become citizens, no time is wasted before relatives redefine old promises and establish new obligations. Failure to provide generous financial assistance to family members upon attaining citizenship is considered a disgrace and sometimes results in subtle ostracism and exclusion from family decision-making. Direct pressure to conform to the family's expectations regarding remittances may come from elders who remind their children of the sacrifices others made to provide the education or financial assistance that made the journey to the United States possible. Family-sponsored migration is a major aspect of African migration. Those who are selected by their family for educational sponsorship abroad are expected to assist other family members once they have completed their studies and have obtained gainful employment. Infrequently but not rarely, the entire family may reject a newly naturalized immigrant for not providing material assistance to family members. One immigrant with citizenship status who failed to remit money to his relatives for a whole year described his experiences on returning home:

Upon [my arrival] in my village, my family treated me royally during the first three days. Immediately after that, the hospitality and services began to diminish. The lavish cooking slowed. After one week, I would be lucky if I got one hot meal. My whereabouts [were] of no concern to anyone. My sisters stopped cleaning my room. And I was shocked when my father said to me: "When you die, make sure you are buried in America."

In American discourse on immigrants, there is a widely held belief that immigrants apply for legal status to become eligible for welfare benefits. Public culture and ideology reinforce this view, which can result in the passage of legislation preventing immigrants from receiving public assistance. Among African immigrants, the opportunity to receive social benefits is not a major reason for acquiring naturalized status. Nearly 70 percent of the immigrants surveyed indicated that the opportunity to become eligible for public support did not influence the decision to become naturalized.

The majority of the immigrants do consider the benefits of citizenship, but only a small proportion will file to become naturalized. As indicated, for a majority of the immigrants, having a green card is considered sufficient legal status. Reasons cited by the immigrants for not applying for naturalization included lack of time to prepare for the citizenship examination, feelings of patriotism associated with the homeland, and the perception that with the exception of the right to vote, citizenship does not confer any special privileges to immigrants over and above permanent residency.

The decision not to naturalize is framed by the immigrants' own construction of what one termed the "boundaries of citizenship." The boundaries of citizenship in America are influenced, according to this immigrant, by the degree of racial inclusiveness or exclusiveness in American society. In his words,

Citizenship does not ensure inclusion and protection as long as race determines life chances and economic and political power in the United States. The ethnic and cultural identities that African immigrants bring with them to the United States are bound to lose much of their relevance with increased African naturalization. In America, sometimes, your blackness is held against you; it imposes boundaries and even limits your choices of identity. As long as I remain African, I want to remain free of such boundaries.

Immigrants have strong attachments to the United States. But underneath the bonding, the majority of African immigrants recognize that the persistence of racial categorization and institutionalized discrimination will remain a barrier to their full incorporation as citizens or permanent residents in the affairs of this country.

## THE AFTERMATH OF NATURALIZATION AND POST-RETIREMENT DYNAMICS

What are the long-term goals of African immigrants in this country? Does becoming naturalized imply the intention of staying permanently in the United States? What role, if any, do naturalization and permanent resident status play in shaping the post-retirement activities of African immigrants? Although the majority of respondents perceived that their standard of living was better than that to which they were accustomed in Africa, the survey revealed that nearly 80 percent of the immigrants plan to repatriate to Africa permanently upon their retirement after their children have left home. Immigrants very frequently expressed the desire to be at home in their birthplace after retirement, with relatives and friends. This applied irrespective of immigrants' educational, professional, and socioeconomic status. Most immigrants were eager to discuss retirement and long-term goals. Plans being made toward retirement in Africa included purchasing or building a home and establishing a business.

Economic factors dominate the immigrants' decision whether to live permanently in the United States or return to Africa after retirement. The survey revealed that among those whose yearly incomes range between $30,000 and $50,000, the desire to return to Africa is more prevalent than among those whose income falls between $20,000 and $29,000. Home ownership in Africa is also a determinant of the decision whether or not to repatriate. In general, those immigrants who already own a house in Africa are more likely to consider repatriation than those who do not. The homes are usually rented out and the income used for the educational expenses of extended family members, supporting the elderly, or investing in a business.

The decision to repatriate is influenced by three additional factors: the frequency and length of visits made to Africa while a permanent resident or a naturalized citizen, the number of siblings and relatives already in the United States, and the establishment or absence of a family-operated business in Africa. In addition, repatriation is influenced by the age and number of children in the household, the nationality of the spouse, and the anticipated cost of relocation and other financial considerations. The desire to relocate was found to be higher among immigrants who make yearly visits home, who have fewer than five relatives already in the United States, and who have established a business venture in Africa. While job satisfaction, educational attainment, and occupation are all significant in predicting post-retirement plans, these factors are outweighed by the actual amount saved toward retirement and the financial vehicles in which the savings are invested or held. Immigrants who own stocks, annuities, and bonds, unlike those whose savings are in treasury bills and passbook accounts, tend to be more committed to returning to Africa permanently.

Immigrants' desire to move to Africa upon retirement is not much influenced by length of stay in the United States or by immigration status. Financial exigencies and the amount of money available have a greater significance in predicting retirement initiatives. Since the majority of immigrants do not plan to stay in the United States permanently, most take steps to set up a savings plan that will facilitate their plans to repatriate to Africa.

A group of Ghanaian and Nigerian immigrants in Atlanta have formed a *susu* (savings club) to fund projects in Accra and Lagos that will provide economic support once they arrive home. This savings club started in 1989 with twenty-five members ranging from taxi drivers to engineers. Since the group's first meeting at a suburban Atlanta home, membership has risen to fifty-three, with another twenty-six waiting to join at the time of my study. An initial deposit of $25 is required to join the savings club. Thereafter, a mandatory deposit of $50 must be made every two weeks. When members fall behind in their payments, they are not automatically dropped from the club, however, as loss of income due to unemployment and family problems are taken into consideration.

One-third of the total assets are invested in economic ventures in the Atlanta area, with the rest going back to Ghana or Nigeria in the form of capital or business formation. The driving force behind the savings club is to ensure that upon their return home, the immigrants will not be put to shame by extended family members who have come to expect so much from them. One immigrant said, "if I am not able to put together sufficient resources, do something meaningful back home before or after I return, then I might as well stay here. And when I die, I might as well be buried here in the United States." Another club member indicated that the reception he receives during visits home is linked to how long he will be able to provide for family members. Irrespective of the motivations for joining, one fact seems clear. To assure economic security for themselves and their families, the immigrants recognize the necessity of setting aside part of their earnings for use when they leave the workforce.

Most of the survey respondents are using passbook savings, bonds, and treasury bills to save for their retirement. Only 15 percent of the respondents mentioned investments in stocks and growth funds. The better educated immigrants were most likely to invest in stocks and equities. Generally, those who indicated they would prefer to retire in Africa were confident that they would have sufficient resources to meet their retirement needs. One respondent indicated that she had recently spent about $10,000 to purchase a house in Africa to serve as her retirement home. According to her, "one does not need to have a lot of money to retire in Africa because of the strong value of the American dollar relative to currencies in Africa. You know in Ghana, the American dollar is officially over two thousand times the local Ghanaian currency."

In discussions of the long-term goals of the immigrants, the term "free hustler" emerged. As used in the African immigrant community, this term describes a small but growing number of African immigrants who have permanent resident status or, in a few cases, are naturalized. Primarily Nigerians, Ghanaians, Liberians, and, more recently, South Africans, these immigrants initially came to the United States to pursue education but were unsuccessful because of insufficient funds. Always in a state of transnational transition, these immigrants have no ties to a specific country, nor do they have a fixed business address or location. Their economic mainstay is the import-export business; they often buy the much-needed foreign consumer items that urban Africans and the growing middle class have become dependent upon. They sell these items to retailers and middlemen and then use the proceeds to buy African consumer items for sale to African immigrants all over the world. This group of immigrants prefers to reside in one of three Western countries—the United States, Canada, and Great Britain—even though a few have succeeded in making inroads into Asian capitals. They choose locations where they can secure access to international consumer markets in which they can purchase items in bulk for shipment to Africa.

Often using the United States as a base from which to conduct their businesses, these immigrants operate largely outside the African immigrant kinship bonds, using the immigrant networks only when it suits their economic and cultural interests. Preferring to maintain their designation as alien registrants, this group of African immigrants generally has no immediate plans to repatriate to a specific country or to seek U.S. citizenship status.

## IMPLICATIONS OF NATURALIZATION: IMPACT ON AFRICA

At first glance, one might opine that the migration of Africa's skilled and unskilled labor to the United States has no obvious value to the immigrants' countries of origin. As a continent undergoing economic and political transformation, Africa needs to mobilize every available human and capital resource in the drive toward self-sufficiency and economic independence. Since emigrants from Africa tend to be young, usually in their twenties and thirties, and many are skilled or highly educated, their departure seems bound to have a deleterious impact on development.

Whatever the economic and political problems confronting the African nations today, there is little doubt, however, that the Africans who are migrating to the Western industrialized countries will play a major role in shaping the future direction of the continent. Whether or not they become citizens of the countries to which they migrate, they influence the political, cultural, and economic organization of their home countries. Those who return home become agents of social, cultural, economic, and political transformation. They often introduce commercial and entrepreneurial innovations, form new political parties, advocate the democratization of social institutions, and foster the creation of a civil society in which basic human rights are guaranteed, and governments do not subvert constitutional rights. Immigrant returnees become representatives and symbols of the culture or societies from which they have returned. In both urban and rural Africa, returning immigrants introduce new consumer items to the rural and urban landscapes, create aspirations hitherto unknown in the rural and urban cultures, and sometimes play major roles in changing fertility patterns and gender role expectations. The resourcefulness, perseverance, and fortitude of immigrants coupled with the monies that they bring back home provide the communities to which they return with economic vitality, regeneration of ideas, and a reconfiguration of the social contract. Returning immigrants are accorded a high status and prestige, a social capital which most exploit for their benefit as well as their community's benefit.

When they visit home, no matter the duration, or come home permanently, Africans who have become naturalized citizens of the United States are perceived as elites. They are viewed as propagators of innovation and even as leaders of opposition to be "contained" by the national government. Naturalized American citizens of African descent are fast becoming agents of social, cultural, economic, and political change in their home countries. Their awareness of democracy in America gives them a unique prism through which to filter local politics. They bring new ideas about commerce and business, for which their governments do not have the resources or the capital. More importantly, they become political power brokers whose participation in the political process promotes diversity of ideas. Astute local politicians incorporate returnees' ideas into their political platforms and agendas. Returnees form national associations according to the higher education institutions they attended in the United States. That gives them a voice and political legitimacy. From their ranks will emerge future political leaders. To ensure their financial and political support, some governments have rewarded returnees, especially the well-educated, with ministerial appointments and senior positions. This form of political co-optation does not imply that the returnees bow to the official political line. In fact, most of them have their own political ambitions and break away to organize political resistance movements. Governments that resist their input risk the peril of opposition and eventual political suicide. In Ghana as well as Nigeria, some who have returned from the United States have formed political parties to challenge unpopular regimes.

The evolving pattern of connections that the returnees are forging with the central governments of Africa is an unfinished matter whose end state will determine the political and economic destinies of the African countries on the world stage. The contact with America becomes a valued asset that eventually will determine the definition of national objectives and priorities in Africa as a whole. In the words of one immigrant, now a naturalized citizen residing in New Brighton, a suburb of Minneapolis, "America has already won the hearts and minds of most of Africa's youths without having to fire a single shot. Their embrace of American values bodes well for this country in the long term. Their perceptions of America as a land of opportunity are confirmed by the presence of their African relatives who travel to and fro between the two continents."

Whether or not they naturalize, Africans do not abandon their ancestral homes. They do not consider that their absence diminishes their spiritual ties with the motherland. Actually, becoming citizens of the United States even strengthens their ties to the motherland because their new status in America provides them with political power and economic advantages at home. They contribute equally to the development of their adopted home, the United States, and to that of their places of birth. Certainly, this is the dominant viewpoint among the immigrants surveyed. They believe strongly that as Africa gradually opens up to world commerce and as trade agreements are made between the United States and Africa, the African immigrants are going to provide links to Africa, providing valuable insights into new markets for American companies and businesses.

The portrait of America painted for the citizens of Africa by Africans currently residing in the United States is not, however, always a glowing one. To discourage African youths from migrating in droves to the West and to focus their collective energies on the promotion of economic self-reliance, some returnees as well as visiting migrants disseminate information about the dark spots in America, the racial polarization, anti- immigrant sentiments, crime, violence, poverty of the urban underclass, moral decay, and subordinate roles played by immigrants. But in the minds of a great many Africans, the United States remains a land of opportunity, a place where people temporarily sojourn until such time as they make something out of themselves, no matter how big or small, and then return home. This is the image of America that remains etched on the minds of Africa's youths, educated or uneducated. Most young Africans view emigration from Africa to the West, especially the United States, as their hope of economic fulfillment, personal satisfaction, and self-enrichment. As sojourners in an alien land, the majority of the African immigrants in this study plan a temporary or permanent return home. The unanswered question is whether African governments can formulate policies to reduce the brain drain of its human resources. Will the future expansion of higher education without a corresponding increase in job opportunities for graduates exacerbate the brain drain problem? Will the African governments institute internal controls to limit the number of Africans who can emigrated? An equally significant issue is whether America can tolerate more immigrants. And even if it can, there are many unknowns and uncertainties awaiting future immigrants to this country. Documenting their individual and collective experiences will continue to be fertile ground for social scientists.

# Chapter 9

# The Future of African Immigration to the United States

Transnational migration is not a new phenomenon among Africans. Evidence abounds of centuries of voluntary migration by people of African ancestry inside and outside Africa. In countries where they have settled, Africans have contributed significantly to the ethnic landscape by importing their rich cultures while at the same time they have been influenced by the cultures of their host societies.

The migration of people across international boundaries reflects complex motivations and processes. Even more complex and difficult to delineate are the processes by which immigrants come to form, define, and negotiate relationships with members of a host society. Previous research into the dynamics of transnational migration has yielded abundant information about the motivations for moving and the social conditions associated with the host and source societies that trigger movement. Research has led to an understanding of how globally structured inequality fuels movement to destinations of high capital formation; of national policies regulating admission of immigrants; public sentiments regarding immigration; the economic, social, political, and cultural contributions of immigrants to host as well as source societies; and the adaptive adjustment mechanisms that immigrants employ upon arriving at their destinations.

Using ethnographic and quantitative approaches, this study has presented a dynamic portrait of how African immigrants construct membership in American society and negotiate the complex contours of their experiences in the United States. The study provides a detailed sociological understanding of the making of African immigrant social and cultural communities in the United States and the continuities in the adaptive roles played by these immigrants.

What emerges from the study is that Africans who come to America are resourceful, assiduous, and industrious. Like other participants in the new global movement of labor, Africans are driven by the desire to succeed materially and are bonded together by one collective dream: to improve upon their lives and the lives of their extended family members at home and to assist in the economic development of their home countries. From their perspectives, America has afforded them opportunities that their home countries have yet to offer.

Consciousness of their African identity and heritage sustains them in their quest for a better life. They are under strong pressure from extended family members at home to become successful. Their achievements are celebrated by pomp and festivity. In their home countries, the social capital that accrues to their relations from their residence in the United States is very high. It confers status and prestige on the immigrant's immediate as well as extended family. The immigrant's experience is shared by the entire family. For the immigrant, this support creates a sense of both security and responsibility. This means that immigrant goals and aspirations are defined with the interest of the community of family members in mind. The knowledge of collective security assures immigrants that although they are far away from home, they are never alone in their daily struggles for a better life in the United States.

The majority of the African immigrants come from countries where genuine democracy has been stillborn and economic development has been obstructed. Their migration has also been explained by external geopolitical, economic, and cultural forces set in motion by the industrialized countries. Through colonization, and the penetration of emerging nations' economies by capitalist monopolies eager to accumulate wealth and resources on a global scale, the developed countries came to view the emerging nations as appendages of the developed nations' economic systems. Emerging nations became peripheral economies that revolved around the more technologically advanced core economies of the West. The peripheral countries became dependent on the core countries for much-needed, but constantly scarce, consumer goods. In return, through their global economic and financial networks, the core countries made policies for the marketing of raw materials produced by the underdeveloped countries.

A system of European education was put in place by colonizers who taught Africans to scorn and relinquish their cultural heritage. Africans were taught to look to the West as the embodiment of civilization, science, progress, and technology. The educational curriculum was and is still not designed to provide solutions to African problems. The function of the Euro-based system of education was to westernize Africa and bring it to the standard of Western "civilization." The products of this educational system, therefore, looked beyond Africa, mainly to Western Europe and America, for psychological fulfillment and economic enrichment. A tradition and ethos of personal ambition, drive, and self-sacrifice was stressed for social mobility. The institutions of learning have trained young, aspiring Africans in the arts and sciences, but the economies of Africa have not been expanding rapidly enough to absorb their graduates. The result is migration to the West, chiefly to England, Canada, and the United States, to pursue advanced education, to join family members, and to make money.

African immigrants participate in the host society without becoming assimilated. Participation occurs only to the extent that it facilitates the achievement of cultural and economic goals, mainly the pursuit of education and access to the labor market. This kind of selective adaptation is deliberate and designed chiefly to minimize social contacts with the host society. The African immigrants engage the host society selectively, confining themselves to those carefully chosen domains of the host society that render them more likely to accomplish their goals. This predetermined cultural territoriality defines the social space of the African immigrants, and it is from within such a territory that every engagement with the host society originates. When the immigrants look for work, they do so within the predetermined territory composed of friends, associates, and relatives who themselves are immigrants. When immigrants operate their own economic ventures, their clients are also drawn from within this cultural territory. It is within the context of this territory that bonds of affinity, real, and fictive kinships are formed and nurtured.

As a group, the Africans attach great value to education. At home in Africa, many of the immigrants had taken advantage of public education by completing secondary and postsecondary educational programs modeled after the British or French systems of education. At the point of entering the United States, many, therefore, have achieved a level of educational attainment and commitment to higher education that is enviable in relation to both minority and majority groups in the United States. Africans attach a high value to education, recognizing advanced education as a major vehicle for achieving social mobility in the United States. Irrespective of their cultural backgrounds, Africans are socialized into adopting long-term perspectives. The majority of the immigrants will follow the pathway of education, employment, and family formation in that order. Educational goals are often pursued with one objective in mind—that America rewards citizens and non-citizens alike who avail themselves of its educational opportunities.

African immigrants in general recognize the insidiousness of racism and discrimination in many spheres of social encounter in the United States. But this does not affect their efforts to achieve higher educational qualifications and enter the labor market. The immigrants tend to develop a deep sense of guarded appreciation for the American ethos that eventually rewards accomplishments, even those of marginalized non-white groups. Through education, many become competitive in the labor market. With the status that they negotiate through their educational achievements, Africans become a part of the ethos that defines the cultural ideology of the American dream.

Because they perceive themselves as powerless and marginal, African immigrants hardly participate in the American political system. In addition, their reluctance to participate may, perhaps, be traced to African cultural expectations of the relationship between strangers and their hosts. The African cultural ethos discourages meddling in the internal affairs of migrants' temporary homes. Matters of politics and social debates are best left to the citizens of the host society. As sojourners, Africans, wherever they go, prefer to pay tribute, offering gifts and acknowledging their subordinate status and the generosity of the host society in accepting them. While the immigrants follow social debates on issues of importance to Americans in order to find out who the power brokers are, overall they remain aloof, as bystanders who refrain from behaviors that will raise the anger of the host society or challenge the status quo, even if the status quo is unjust and discriminatory.

To minimize their marginality and political impotence and to ensure their survival in America, the immigrants rely on strong kinship bonds and mutual aid associations. These bonds and associations serve as protection against the persistent racism and discrimination associated with being black and foreign in America. The immigrants negotiate the terrain of racism by establishing and nurturing pan-ethnic loyalties that help define the context of their relationships to the larger society. Even when they achieve a high social status in the United States, African immigrants remain convinced about one fact: that they cannot become full members of society as long as blacks in general remain marginalized and ghettoized and racism remains entrenched in the American psyche. From the immigrants' perspective, blacks (whether they have come to America voluntarily or involuntarily) will always be perceived as a threatening and problematic people who have to be contained or tolerated. Acceptance of this by the immigrants enables them to look for strategies to help them deal with the daily hardships of underclass membership.

The immigrants' physical and cultural attributes offer them no protection at all. Lumped together with their American-born black kinsmen and women into the same white-perceived category of economic and social subserviency, the immigrants try, albeit unsuccessfully, to differentiate themselves from American-born blacks. There are shared, but subtly vocalized, perceptions among the immigrants that their voluntary migration to America, unlike the forced migration of earlier Africans to America, is an effort to renew the black African presence in the United States by changing the terms of the original relationship created by the enslavement and racism that characterized previous social interactions between whites and blacks in America. To the majority of African immigrants, therefore, the successful creation of their presence in America rewrites the encounter between black and white America. This time, Africans must stress their citizenship in a world community where there is recognition of equality, justice, fairness, and liberty—those same rights that European immigrants to America have already sought and won.

Though physically present in America, spiritually the immigrants identify with Africa and with issues pertaining to the African continent. Being permanent residents or naturalized citizens in the United States does not diminish their attachment to and affiliation with Africa. To most, their adopted home in America is temporary. The belief that one day economic and political conditions in Africa will improve and they will be able go home sustains the immigrants. The majority of them have one foot in their adopted home but the other in Africa. They actively engage in all spheres of life in Africa, awaiting the best moment to seize any new opportunities and meet any challenges that may arise. Their sojourn in America is predicated upon economic, social, and political forces at home.

By making regular financial contributions to their families at home, these immigrants have bought a place at the table of African social, political, and economic discourse. Even from afar, their voices are heard; their investments in business ventures, their regular visits, and the networks of contacts that they nurture back home legitimize their role and make them equal partners in family decision-making. The impact of their presence in America is not found in their day-to-day activities, but rather in their ideas, innovations, and material contributions toward the development of Africa. And from their domiciles in the United States, they share themselves and their resources with extended family members and acquaintances at home. In this way, their immigrant experiences find expression and meaning in the many lives in Africa that they touch, in the hopes that they help to renew, and the aspirations that they help to create. Structuring their immigrant experiences in America in such a way that they do not have to engage the greater body politic, the immigrants are leading compartmentalized lives. Such restricted lives offer fewer risks and keep the immigrants focused on their goals—higher education, access to employment, savings, and then, ultimately, the return home to Africa.

The relationships that the immigrants form with other blacks, especially American-born blacks, are very difficult to delineate. Though bonded together by their diasporic experiences and heritage, the two groups are yet to develop a meaningful and mutually sustaining affinity that transcends symbolic enthusiasms and the romanticization of African ideals. The immigrants choose their network of relations carefully, often confining their associations to other immigrants of the African diaspora, especially from the Caribbean basin. Intra-immigrant bonds formed along ethnic lines tend to be very strong. Bonds are also formed to nurture national and pan-African ideals.

The second and third generations, as expected, are becoming more assimilated than their parents and grandparents. The immigrant children remain cognizant of the pressures, especially the economic and cultural obstacles, that confronted their parents and grandparents upon their arrival in America. The sacrifices made by immigrant parents to ensure a better life for their children in America, coupled with their strong work ethic, have been pivotal in defining the expectations that the immigrants bring to their experiences in the United States. These expectations include hard work, education, self-reliance, and economic empowerment.

The parents hope that their children will maintain the strong African cultural heritage and the same commitment to hard work qualities that ensured the parents' survival in America. But conflicts between the first and second generations are beginning to tear the kinship fabric of some families. The teenage children of the immigrants, having been born in this country, define themselves culturally more as Americans than as Africans. For some teenagers, this means that American, as opposed to African, culture has become the lens through which they construct and interpret social reality. The choices made by the children in such areas of culture as clothing, language, music, relationships, and world view have become major sites of conflict. For some parents, the choices of their children symbolize a rejection of traditionally proven African cultural values even though, educationally, these children are performing very well, to the pride of their parents. The parents prefer that their children should be selective of American culture rather than embracing wholesale, unfettered assimilation.

## LOOKING AHEAD TO THE FUTURE OF AFRICAN IMMIGRATION TO THE UNITED STATES

The future direction of African migration to the United States will depend on political and economic conditions both in Africa and in the West. The continuous population pressures along with deteriorating economic and political conditions will cause millions of people from Africa and other areas of the world to cross national borders and seek economic and political security in the developed world. In the early 1990s, a total of at least one hundred million migrants and refugees worldwide lived outside their countries of citizenship. About one-half are living in the industrialized countries (Russell and Teitelbaum, 1992). Future U.S. immigration policies will become critical in determining the future patterns of African emigration to this country. Expected shifts in immigration policies emphasizing skills and family reunification will further promote African migration to this country.

The dynamics of this migration for both the receiving and the sending countries are very difficult to predict. But one thing is certain. Such emigration will necessitate bilateral and multilateral agreements between the United States and the principal countries of African emigration. As Jasso and Rosenzweig (1990) noted, the sheer volume of people currently living in the developing countries who would like to emigrate to the United States exceeds, by far, the number that America can afford to accept. This means that entry will be limited to those with skills, family ties, and capital to invest. Where necessary, bilateral agreements can be made between the United States and African countries to ensure the return home of students after the completion of their studies.

The long-term regeneration of economic and industrial activities and the establishment of democratic institutions in Africa are expected to increase Africa's contacts with the United States. With its dominant global economic position, the United States stands to gain as markets in Africa become more open to global trade and African industrial production reaches the level of contemporary Asia. With a population about to reach seven hundred million, and a growth rate of about 3 percent per annum, the sheer size of the potential African market cannot be overlooked. The United States will have to develop a more comprehensive African foreign policy. This must go beyond existing American policies that have been limited principally to family planning, fertility reduction, and the containment of unpopular regimes. Access to appropriate and proven technology, as well as global capital from the United States and other Western democracies, is needed to revamp the crumbling infrastructure of Africa and its stagnant economies.

For their part, the governments of Africa must develop policies designed to stem the tide of well-educated Africans emigrating to the United States and other Western countries. A first approach must stress economic and industrial expansion using local human and natural resources. This must be accompanied by a gradual improvement in the infrastructure of all economic sectors, especially the infrastructure of the rural areas where the mass of the population resides. Current policies of urban development and rural neglect have worsened the plight of Africa's rural population. They have not made the economic and social conditions of the urban centers any better. If anything, they have worsened the plight of urban dwellers, making them overly dependent on imported consumer goods and creating expectations that cannot be met under existing conditions. The disproportionate allocation of industrial and other economic projects to urban centers continues to force the rural population to seek opportunities in urban centers that have already seen an enormous increase in population for whom social services need to be provided.

Policies designed to keep people in rural areas must be multifaceted. Their aim must be to raise the standard of living of the rural poor by extending basic social, economic, and cultural necessities such as hospitals and clinics, pipe-borne water, quality housing, surfaced feeder roads, and electricity to the depressed rural communities. Rural population retention policies aimed at diversifying the monocultural economies of rural Africa are sorely needed. The bulk of the food consumed by the urban population is produced in the rural areas, yet the farmers do not have access to long-term, sustained support from their national governments. The result is that the farmers are left on their own to spend their meager resources on tools, fertilizers, and high-yielding seeds. They must also deal with a distribution and marketing system that has always favored the middleman. Even where agricultural produce-marketing boards exist, farmers are not always given fair market prices. Delays in the processing of returns from the sale of their harvests add to their frustration.

To facilitate the processing of agricultural raw materials into semi-finished or finished goods for rural consumption and possibly for export, the development of simple but appropriate technologies that are not capital intensive is critical in the diversification of the rural economy. This way, young people leaving school in the rural areas would have access to job opportunities in the rural economy without having to move to try to find employment in a saturated urban labor market. Rural population retention through vigorous rural economic development is imperative. In sum, proactive economic policies aimed at harnessing and mobilizing the human and natural resources of the rural areas will ensure that these areas will become self-sustaining. Such measures will go a long way toward retaining population, thereby minimizing transnational migration in search of greener pastures.

Stable democratic institutions committed to order and the rule of law must be nurtured. Political accountability must be sought at all levels of governance. The political terror unleashed by unpopular regimes in Africa to quash opposition has had a deleterious impact on most Africans' views of their governments. Constructive opposition to the government in power is yet to be recognized by political office holders as integral to democracy. Civilian as well as military regimes have shored up their regimes by silencing political dissent, often by using the state-owned media and military and paramilitary structures. Incorporating legitimate opposition and ethnic minorities into the political decision-making process must be accorded the highest priority. Hitherto, the exclusion of minority groups from political decision-making has been one of the major causes of civil wars on the continent. Political instability and the violence it breeds are at the core of Africa's problem with refugees and other uprooted people. The need to flee from the violence that targets defenseless citizens is a major determinant of the international population movement out of the continent. The legitimization of violence at the national level as a means of conflict resolution has also added to the out-migration. Political socialization and campaigns to educate people about their civil rights and what they should expect of their leaders are central to nation-building. This would foster political account-ability and make political regimes realize that the ultimate source of power is the people, not the office holders.

Political suspicion of elites and wealthy individuals is commonplace in Africa. Often, such people are viewed as a problem instead of a solution. Immigrants with capital to invest are reluctant to come home for fear of having their wealth confiscated without due process. In a political climate of fear, intimidation, and political corruption, businesses and institutions of higher learning become reluctant to provide the capital and ideas that are needed to solve national problems. The mass mobilization of people to achieve national and collective goals has failed woefully. In place of politi-cal freedom and economic prosperity, political terror and economic misery reign. Political terror and economic stagnation do not foster political confi-dence in the international community. Businesses take their investments and ideas to other countries. The institution of one-party rule and life-long presidencies, also common political phenomena in Africa, has served fur-ther to encourage disillusionment and despair, leading to migration.

The number of both educated and unskilled Africans who are leaving their countries to come to the West is growing. University graduates, teach-ers, and professors are leaving in droves, even if they find themselves in the major cities of the West driving taxis. Establishing confidence in Africa's economic and political systems is a daunting task. By dint of hard work, Af-rican immigrants have distinguished themselves wherever they have gone. The majority are proud of and love their motherland. They would like to return home and play an active role in the process of nation-building. This return of human resources and the capital that they possess will not oc-cur unless a favorable political and economic climate is created where the rule of law prevails, civility and legality are cherished, political dissent is tolerated, and institutions fostering human rights are nurtured. Africa is rich in human and natural resources with much to offer the commonwealth of humanity. The gigantic task of bringing about the continent's social, eco-nomic, and political development will have to be undertaken with signifi-cant international assistance from the West. Such international assistance should be liberal and not burden the emerging nations with foreign debt. Meanwhile, the African nations will have to take measures to curb political and economic corruption, establish stable democratic institutions, promote the rule of law, recognize human rights, and provide accountability at all levels of governance. Africa and Africans are capable of meeting this chal-lenge. And this they will have to do.

# Appendix: Figure, Tables, and Survey Questionnaire

**Figure 1**
**Africans Legally Admitted to the United States, 1980–1993**

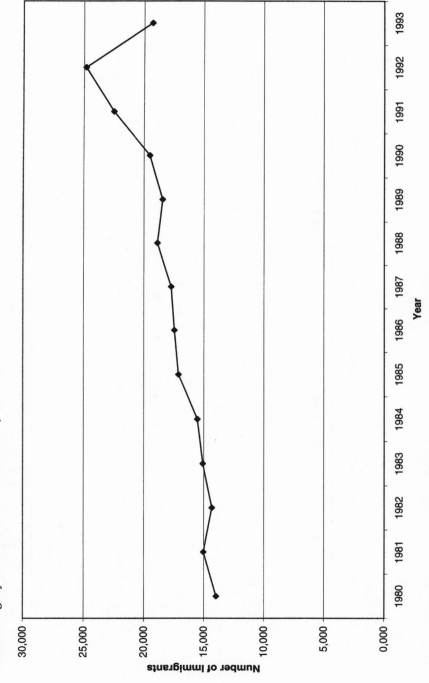

*Source:* U.S. Immigration and Naturalization Service, Immigrant Tape Files: 1980–1993.

153

**Table 1**
**African Immigrants Legally Admitted as Permanent Residents by Country of Birth, 1980–1993**

| Country of Birth | N | % | Country of Birth | N | % | Country of Birth | N | % |
|---|---|---|---|---|---|---|---|---|
| Angola | 1,762 | 0.7 | Cape Verde | 10,761 | 4.3 | Benin | 275 | 0.1 |
| Congo | 132 | 0.1 | Djibouti | 136 | 0.1 | Botswana | 197 | 0.1 |
| Gambia | 590 | 0.2 | Egypt | 41,978 | 17.0 | Cameroon | 1,904 | 1.0 |
| Guinea | 544 | 0.2 | Ghana | 15,862 | 6.4 | Ethiopia | 39,605 | 16.0 |
| Madagascar | 302 | 0.1 | Libya | 2,981 | 1.2 | Kenya | 10,095 | 4.1 |
| Ivory Coast | 1,329 | 0.5 | Mali | 241 | 0.1 | Liberia | 9,135 | 3.7 |
| Mauritius | 660 | 0.3 | Morocco | 10,423 | 4.2 | Malawi | 592 | 0.2 |
| Niger | 344 | 0.1 | Senegal | 1,500 | 0.6 | Mozambique | 881 | 0.4 |
| Nigeria | 38,546 | 16.0 | Seychelles | 457 | 0.2 | Sierra Leone | 6,129 | 2.5 |
| South Africa | 22,328 | 9.0 | Swaziland | 134 | 0.1 | Somalia | 3,393 | 1.4 |
| Sudan | 3,676 | 1.5 | Togo | 282 | 0.1 | Tunisia | 800 | 0.3 |
| Tanzania | 5,032 | 2.0 | Zambia | 2,294 | 0.9 | Uganda | 4,637 | 2.0 |
| Republic of Congo | 1,701 | 0.7 | Zimbabwe | 2,943 | 1.2 | Other | 1,145 | 0.4 |
| **Totals** | | | | | | | 245,726 | 100.0 |

*Source:* U.S. Immigration and Naturalization Service, Immigrant Tape Files: 1980–1993.

Table 2
**African Immigrants Admitted Legally by Category of Admission, 1980–1993**

| Class of Admission | N | % |
|---|---|---|
| Spouse of U.S. citizen | 82,059 | 54.2 |
| Child of U.S. citizen | 5,554 | 3.6 |
| Parent of U.S. citizen | 6,470 | 4.3 |
| Second preference: spouse of lawful permanent resident | 8,328 | 5.5 |
| Unmarried son or daughter of lawful permanent resident | 12,512 | 8.3 |
| Third preference: professional or highly skilled immigrant | 4,907 | 3.2 |
| Spouse of third preference alien | 2,687 | 2.0 |
| Child of third preference alien | 2,604 | 1.7 |
| Fifth preference | 8,111 | 5.4 |
| Spouse of fifth preference alien | 4,604 | 3.0 |
| Child of fifth preference alien | 6,689 | 4.4 |
| Asylee | 6,036 | 4.0 |
| Spouse of an asylee | 674 | 0.4 |
| **Totals** | **151,235** | **100.0** |

*Source*: U.S. Immigration and Naturalization Service, Immigrant Tape Files: 1980–1993.

Table 3
**States of Residence for African Immigrants, 1970–1990**

| State of Residence | N | % | State of Residence | N | % |
|---|---|---|---|---|---|
| California | 2,774 | 18.7 | New Jersey | 870 | 5.9 |
| Connecticut | 161 | 1.1 | New York | 2,228 | 15.0 |
| Georgia | 717 | 4.8 | Ohio | 318 | 2.1 |
| Florida | 324 | 2.2 | Pennsylvania | 521 | 3.5 |
| Illinois | 624 | 4.2 | Texas | 902 | 6.1 |
| Maryland | 667 | 4.5 | Virginia | 529 | 3.6 |
| Massachusetts | 469 | 3.2 | Washington | 241 | 1.6 |
| Michigan | 384 | 2.6 | Crossed boundaries | 94 | 0.6 |
| Minnesota | 189 | 1.3 | Other states | 2,815 | 19.0 |
| **Totals** | | | | **14,827** | **100.0** |

*Source*: Figures computed from Census of the United States, 1970–90.

**Table 4**
**Metropolitan Areas of Residence for African Immigrants,**
**1970–1990**

| Metro Area | N | % |
|---|---|---|
| Atlanta area | 206 | 1.4 |
| Boston area | 260 | 1.8 |
| Chicago–Northwest Indiana area | 377 | 2.5 |
| Dallas–Ft. Worth–Arlington | 269 | 1.8 |
| Houston | 224 | 1.5 |
| Los Angeles area | 215 | 1.5 |
| Long Beach | 831 | 5.6 |
| Minneapolis–St. Paul | 123 | 0.8 |
| Philadelphia–Wilmington–Trenton | 286 | 1.9 |
| San Francisco–Oakland | 342 | 2.3 |
| San Jose | 159 | 1.1 |
| Washington, D.C.–Maryland–Virginia | 745 | 5.0 |
| No place declared | 4,951 | 33.4 |
| All other places combined | 5,849 | 39.4 |
| **Totals** | **14,837** | **100.0** |

*Source*: Figures computed from Census of the United States, 1970–90.

**Table 5**
**Total Family Income: Africans in the United States, 1970–1990**

| Total Family Income | N | % | Total Family Income | N | % |
|---|---|---|---|---|---|
| Under $10,000 | 3,361 | 23.0 | $60,000–69,999 | 543 | 3.7 |
| $10,000–19,999 | 3,453 | 23.7 | $70,000–79,999 | 446 | 3.1 |
| $20,000–29,999 | 2,348 | 16.1 | $80,000–89,999 | 216 | 1.5 |
| $30,000–39,999 | 1,567 | 10.7 | $90,000–99,999 | 115 | 0.8 |
| $40,000–49,999 | 1,025 | 7.0 | $100,000+ | 713 | 4.9 |
| $50,000–59,999 | 805 | 5.5 | | | |
| **Totals** | | | | **14,592** | **100.0** |

*Source*: Figures computed from Census of the United States, 1970–90.

**Table 6**
**Fluency in English: Africans in the United States, 1970–1990**

| Fluency in English | N | % | Fluency in English | N | % |
|---|---|---|---|---|---|
| Does not speak English | 73 | 0.5 | Yes, speaks well | 1,165 | 7.9 |
| Yes, speaks only English | 4,942 | 33.3 | Yes, but not well | 323 | 2.2 |
| Yes, speaks very well | 3,352 | 22.6 | Not applicable | 4,972 | 33.5 |
| **Totals** | | | | **14,827** | **100.0** |

*Source*: Figures computed from Census of the United States, 1970–90.

**Table 7**
**Family Size: Number of Family Members at Home, 1970–1990**

| Family Size | N | % | Family Size | N | % |
|---|---|---|---|---|---|
| One family member present | 2,023 | 13.6 | Seven | 623 | 4.2 |
| Two | 1,970 | 13.3 | Eight | 184 | 1.2 |
| Three | 2,331 | 15.7 | Nine | 135 | 0.9 |
| Four | 3,336 | 22.5 | Ten | 50 | 0.3 |
| Five | 2,650 | 17.9 | Eleven | 55 | 0.4 |
| Six | 1,470 | 9.9 | | | |
| **Totals** | | | | **14,872** | **99.9** |

*Source*: Figures computed from Census of the United States, 1970–90.

## SURVEY QUESTIONNAIRE

Respondent I.D. Number: _____

1. Sex

      01___ male                02___ female

2. How old are you? (Please check one of the following.)

| | | | |
|---|---|---|---|
| 01___ | 10–19 | 06___ | 60–69 |
| 02___ | 20–29 | 07___ | 70–79 |
| 03___ | 30–39 | 08___ | 80 and above |
| 04___ | 40–49 | 09___ | don't know |
| 05___ | 40–59 | 10___ | no answer |

3. Country of birth

| | | | |
|---|---|---|---|
| 01___ | Ghana | 16___ | Mali |
| 02___ | Nigeria | 17___ | Egypt |
| 03___ | Liberia | 18___ | Somalia |
| 04___ | Sierra Leone | 19___ | Ethiopia |
| 05___ | Togo | 20___ | Chad |
| 06___ | Senegal | 21___ | Guinea |
| 07___ | Ivory Coast | 22___ | Zambia |
| 08___ | Kenya | 23___ | Zimbabwe |
| 09___ | Uganda | 24___ | South Africa |
| 10___ | Tanzania | 25___ | Lesotho |
| 11___ | Botswana | 26___ | Cameroon |
| 12___ | Sudan | 27___ | Malawi |
| 13___ | South Africa | 28___ | Madagascar |
| 14___ | Burkina Faso | 29___ | Cape Verde |
| 15___ | Niger | 30___ | Zaire (Democratic Republic of Congo) |

4. From what source(s) did you obtain information about the U.S. prior to your immigration? (Please check all that apply.)

      01___ from relatives already in the U.S.
      02___ from friends already in the U.S.
      03___ from the U.S. Information Service back home
      04___ from TV, radio, and print media
      05___ from friends/relatives who have visited the U.S.
      06___ from the library
      07___ other sources (please specify) _____
      08___ don't know
      09___ no answer

5. Did you enter the U.S. directly from Africa?

  01_____yes         03_____don't know

  02 _____no         04_____no answer

6. If no, in what other country (countries) did you reside prior to immigrating to the U.S.? (Please list all that apply.)

_____    _____    _____    _____

7. Now that you have been in the U.S. for some time, how accurate/reliable was the information you received about the U.S. prior to coming here?

  01___very accurate/reliable     04___don't know

  02___somewhat accurate/reliable   05___no answer

  03___not accurate/reliable

8. Which of the following comes closest to describing the type of place in which you were living in Africa?

  01____rural area        05____very large city

  02____small town       06____don't know

  03____large town or small city   07____no answer

  04____medium-sized city

9. While living in Africa, did you engage in rural-to-urban migration?

  01____yes          03____don't know

  02____no           04____no answer

10. If yes, did you move for any of the reasons below? (Please check all that apply.)

  01____educational       04____remain or unite with relatives

  02____financial/economic    05____other (please specify)___

     (earn more money)    06____don't know

  03____political         07____no answer

11. Which of the following best describes your occupation while in Africa?

  01____professional/administrative   10____student

  02____managerial/administrative   11____clergy

  03____technical/administrative    12____disabled

  03____sales/business       13____unemployed

  05____craft/licensed craft     14____petty trader

  06____manufacturing/production   15____housewife

  07____clerical         16____other (please specify)

  08____service (driver, food service  17____don't know

     personnel, barber/beautician, etc.)  18____no answer

  09____farming/fishing/animal husbandry

12. How old were you when you immigrated to the U.S.?

| | | | |
|---|---|---|---|
| 01____under 9 years | | 07____between 35 and 39 years | |
| 02____between 10 and 14 years | | 08____between 40 and 44 years | |
| 03____between 15 and 19 years | | 09____between 45 and 49 years | |
| 04____between 20 and 24 years | | 10____50 years and above | |
| 05____between 25 and 29 years | | 11____don't know | |
| 06____between 30 and 34 years | | 12____no answer | |

13. In what year did you immigrate to the U.S.?_____

14. What was your most important reason for immigrating to the U.S.?
01____educational
02____financial
03____political (example: as refugee or political prisoner)
04____religious
05____unite with relatives
06____other (please specify) _____
07____don't know
08____no answer

15. In preparing to leave Africa, would you consider your experience with your government to have been
01_____not difficult          04_____don't know
02_____somewhat difficult     05_____no answer
03_____very difficult

16. Would you consider your immigration to be family sponsored? (family contributions to assist your travel and resettlement)
01 _____yes          03_____ don't know
02 _____no           04_____ no answer

17. Was your immigration sponsored by any of the following? (Please check all that apply.)
01_____government                 06_____other (please specify)____
02_____religious organization     07_____don't know
03_____employer                   08_____no answer
04_____educational institution
05_____non-profit, philanthropic, or charitable organization

18. On which type of visa did you first travel to the U.S.?
01_____visitors     05_____business
02_____student      06_____don't know
03_____refugee      07_____no answer
04_____exchange

160

19. When you first came to the U.S. to live, did any of the following travel with you?

      01____family member(s) only           04____came alone

      02____friend(s) only                  05____don't know

      03____both family and friends        06____no answer

20. When you first came to the U.S. to live, did you have family or friends already living here?

      01____family members only         04____neither

      02____friends only                05____don't know

      03____both family and friends        06____no answer

21. Were any of these (family members or friends) U.S. citizens at that time?

      01____yes                       03____don't know

      02____no                      04____no answer

22. Have you been living in this city since you arrived in the U.S.?

      01____yes                       03____don't know

      02____no                      04____no answer

23. If no, which city or cities in the U.S. did you live? (Please list all that apply.)

     _____       _____       _____       _____

24. For what reason(s) did you move to this city? (Please check all that apply.)

      01____seek better job opportunities      08____don't know

      02____seek better educational opportunities   09____no answer

      03____to be closer to friends and relatives

      04____warmer climate

      05____take advantage of recreational opportunities

      06____lower taxes

      07____other (please specify) _____

25. Do you intend to move again?

      01____yes                       03____don't know

      02____no                      04____no answer

26. If yes, for what reason(s) will you consider moving? (Please check all that apply.)

      01____seek better job opportunities      08____don't know

      02____seek better educational opportunities   09____no answer

      03____to be closer to friends and relatives

      04____warmer climate

      05____take advantage of recreational opportunities

      06____lower taxes

      07____other (please specify)____

27. In comparison with the immigrants who came to the U.S. during the 1800s and 1900s and those who are now arriving, would you say that (Please check all that apply.)

01____Immigrants of 1800s and 1900s had better economic opportunities than those now coming in.

02____New immigrants have better economic opportunities than those before.

03____Previous and current immigrants have the same economic opportunities.

04____Generally, all immigrants face economic hardships and discrimination but with time become assimilated.

05____don't know

06____no answer

28. The degree of *residential* segregation confronting American-born blacks is no different from that facing foreign-born black African immigrants.

01____strongly agree          04____strongly disagree
02____agree                   05____don't know
03____disagree

29. The degree of *economic* segregation confronting American-born blacks is no different from that facing foreign-born black African immigrants.

01____strongly agree          04____strongly disagree
02____agree                   05____don't know
03____disagree                06____no answer

30. The high-paying jobs in manufacturing and industrial work that supported middle-class families are being replaced by low-paying jobs in the service sector. How concerned are you about this shift?

01____very concerned          04____don't know
02____somewhat concerned      05____no answer
03____not concerned

31. To become highly marketable, immigrants should hold advanced degrees in the arts and sciences.

01____strongly agree          04____strongly disagree
02____agree                   05___don't know
03____disagree                06____no answer

32. To remain competitive in the labor market, immigrants should engage in continuing education to sharpen their skills.

01____strongly agree          04____strongly disagree
02____agree                   05____don't know
03____disagree                06____no answer

33. To remain competitive in the labor market, immigrants should attain educational levels higher than that of the general American population.

    01____strongly agree          04____strongly disagree
    02____agree                  05____don't know
    03____disagree             06____no answer

34. Does the company/organization you work for provide on-the-job training for its workers?

    01___yes                  03___don't know
    02___no                   04___no answer

35. Does the company/organization you work for provide tuition assistance or reimbursement for continuing education?

    01___yes                  03___don't know
    02___no                   04___no answer

36. If yes, do you take advantage of that benefit?

    01___yes                  03___don't know
    02___no                   04___no answer

37. If no, why? (Please check all that apply.)

    01___prefer to spend more leisure time with family
    02___work schedule conflicts
    03___I plan to take advantage of this benefit at a future time
    04___further education will not make much difference in my pay
    05___further education will not affect my chances of being promoted
    06___other (please specify) _____
    07___don't know
    08___no answer

38. In what year did you get your permanent resident status?_____

39. Are you now a U.S. citizen?

    01_____yes                03_____don't know
    02_____no                 04 _____no answer

If you answer no to question 39, skip the next question and go to question 45.

40. Are you currently registered to vote in the U.S.?

    01_____yes                03_____don't know
    02 _____no                04_____no answer

41. Did you vote in the 1992 presidential elections?

    01_____yes                03_____don't know
    02 _____no                04_____no answer

42. If yes, for whom did you vote in 1992?

01_____George Bush          04_____other (please specify)__
02_____Bill Clinton          05_____don't know
03_____Ross Perot           06_____no answer

43. Did you vote in the 1996 presidential elections?

01_____yes                  03_____don't know
02_____no                   04_____no answer

44. If yes, for whom did you vote in 1996?

01_____Bill Clinton         04_____other (please specify) __
02_____Bob Dole             05_____don't know
03_____Ross Perot           06_____no answer

45. Did you participate in the political process by voting in your home country?

01_____yes                  03_____don't know
02_____no                   04_____no answer

46. If you are now a U.S. citizen, do you usually think of yourself as a (n)

01____Democrat              04____other (please specify) ___
02____Republican           05____don't know
03____independent          06____no answer

47. If you are not a U.S. citizen, do you plan to apply for citizenship some time in the future?

01_____yes                  03_____don't know
02 _____no                  04_____no answer

48. Since coming to the U.S., have you returned to your home country for a visit?

01_____yes                  03_____don't know
02 _____no                  04_____no answer

49. Do you make regular (at planned intervals) visits to your home country?

01_____yes                  03_____don't know
02 _____no                  04_____no answer

50. If yes, what are those intervals?

01____every six months     05____every three years
02____every year           06____every four years
03____every eighteen months 07____don't know
04____every two years      08____no answer

51. Do you plan to return to Africa to live permanently?

01_____yes                  03_____don't know
02 _____no                  04_____no answer

52. If yes, when do you plan to leave?
        01____before retirement           04____other (please specify)
        02____after retirement            05____don't know
        03____after my children are grown    06____no answer
                and left home

53. Are you currently saving money to support yourself and your family when you retire?
        01_____yes                   03_____don't know
        02 _____no                 04_____no answer

54. If yes, how is the money being invested? (Please check all that apply.)
        01____stocks              06_____passbook savings
        02____certificates of deposit     07_____other (please specify)
        03____annuities           08_____don't know
        04____bonds              09_____no answer
        05____treasury bills

55. Do you currently own a house in your country of origin?
        01_____yes                   03_____don't know
        02 _____no                 04_____no answer

56. If yes, is this house being rented or inhabited by relatives?
        01____being rented          04____don't know
        02____being inhabited by relatives   05____no answer
        03____other (please specify) _____

57. If house is being rented, how is the rent money being used?
        01____to support extended family members (education, healthcare needs,
                emergencies)
        02____to operate a business
        03____savings in a bank
        04____invested
        05____other (please specify) _____
        05____don't know
        06____no answer

58. If you do not own a house at home, are you making plans to build or purchase one?
        01____planning to build one       04____don't know
        02____planning to purchase one   05____no answer
        03____planning to rent one when I retire

59. What was the highest level of education you acquired in Africa?
      01____less than secondary school
      02____secondary school
              (indicate whether "O" or "A" level certificate) _____
      03____technical school/teacher training
      04____baccalaureate degree
      05____master's
      06____Ph.D.
      07____don't know
      08____no answer

60. If you have continued your education in the U.S., what is the highest level acquired here?

| | |
|---|---|
| 01____less than secondary school | 05____master's |
| 02____secondary school | 06 ____Ph.D. |
| 03____technical school/teacher training | 07____don't know |
| 04____baccalaureate degree | 08____no answer |

61. How did you obtain information about the school that you attended in the U.S.?
(Please check all that apply.)
      01____from newspapers, magazines, newsletters, professional journals
      02____from friends
      03____from educational fairs
      04____from the library
      05____from relatives
      06____from other sources (please specify) _____
      07____don't know
      08____no answer

62. How does your level of education compare with that of your parents?
Is it higher, the same, or lower?

| | |
|---|---|
| 01____higher | 04____don't know |
| 02____same | 05____no answer |
| 03____lower | |

63. Which of the following best describes your present employment situation?

| | |
|---|---|
| 01___working full-time | 07____retired |
| 02___working part-time | 08 ___disabled |
| 03___temporarily laid off | 09____other  (please specify) |
| 04___jobless and looking for work | 10____don't know |
| 05___a student | 11____no answer |
| 06___a homemaker | |

64. Are you self-employed on a full-time basis?
    01 _____ yes                               03 _____ don't know
    02 _____ no                                04 _____ no answer

65. If yes, was the capital/funding for your business provided by
    01 _____ bank/financial institution      05 _____ government (Small
    02 _____ own personal savings                     Business Administration Loan)
    03 _____ relatives/family members        06 _____ don't know
    04 _____ friends                         07 _____ no answer

66. How difficult was it to raise the capital/funds for your business?
    01 _____ very difficult                  04 _____ easy
    02 _____ difficult                       05 _____ don't know
    03 _____ very easy                       06 _____ no answer

67. Are you employed on a part-time basis?
    01 _____ yes                              03 _____ don't know
    02 _____ no                               04 _____ no answer

68. Select the category that best describes your present occupation.
    01 _____ professional/administrative   09 _____ farming/fishing/animal husbandry
    02 _____ managerial/administrative     10 _____ clergy
    03 _____ technical/administrative      11 _____ other (please specify) _____
    04 _____ sales                         12 _____ don't know
    05 _____ craft/licensed craft          13 _____ no answer
    06 _____ manufacturing/production
    07 _____ clerical
    08 _____ service (driver, food service personnel, barber/beautician, etc.)

69. In which of the following sectors do you work?
    01 _____ government                     06 _____ religious organization
    02 _____ military                       07 _____ charitable organization
    03 _____ private industry               08 _____ other (please specify)
    04 _____ education                      09 _____ don't know
    05 _____ self-employment                10 _____ no answer

70. How did you obtain information about your current job? (Please check all that apply.)
    01 _____ from newspapers, magazines, newsletters, professional journals
    02 _____ from friends
    03 _____ from job fairs
    04 _____ from an employment agency
    05 _____ from relatives
    06 _____ from other sources (please specify)
    07 _____ don't know
    08 _____ no answer

71. What is your individual annual income?

| | |
|---|---|
| 01____ $10,000–14,999 | 10____ $55,000–59,999 |
| 02____ $15,000–19,999 | 11____ $60,000–64,999 |
| 03____ $20,000–24,999 | 12____ $65,000–69,999 |
| 04____ $25,000–29,999 | 13____ $70,000–74,999 |
| 05____ $30,000–34,999 | 14____ $75,000–79,999 |
| 06____ $35,000–39,999 | 15____ $80,000–84,999 |
| 07____ $40,000–44,999 | 16____ $85,000 and above |
| 08____ $45,000–49,999 | 17____ don't know |
| 09____ $50,000–54,999 | 18____ no answer |

72. Do you currently receive income, benefits, or services from any of the following? (Please check all that apply.)

01____ Social Security
02____ Aid to Families with Dependent Children (AFDC)
03____ food stamps
05____ Medicaid or Medicare
06____ educational assistance programs
07____ veteran's benefits
08____ housing subsidy
09____ any other government assistance program? (Please specify)____
10____ don't know
11____ no answer

73. What is your marital status?

| | |
|---|---|
| 01____ single, never married | 05____ widowed |
| 02____ married | 06____ don't know |
| 03____ divorced | 07____ no answer |
| 04____ separated | |

74. Is your spouse

| | |
|---|---|
| 01___ African | 04___ white |
| 02___ black American | 05___ other |
| 03___ black, not born in Africa or the U.S. | (please specify) ____ |

75. Has your spouse ever worked for pay in the U.S.?

| | |
|---|---|
| 01____ yes | 03____ don't know |
| 02 ____ no | 04____ no answer |

168

76. Which of the following best describes your spouse's employment situation?

01_____working full-time      07_____retired
02_____working part-time      08_____disabled
03_____temporarily laid off   09_____other (please specify)
04_____jobless and looking for work  10_____don't know
05_____a student              11_____no answer
06_____a homemaker

77. Select the category that best describes your spouse's present occupation.

01___professional/administrative   08___service (driver, food service
02___managerial/administrative          personnel, barber/beautician, etc.)
03___technical/administrative      09___farming/fishing/animal husbandry
04___sales                         10___other (please specify)
05___craft/licensed craft          11___don't know
06___manufacturing/production      12___no answer
07___clerical

78. What is your spouse's highest level of education?

01___less than secondary school    05___master's
02___secondary school              06___Ph.D.
03___technical school/teacher training  07___don't know
04___baccalaureate degree          08___no answer

79. Was this level of education achieved in the U.S.?

01_____yes      03_____don't know
02_____no       04_____no answer

80. Do your children under 18 years old attend a public or a private school?

01___public     03___don't know
02___private    04___no answer

81. If they attend a private school, about how much do you spend per academic year?

01___under $1,000                  06___$9,000 and $10,000
02___between $1,000 and $2,000     07___over $10,000
03___between $3,000 and $4,000     08___don't know
04___between $5,000 and $6,000     09___no answer
05___between $7,000 and $8,000

82. How many people reside in your household, including yourself?

01___one        05___five
02___two        06___six or more
03___three      07___don't know
04___four       08___no answer

83. What are the other residents' relationships to you? (Please check all that apply.)

01___spouse  07___cousins
02___parent(s)  08___parents-in-law
03___children  09___other in-laws
04___siblings  10___other relatives
05___aunts/uncles  11___don't know
06___nieces/nephew  12___no answer

84. Are any of the above U.S. citizens?

01 ____yes  03_____don't know
02 ____no  04_____no answer

85. If yes, are they

01___spouse  05___other (please specify)
02___parent  06___don't know
03___children  07___no answer
04___siblings

86. What is your combined household annual income per year?

01____$10,000–$14,999  10____$55,000–$59,999
02____$15,000–$19,999  11____$60,000–$64,999
03____$20,000–$24,999  12____$65,000–$69,999
04____$25,000–$29,999  13____$70,000–$74,999
05____$30,000–$34,999  14____$75,000–$79,999
06____$35,000–$39,999  15____$80,000–$84,999
07____$40,000–$44,999  16____$85,000 and above
08____$45,000–$49,999  17____don't know
09____$50,000–$54,999  18____no answer

87. Do you provide financial support for relatives in Africa?

01_____yes  03_____don't know
02_____no  04_____no answer

88. If yes, do you provide this support

01_____on a regular basis  03_____don't know
02 ____as requested by family  04_____no answer

89. If on a regular basis, how often do you provide support?

01___once every month  06____once every six to eleven months
02___once every two months  07____once every year
03 ___once every three months  08____don't know
04___once every four months  09____no answer
05___once every five months

90. If on a regular basis, on average, how much do you provide per year?

01____ under $499   09____ between $4,000 and $4,499
02____ between $500 and $999   10____ between $4,500 and $4,999
03____ between $1,000 and $1,499   11____ between $5,000 and $5,499
04____ between $1,500 and $1,999   12____ between $5,500 and $5,999
05____ between $2,000 and $2,499   13____ over $6,000 per year
06____ between $2,500 and $2,999   14____ don't know
07____ between $3,000 and $3,499   15____ no answer
08____ between $3,500 and $3,999

91. Monies sent home by black African immigrants to their relatives are vital for the economic and industrial development of Africa.

01____ strongly agree   04____ strongly disagree
02____ agree   05____ don't know
03____ disagree   06____ no answer

92. If on a regular basis, for what purpose is the money to be used? (Please check all that apply.)

01____ investment in family business   05____ add to family's income
02____ education expenses of relative(s)   06____ other (please specify)
03____ build or purchase a home   07____ don't know
04____ medical expenses of relative(s)   08____ no answer

93. Do you plan to have other family members still in Africa come to the U.S. some time in the future?

01____ yes   03____ don't know
02____ no   04____ no answer

94. Many forms in the U.S. use five or six racial/ethnic origin categories. When filling out such forms, how do you designate yourself? (Please check all that you have used.)

01____ black   04____ other
02____ African-American   05____ leave blank
03____ black African-born immigrant (American)

95. How would you describe relationships between American-born blacks and African-born black immigrants in the U.S.? (Please check all that apply.)

01____ very excellent   05____ very poor
02____ excellent   06____ don't know
03____ fair   07____ no answer
04____ poor

96. In your opinion, are the economic conditions of African-born black immigrants higher, about the same, or lower than those of American-born blacks living in the U.S.?

01___ higher
02___ about the same
03___ lower

04___ don't know
05___ no answer

97. In your opinion, are the economic conditions of African-born black immigrants higher, about the same, or lower than those of immigrants from the Caribbean living in the U.S.?

01___ higher
02___ about the same
03___ lower

04___ don't know
05___ no answer

98. In your opinion, are the economic conditions of African-born black immigrants higher, about the same, or lower than those of immigrants from Central and South America living in the U.S.?

01___ higher
02___ about the same
03___ lower

04___ don't know
05___ no answer

99. In your opinion, are the economic conditions of African-born black immigrants higher, about the same, or lower than those of Asian immigrants living in the U.S.?

01___ higher
02___ about the same
03___ lower

04___ don't know
05___ no answer

100. A recent study conducted by Professor Mary Waters from Harvard University, which appeared in the journal *International Migration Review* in 1994, found that foreign-born black immigrants living in the U.S. view themselves as "hardworking," "ambitious," "militant about their racial identities," "not oversensitive or obsessed with race," and "committed to family and education." *The quotes came directly from her study.* Concerning these views, I tend to

01___ strongly agree
02___ agree
03___ disagree

04___ strongly disagree
05___ don't know
06___ no answer

101. In the same study that I just referred to above, it was reported that American-born blacks described foreign-born blacks living in the U.S. as "arrogant," "selfish," "oblivious to racial tension and politics in the U.S.," "exploited in the work place," "unfriendly," and "unwilling to have relations with black Americans." Concerning these views, I tend to

01___ strongly agree
02___ agree
03___ disagree

04___ strongly disagree
05___ don't know
06___ no answer

172

102. Irrespective of where they have come from to settle in the U.S., the economic and living conditions of people of black African ancestry in the U.S. are characterized by racism and discrimination.

01____strongly agree          04____strongly disagree
02____agree                   05____don't know
03____disagree                06____no answer

103. Irrespective of where they have come from to settle in the U.S., the economic and living conditions of people of black African ancestry in the U.S. are characterized by economic deprivation and poverty.

01____strongly agree          04____strongly disagree
02____agree                   05____don't know
03____disagree                06____no answer

104. Irrespective of where they have come from to settle in the U.S., the economic and living conditions of people of black African ancestry in the U.S. are characterized by abundant opportunities and equal access to resources.

01____strongly agree          04____strongly disagree
02____agree                   05____don't know
03____disagree                06____no answer

105. What was your attitude about race relations in the U.S. prior to coming to this country? Would you say that what you knew about race relations in this country was

01___very favorable           04___don't know
02___favorable                05___no answer
03___not favorable

106. Has your attitude about race relations changed since you have been in this country?

01___yes                      03___don't know
02___no                       04___no answer

107. If yes, has this change been

01___for the better           04___don't know
02___for the worse            05___no answer
03___the same

108. Do you have a religious preference?

01____yes                     03____don't know
02____no                      04____no answer

109. If yes, what is your preference?

01_____a traditional African religion     06_____Buddhism
02_____Christianity     07_____other
03_____Islam     08_____don't know
04_____Judaism     09_____no answer
05_____Hinduism

110. Are your religious practices in the U.S. the same or similar to those in Africa?

01_____yes     03_____don't know
02_____no     04_____no answer

111. If no, do you practice some other religion in the U.S.?

01_____yes     03_____don't know
02_____no     04_____no answer

112. How concerned are you personally about race relations in the U.S.?

01_____very concerned     04_____not concerned at all
02_____somewhat concerned     05_____don't know
03_____not very concerned     06_____no answer

113. Are most of your friends and associates

01_____fellow Africans     04_____whites
02_____black Americans     05_____other (please specify)_____
03_____other blacks     06_____don't know
      (Haitians, Jamaicans, etc.)     07_____no answer

114. Do you associate on a social basis with black Americans?

01_____yes     03_____don't know
02_____no     04_____no answer

115. If yes, how important is the association to you?

01_____very important     04_____not important at all
02_____important     05_____don't know
03_____not very important     06_____no answer

116. Do you associate on a social basis with white Americans?

01_____yes     03_____don't know
02_____no     04_____no answer

117. If yes, how important is the association to you?

01_____very important     04_____not important at all
02_____important     05_____don't know
03_____not very important     06_____no answer

118. Is there a network of mutual aid among immigrants from your home country?
   01_____yes                          03_____don't know
   02_____no                           04_____no answer

119. If yes, what is the purpose of the mutual aid network? (Please check all that apply.)
   01_____to assist new immigrants to settle in the U.S.
   02_____to provide funds to establish a business
   03_____to assist immigrants in times of emergencies such as illness or death
   04_____to pay for the legal expenses of immigrants who get into trouble
              with the law
   05_____to pay for the cost of organizing parties, cultural/festive events
   06_____to donate funds to charitable organizations
   07_____to assist immigrants to locate jobs/employment
   08_____other (please specify) _____
   09_____don't know
   10_____no answer

120. Is there a national association of immigrants from your home country?
   01_____yes                          03_____don't know
   02_____ no                          04_____no answer

121. If yes, are you a member of this association?
   01_____yes                          03_____don't know
   02_____ no                          04_____no answer

122. For what reason(s) was this association formed? (Please check all that apply.)
   01_____to assist new immigrants to settle in the U.S.
   02_____to provide funds to establish a business
   03_____to assist immigrants in times of emergencies such as illness or death
   04_____to pay for the legal expenses of immigrants who get into trouble
              with the law
   05_____to pay for the cost of organizing parties, cultural/festive events
   06_____to donate funds to charitable organizations
   07_____to assist immigrants locate jobs/employment
   08_____to support political parties back home
   09_____other (please specify) _____
   10_____don't know
   11_____no answer

123. Are there specific African festivals/cultural events that you celebrate in the U.S.?
   01_____yes                          03_____don't know
   02_____ no                          04_____no answer

124. Do you participate in these festivals/cultural events?

01____yes                                        03____don't know
02____no                              ·          04____no answer

125. If yes, how often are these festivities/cultural events held?

01___once a month                                05___once a year
02___once every three months                     06___don't know
03___once every six months                       07___no answer
04___once every nine months

126. How about your children? Do they also participate in these festivals/cultural events?

01___yes                                         03___don't know
02___no                                          04___no answer

127. What is the purpose of the festivities/cultural events? (Please check all that apply.)

01___to celebrate African culture
02___to observe a religious ritual
03___to socialize with others from your home country
04___to enable your children to learn about their heritage
05___other (please specify)

128. What is the main language of conversation you use at home? (Please check all that apply.)

01___African language/dialect                    04___other (please specify)
02___English                                     05___don't know
03___French                                      06___no answer

129. Are your children fluent in the African language you speak?

01___yes                                         03___don't know
02___no                                          04___no answer

130. Which of the following is your major source of information about current events in Africa? (Please check one.)

01_____television                                07_____don't know
02_____radio                                     08_____no answer
03_____African newspapers/magazines
04_____other newspapers/magazines (please specify) _____
05_____personal correspondence
06_____internet/world wide web

131. Aside from the source you checked above, please check any of your other sources of information about current events in Africa.

01_____television                         07_____don't know
02_____radio                              08_____no answer
03_____African newspapers/magazines
04_____other newspapers/magazines (please specify) _____
05_____personal correspondence
06_____internet/world wide web

132. What is your perception of U.S. news media portrayal of Africa?

01_____favorable                          04_____don't know
02_____unfavorable                        05_____no answer
03_____neutral

133. If unfavorable, would you attribute this portrayal to

01_____lack of understanding              03_____other (please specify) _____
          about Africa                     04_____don't know
02_____racism                             05_____no answer

134. Do you think African immigrants are discriminated against in the U.S.?

01_____yes                                03_____don't know
02_____no                                 04_____no answer

135. Have you or any member of your family experienced discrimination in the U.S.?

01_____yes                                02_____no
03_____don't know                         04_____no answer

136. Has this happened

01_____hardly ever                        04_____don't know
02_____occasionally                       05_____no answer
03_____frequently

137. In your home country, did you ever participate in politics in any of the following ways? (Please check all that apply.)

01___following politics in the news
02___writing letters
03___distributing literature
04___canvassing/marching
05___fund raising/contributing money
06___voting in elections
07___helping people register and vote
08___never participated in politics
09___don't know
10___no answer

138. In the U.S. have you ever participated in politics in any of the following ways? (Please check all that apply.)

01___following politics in the news
02___writing letters
03___distributing literature
04___canvassing/marching
05___fund raising/contributing money
06___voting in elections
07___helping people register and vote
08___never participated in politics
09___don't know
10___no answer

139. In general has your life been better

01___in the U.S.?                    04___don't know
02___in your home country?           05___no answer
03___other (please specify) _____

140. Which of the following best describes how you see yourself?

01___more as an American                    04___don't know
02___more as a foreign-born black African    05___no answer
03___something else (please specify) _____

141. Which of the following best describes how your children see themselves?

01___more as American(s)                     04___don't know
02___more as foreign-born black African       05___no answer
       immigrant(s)
03___something else (please specify) _____

142. Thinking about your lifestyle now, including your job, your home, and your leisure activities, do you think that when your children are your age, their lifestyle in this country will be

01___better than yours is now        04___don't know
02___about the same as yours is now   05___no answer
03___not as good as yours is now

143. How concerned are you about proposed laws in California or in Congress to limit assistance to legal residents and non-citizens?

01___very concerned       04___don't know
02___somewhat concerned   05___no answer
03___not concerned

144. Since you became a permanent resident, have you had any periods of unemployment that have lasted six months or longer when you were looking for a job, but could not find one?

01_____yes          03_____don't know
02_____no           04_____no answer

145. If you have decided not to apply for U.S. citizenship, please rate by using the number in front of any of the applicable reasons as being (01) very important (02) somewhat important, (03) not very important, or (04) not at all important.

____You plan to return to your home country some day to live there permanently.
____You feel there is discrimination against (black) Africans in the U.S.
____You are afraid of losing the culture of your home country.
____You want to maintain political ties with your home country.
____You think the INS exam will be too difficult.
____You would lose your property rights in your home country.
____You would feel disloyal to your home country.
____You feel you would be mistreated by the INS.
____There are no real benefits to becoming a citizen.
____other (please specify) _____
____don't know
____no answer

146. If you have applied or plan to apply for U.S. citizenship, please rate by using the number in front of any of the applicable reasons as being (01) very important, (02) somewhat important, (03) not very important, or (04) not at all important.

____Citizenship helps you get a better job.
____Citizenship helps you earn more money.
____Citizenship makes you eligible for U.S. government programs.
____Citizenship enables your children to become U.S. citizens.
____Citizenship helps your relatives immigrate to the U.S.
          more quickly.
____Citizenship allows you to vote in U.S. elections.
____Citizenship allows you to participate more equally in American life.
____Citizenship provides greater opportunities for your children's future.
____Citizenship makes your life better overall.
____Citizenship offers you more protection under the law.
____Citizenship offers U.S. citizens worldwide protection.
____Citizenship allows you to travel throughout the world.
____other (please specify) _____
____don't know
____no answer

147. Since you became a U.S. citizen, have you had any periods of unemployment that have lasted six months or longer when you were looking for a job, but could not find one?

01_____yes                              03_____don't know
02_____no                               04_____no answer

Do you think an increase in the number of immigrants who are coming into the country will likely result in the following?

148. Higher economic growth
01_____very likely                      04_____not at all likely
02_____somewhat likely                  05_____don't know
03_____not too likely                   06_____no answer

149. Higher unemployment
01_____very likely                      04_____not at all likely
02_____somewhat likely                  05_____don't know
03_____not too likely                   06_____no answer

150. Difficulties in keeping the country united
01_____very likely                      04_____not at all likely
02_____somewhat likely                  05_____don't know
03_____not too likely                   06_____no answer

151. Racial tension, conflicts, and polarization
01_____very likely                      04_____not at all likely
02_____somewhat likely                  05_____don't know
03_____not too likely                   06_____no answer

152. Do you think that immigrants who are in the U.S. legally should be eligible for government services such as Medicaid, food stamps, or welfare on the same basis as citizens?

01_____eligible                         04_____no answer
02_____not eligible                     05_____not applicable
03_____don't know

153. Do you think that undocumented aliens who are in the U.S. illegally should be eligible for government services?

01_____eligible                         04_____no answer
02_____not eligible                     05_____not applicable
03_____don't know

154. Should illegal immigrants be entitled to work permits?

01_____yes, entitled                    04_____no answer
02_____no, not entitled                 05_____not applicable
03_____don't know

155. Should illegal immigrants be entitled to attend public universities at the same cost as other students?

01_____yes, entitled              04_____no answer
02_____no, not entitled        05_____not applicable
03_____don't know

156. Should illegal immigrants' children qualify as American citizens if born in the U.S.?

01_____yes, entitled              04_____no answer
02_____no, not entitled        05_____not applicable
03_____don't know

157. Overall, how would you rate the quality of services that you have received from the Immigration and Naturalization Service so far?

01_____excellent              04_____don't know
02_____fair                  05_____no answer
03_____poor

158. I take pride in teaching my children about African history and culture.

01_____strongly agree        04_____strongly disagree
02_____agree               05_____don't know
03_____disagree          06_____no answer

159. I stress the value of education to my children and insist on educational excellence.

01_____strongly agree        04_____strongly disagree
02_____agree               05_____don't know
03_____disagree          06_____no answer

160. We have designated times at home each day when we turn off the television and interact with the children.

01_____strongly agree        04_____strongly disagree
02_____agree               05_____don't know
03_____disagree          06_____no answer

161. I believe parents should pass on their ethnic and racial heritage to their children.

01_____strongly agree        04_____strongly disagree
02_____agree               05_____don't know
03_____disagree          06_____no answer

162. I prefer my children to adopt black African ethnic role models.

01_____strongly agree        04_____strongly disagree
02_____agree               05_____don't know
03_____disagree          06_____no answer

163. My family observes African cultural and religious ceremonies.
01___yes                                03___don't know
02___no                                 04___no answer

164. In terms of cultural affinity and identification, my children tend to identify themselves as
01___Americans                          04___don't know
02___African-Americans                  05___no answer
03___black Africans

165. My children tend to associate with other children whose parents are from Africa.
01___yes                                03___don't know
02___no                                 04___no answer

166. My children tend to associate with American-born black children.
01___yes                                03___don't know
02___no                                 04___no answer

167. It makes no difference to me what the racial/ethnic backgrounds of my children's friends are.
01___yes                                03___don't know
02___no                                 04___no answer

168. Family life and quality time spent with my family is
01___very important to me               04___don't know
02___important to me                    05___no answer
03___not very important to me

169. I spend time assisting my children with their school work.
01___yes                                03___don't know
02___no                                 04___no answer

170. In thinking about immigration to the U.S., the immigrant's family is the main base for organizing resources in the pursuit of collective economic advancement.
01___strongly agree                     04___strongly disagree
02___agree                              05___don't know
03___disagree                           06___no answer

171. The interpersonal bonds that exist among black African immigrant families are the key to their economic and political survival in the U.S.
01___strongly agree                     04___strongly disagree
02___agree                              05___don't know
03___disagree                           06___no answer

172. Most of the black African immigrants that I personally know came to the U.S. with substantial human capital in the form of quality education, which facilitates their employment in well-paying jobs.

01___strongly agree 04___strongly disagree
02___agree 05___don't know
03___disagree 06___no answer

173. I am aware of successful black African ethnic immigrant businesses operating in my community. The success of these businesses has come about because of (Please check all that apply.)

01___strong family unit and pooling of family resources
02___self-employment as opposed to government employment
03___family's stress on hard work
04___savings
05___loans from financial institutions
06___black African immigrants arrive in the U.S. with substantial wealth
07___operating at lower costs by using extended family members
08___other (please specify) _____
09___don't know
10___no answer

174. The social capital inherent in black African groups as opposed to individual relationships has been vital for me and my family.

01___strongly agree 04___strongly disagree
02___agree 05___don't know
03___disagree 06___no answer

175. All things considered, how would you describe your marriage?

01___very happy 04___not too happy
02___pretty happy 05___don't know
03___happy 06 ___no answer

176. All things considered, how would you describe your health?

01___very good 04___not too good
02___pretty good 05___don't know
03___good 06___no answer

177. Do you have health insurance providing medical coverage for yourself and your family?

01___yes 03___don't know
02___no 04___no answer

178. If yes, does this cover dental and vision costs?

01___covers only dental 03___don't know
02___covers dental and vision 04___no answer

179. I do not carry a health insurance policy currently because
01___my employer does not provide one     03___don't know
02___I cannot afford the cost at this time     04___no answer

180. If you do not currently have health insurance, do you plan to purchase it in the near future?
01___yes     03___don't know
02___no     04___no answer

181. Taking things altogether, how satisfied are you with your current job?
01___very satisfied     04___don't know
02___satisfied     05___no answer
03___not so satisfied

182. How confident are you in the institutions of justice in this country?
01___very confident     04___don't know
02___confident     05___no answer
03___not too confident

183. Have you had any interactions with the police?
01___yes     03___don't know
02___no     04___no answer

184. If yes, how would you describe your interaction with the police?
01___The officer treated me with respect.     03___don't know
02___The officer did not treat me with respect.     04___no answer

185. In general, do you think sentences imposed on offenders by the courts in your area are
01___ too harsh     04___don't know
02___ just about right     05___no answer
03___ too lenient

186. Within the past five years, were you ever a victim of crime?
01___yes     02___no
03___don't know     04___no answer

187. If yes, what was the type(s) of victimization? (Please check all that apply.)
01___robbery     05___larceny theft
02___burglary     06___arson
03___assault     07___don't know
04___rape     08___no answer

188. Did you report this case to the police?
01___yes     03___don't know
02___no     04___no answer

189. If yes, how would you rate the quality of service that you received from the police?

01___very excellent          05___very poor
02___excellent               06___don't know
03___good                    07___no answer
04___poor

190. Within the past five years, have you personally known someone who was a victim of homicide?

01___yes                     03___don't know
02___no                      04___no answer

191. Was this victim (Please check all that apply.)

01___a friend                04___a co-worker
02___a neighbor              05___don't know
03___a relative              06___no answer

192. In general, I feel very safe in my neighborhood.

01___strongly agree          04___strongly disagree
02___agree                   05___don't know
03___disagree                06___no answer

193. How concerned are you about crime in the U.S.?

01___very concerned          04___don't know
02___somewhat concerned      05___no answer
03___not concerned

194. Overall, how would you characterize the crime problem in your area?

01___getting out of control  04___don't know
02___same as in other places 05___no answer
03___not getting out of control

195. Do you favor or disapprove of laws requiring a background check and a waiting period before a person can purchase a gun?

01___favor                   03___don't know
02___disapprove              04___no answer

196. Do you own a gun at home?

01___yes                     03___don't know
02___no                      04___no answer

197. If yes, for what reason(s) did you acquire this gun? (Please check all that apply.)

01___to protect myself                      04___for sport/recreation
02___to protect my family                   05___don't know
03___because the police are inept/ineffective  06___no answer

198. With the exception of juveniles, the mentally ill, and women who have killed their husbands because they are abused by them, do you favor the death penalty for those who are convicted of murder?

01___yes

02___no

03___don't know

04___no answer

199. As African immigrants and a minority group in the U.S., most of us do not trust the police.

01___strongly agree

02___agree

03___disagree

04___strongly disagree

05___don't know

06___no answer

200. Would you like to see the results from this survey?

01___yes

02___no

03___don't know

04___no answer

Thank you very much for your time and cooperation.

# Bibliography

African Profiles International (July 1996). *Africa Alive in America*. New York: TPA Communication (pp. 13–19).

Amin, S. (1974a). *Colonialism in West Africa*. New York: Monthly Review Press.

Amin, S. (1974b). *Modern Migrations in West Africa*. London: Oxford University Press.

Apraku, Kofi (1991). *African Emigres in the United States*. New York: Praeger.

Arthur, J. (1991). "International Labor Migration in West Africa." *African Studies Review* 34(3): 65–87.

Asika, Nkiru (August 24, 1997). "Africans, African-Americans Say Color Doesn't Ensure Unity. Cultural Barriers Can Even Breed Hostility." *Atlanta Journal and Constitution*: B7.

Attah-Poku, Agyemang (1996). *The Socio-Cultural Adjustment Question: The Role of Ghanaian Immigrant Associations in America*. Brookfield, Vt.: Ashgate.

Bach, R. L. (1993). *Changing Relations: Newcomers and Established Residents in U.S. Communities*. New York: Ford Foundation.

Bashi, V., and McDaniel, A. (1997). "A Theory of Immigration and Racial Stratification." *Journal of Black Studies* 27(5): 668–682.

Beijbom, U. (1971). *Swedes in Chicago: A Demographic and Social Study of the 1846–1880 Immigration*. Chicago, Ill.: Chicago Historical Society.

Bennett, Lerone, Jr. (1975). *The Shaping of Black America*. New York: Penguin.

Bernard, W. S. (1936). "Cultural Determinants of Naturalization." *American Sociological Review* 1: 943–953.

Bonacich, E. (1973). "A Theory of Middleman Minorities." *American Sociological Review* 38: 583–594.

Borjas, G. (1989). "Economic Theory and International Migration." *International Migration Review* 23(3): 457–485.

Borjas, G. (1990). *Friends or Strangers*. New York: Basic Books.

Bouvier, L., and Gardner, R. (1986). "Immigration to the United States: The Unfinished Story." *Population Bulletin*. Washington, D.C., Population Reference Bureau.

Bryce-Laporte, R. S. (1973). "Black Immigrants." In *Through Different Eyes*, P. I. Rose, S. Rothman, and W. J. Wilson, eds. New York: Oxford University Press (pp. 44–61).

Butcher, Kristin (1994). "Black Immigrants in the United States: A Comparison With Native Blacks and Other Immigrants." *Industrial and Labor Relations Review* 47 (2): 265–284.

Census of the United States, 1970–90. *Census of Population: Social and Economic Characteristics*, Washington D.C.: U.S. Department of Commerce (Government Printing Office).

Chabal, P., and Daloz, J. P. (1999). *Africa Works: Disorder as Political Instrument*. Bloomington: Indiana University Press.

Chiswick, B. (1986). "Is the New Immigration Less Skilled than the Old?" *Journal of Labor Economics* 2: 168–191.

Dodoo, Nii-Amoo (1991a). "Blacks and Earnings in New York State." *Sociological Spectrum* 11: 203–212.

Dodoo, Nii-Amoo (1991b). "Earning Differences Among Blacks in America." *Social Science Research* 20(2): 93–108.

Dodoo, Nii-Amoo (1991c). "Minority Immigrants in the United States: Earnings Attributes and Economic Success." *Canadian Studies in Population* 18(2): 42–55.

Evans, M. D. (1988). "Choosing To Be A Citizen: The Time-Path of Citizenship in Australia." *International Migration Review* 21: 390–405.

Feagin, Joe, and Feagin, C. B. (1986). *Discrimination American Style: Institutional Racism and Sexism*. Malabar, Fla.: Robert Krieger.

Foner, N. (1979). "West Indians in New York City and London: A Comparative Analysis." *International Migration Review* 13(2): 284–297.

Foner, N. (1985). "Race and Color: Jamaican Migrants in London and New York City." *International Migration Review* 19(4): 708–727.

Garcia, J. (1981). "Political Integration of Mexican Immigrants: Exploration into the Naturalization Process." *International Migration Review* 15: 608–625.

Glaser, W. (1978). *The Brain Drain: Emigration and Return*. Oxford and New York: Pergamon Press.

Gordon, April (1998). "The New Diaspora—African Immigration to the United States." *Journal of Third World Studies* 15(1): 79–103.

Gordon, M. (1964). *Assimilation in American Life*. New York: Oxford University Press.

Greenwood, M. J. (1983). "The Economics of Mass Migration From Poor to Rich Countries: Leading Issues of Fact and Theory." *American Economic Review* 73(2): 173–177.

Grubel, H., and Scott, A. D. (1977). *The Brain Drain: Determinants, Measurement and Welfare Effects*. Waterloo, Canada: Wilfrid Laurier Press.

Guest, A. M. (1980). "The Old-New Distinction and Naturalization: 1900." *International Migration Review*, 14: 492–510.

Haines, D., ed. (1985). "Toward Integration into American Society." In *Refugees in the United States: A Reference Handbook*, Westport, Conn.: Greenwood Press.

Haines, D., ed. (1996). *Refugees in America in the 1990s*. Westport, Conn.: Greenwood Press.

Haines, D., Rutherford, D., and Thomas, P. (1981). "Family and Community Among Vietnamese Refugees." *International Migration Review* 15(1): 310–319.

Healey, J. F. (1998). *Race, Ethnicity, Gender, and Class*. Thousand Oaks, Calif.: Pine Forge.

*Integrated Public Use Microdata Series*. Historical Census Projects, University of Minnesota.

Jasso, G., and Rosenzweig, M. R. (1990). *The New Chosen People: Immigrants in the United States*. New York: Russell Sage Foundation.

Jones, M. A. (1992). *American Immigration*. Chicago, Ill.: University of Chicago Press.

Kalmijn, M. (1996). "The Socioeconomic Assimilation of Caribbean American Blacks." *Social Forces* 74(3): 911–930.

Kasinitz, P. (1992). *Caribbean New York: Black Immigrants and the Politics of Race*. Ithaca, N.Y.: Cornell University Press.

Kebbede, Girma. (1992). *The State and Development in Ethiopia*. Atlantic Highlands, N.J.: Humanities Press.

Kibria, N. (1994). "Household Structure and Family Ideologies: The Dynamics of Immigrant Economic Adaptation Among Vietnamese Refugees." *Social Problems* 41: 81–96.

Lee, Everett (1966). "A Theory of Migration." *Demography* 3(1): 47–57.

Little, K. L. (1965). *West African Urbanization*. Cambridge, England: Cambridge University Press.

Little, K. L. (1974). *Urbanization as a Social Process: An Essay on Movement and Change in Contemporary Africa*. London: Routledge and Kegan Paul.

Lowenthal, D. (1972). *West Indian Societies*. New York: Oxford University Press.

Mabogunje, A. L. (1970). "Systems Approach to a Theory of Rural-Urban Migration." *Geographical Analysis* 2: 1–17.

Mabogunje, A. L. (1972). *Regional Mobility and Resource Development in West Africa*. Montreal, Canada: McGill University Press.

Martin, Phillip (1994). "Good Intentions Gone Awry: Immigration Reform Control Act (1986) and United States Agriculture." *Annals of the American Academy of Political and Social Science* 534: 44–57.

Martin, P., and Midgley, E. (1994). "Immigration to the United States: Journey to an Uncertain Destination." *Population Bulletin* 49(2). Washington, D.C.: Population Reference Bureau.

McDaniel, A. (1995). "The Dynamic Racial Composition of the United States." *Daedalus* 124(1): 179–198.

Millman, J. (1997). *Other Americans: How Immigrants Renew Our Country, Our Economy, and Our Values*. New York: Viking Penguin.

Model, Suzanne (1991). "Caribbean Immigrants: A Black Success Story?" *International Migration Review* 25(2): 248–276.

Mortimer, Delores, and Bryce-Laporte, Roy (1981). *Female Immigrants to the United States: Caribbean, Latin American, and African Experiences*. Research Institute on Immigration and Ethnic Studies, Washington, D.C.: Smithsonian Institution.

*National Advisory Commission on Civil Disorders* (1968). Washington, D.C.: Government Printing Press.

Nickel, Herman (January 31, 1990). "Democracy or Disaster for Africa." *Wall Street Journal*: A18.

Nyerere, Julius (1968). *Freedom and Socialism: A Collection of Writings and Speeches, 1965–1967*. London: Oxford University Press.

Ong, P., Cheng, L., and Evans, L. (1992). "Migration of Highly Educated Asians and Global Dynamics." *Asian and Pacific Migration Journal* 1(3–4): 543–567.

Pachon, H. P., and DeSipio, L. (1994). *New Americans by Choice: Political Perspectives of Latino Immigrants*. Boulder, Colo.: Westview Press.

Park, R. (1928). "Human Migration and the Marginal Man." *American Journal of Sociology* 33: 881–893.

Peil, Margaret (1995). "Ghanaians Abroad." *African Affairs* 94(376): 345–368.

Portes, A., and Bach, R. (1985). *Latin Journey: Cuban and Mexican Immigrants in the United States*. Berkeley: University of California Press.

Portes, Alejandro (1994). "Introduction: Immigration and Its Aftermath." *International Migration Review* 28(4): 632–639.

Portes, Alejandro, and Curtis, J. (1987). "Changing Flags: Naturalization and Its Determinants among Mexican Immigrants." *International Migration Review* 21: 352–371.

Portes, Alejandro, McLeod, S., and Parker Robert (1978). "Immigrant Aspirations." *Sociology of Education* 51(4): 241–260.

Portes, Alejandro, and Zhou, Min (1996). "Self-Employment and the Earnings of Immigrants." *American Sociological Review* 61: 219–230.

"Race in America: Black Like Me" (May 11, 1996). *The Economist* 339(7965): 29–28.

Rogg, Eleanor (1971). "The Influence of a Strong Refugee Community on the Economic Adjustment of Its Members." *International Migration Review* 5(4): 474–481.

Ronningen, Barbara (1996). *International Migration to Minnesota*. Working Paper 96–99. St. Paul, Minn.: Office of State Demographer.

Russell, S. S., and Teitelbaum, M. (1992). *International Migration and International Trade*. World Bank Discussion Paper (Number 160). Washington, D.C.: World Bank.

Shack, William (1978). "Open Systems and Closed Boundaries: The Ritual Process of Stranger Relations in New African States." In William Shack and Elliot Skinner, eds., *Strangers in African Societies*. Berkeley: University of California Press.

Sowell, Thomas (1983). *The Economics of Politics and Race: An International Perspective*. New York: Quill.

Speer, Tibbett (1995). "A Cracked Door: United States Policy Welcomes Only Africa's Brightest and Richest." *Emerge* 6(9): 6.

Takougang, Joseph (1995). "Black Immigrants to the United States." *Western Journal of Black Studies* 19(1): 50–57.

Thompson, V. B. (1987). *The Making of the African Diaspora in the Americas: 1441–1900.* New York: Longman.

Todaro, M. (1969). "A Model of Labor Migration and Urban Unemployment in Less Developed Countries." *American Economic Review* 59(1): 138–148.

Todaro, M., and Stilkind, J. (1981). *City Bias and Rural Neglect: The Dilemma of Urban Development.* New York: Population Council.

U.S. Bureau of the Census (1990). Table 144: Place of Birth of Foreign-Born Persons. Washington, D.C.: U.S. Department of Commerce (Government Printing Office).

U.S. Committee for Refugees (1994). *Refugee Reports.* Washington, D.C.: American Public Welfare Association.

U.S. Immigration and Naturalization Service (1996). *Immigration to the United States in Fiscal Year 1996.* Table 6: Immigrants Admitted by Major Category of Admission and Region and Selected Country of Birth. Washington, D.C.: U.S. Department of Justice.

U.S. Immigration and Naturalization Service. Immigrant Tape Files: 1980–1993. Washington, D.C.: U.S. Department of Justice.

U.S. Immigration and Naturalization Service. INS Statistics. Table 5: Immigrants Admitted by Region and Selected Country of Birth: Fiscal Years 1994–1996. Washington, D.C.: U.S. Department of Justice.

U.S. Immigration and Naturalization Service. Aliens Legally Admitted to the United States: 1993–1996. Washington, D.C.: U.S. Department of Justice.

Waters, M. C. (1994). Ethnic and Racial Identities of Second Generation Black Immigrants in New York City." *International Migration Review* 28(2): 795–820.

Wilson, W. J. (1980). *The Declining Significance of Race.* 2d edition. Chicago, Ill.: University of Chicago Press.

Woldemikael, Tekle, ed. (1996). "Ethiopians and Eritreans." *In Refugees in America in the 1900s.* Westport, Conn.: Greenwood Press (pp. 147–169).

Wong, M. (1985). "Post-1965 Immigrants: Demographic and Socioeconomic Profile." In *Urban Ethnicity in the United States: New Immigrants and Old Minorities.* L. Maldonado, and J. Moore, eds. Beverley Hills, Calif.: Sage.

Wynn, Ron (1995). "Immigration Woes." *Tennessee Tribune* 5(7): 11–12.

Zachariah, K. C., and Conde, J. (1981). *Demographic Aspects of Migration in West Africa.* Washington, D.C.: World Bank.

Zanden, Vander J. (1983). *American Minority Relations.* 4th edition. New York: Alfred A. Knopf.

# Index

## About the Author

JOHN A. ARTHUR is Professor of Sociology and Criminology at the University of Minnesota, Duluth Campus. He has major interests in international migration, comparative criminology, and criminal justice systems. Professor Arthur has authored and co-authored numerous journal articles and written several book chapters.